Most of you have read newspaper or magazine columns which tell you a little about yourself, according to your astrological "sign." In such columns, your "sign" refers to the segment of the sky in which the Sun appeared to be (as seen from Earth) at the time and place of your birth. Most of you know which sign your Sun is in, but may not be aware that the Moon and the planets also were positioned in one or another of the twelve astrological signs at your birth, and that these heavenly bodies and their placements also influence you. This is why a mere Sun-sign interpretation is likely to describe some of your character traits, attitudes and behaviors, but not all of them.

Conventional Western astrology deals with the influence of the Sun, the Moon and the eight known planets of our solar system. It considers the signs in which these bodies are placed, which sectors or "houses" of the birth chart they occupy, and their "aspects" or relationships to each other. In addition to these features, some astrologers look at the smaller heavenly bodies known as asteroids which exist mainly between the orbits of Mars and Jupiter; others examine the positions of the stars. Some astrologers believe there are more planets in our solar system than scientists currently realize, and some also interpret these suspected planets. There are also numerous sensitive points in the birth chart and interrelationships between the various chart components, all of which have specific influences and which combine to produce a complete and totally unique astrological portrait of an individual.

Even all of this is only a beginning. Astrology's multi-dimensional, infinitely complex nature makes the study and practice of it virtually endless—and astrologers are discovering new facets every day. There are many types of astrological charts, each of which has a special use. For instance, you can cast a chart for the birth of a business, a country, a relationship or an event. You can compare the charts of two people to see how one will affect the other. You can take your birth (or natal) chart and "progress" it to see how things change over time. And on, and on.

This book examines the twelve signs of the zodiac and the known planets, from a Western perspective, and considers them only in terms of the birth chart. (For simplicity's sake, the Sun and Moon usually are referred to as planets, too, although sometimes a distinction is made and they are called the "lights"). For as you can see, this much alone is quite voluminous. As you become more fascinated with the ancient science/art of astrology and more adept at its applications, you will probably want to read other books, including some of the ones in this series, in order to come to a deeper and more complete understanding of your own chart and the charts of others.

Even after you have become quite proficient at chart interpretation, and even when you have considered carefully the hundreds of components that comprise any individual birth chart, there is still one other important factor to remember: free will. Though a birth chart provides a phenomenal amount of information about a person's strengths, weaknesses, talents, proclivities, hidden agendas, problem areas, past, etc., that person still has the final say about how s/he will use his/her chart. Thus, even the best astrologer cannot always tell how a given individual will choose to manifest the basic energies with which s/he was born.

In my experience I have found that the more aware and integrated an individual is, the less likely s/he is to demonstrate blatantly the most obvious characteristics of the birth chart. Such a person might handle those energies in a more subtle or internalized manner, rather than displaying them outwardly. There also are many ways to express basic astrological energies, and usually the destructive expressions of a trait are simply exaggerations of the same trait that is constructive when used more moderately. We can only see possibilities, tendencies and likelihoods in any individual birth chart, and most of us don't fulfill the potentials of our charts. Nothing is ordained, nothing is "fated" and immutable. You are in charge of—and responsible for—your own life and what you do with it. As an old astrological saying puts it, "the stars do not compel, they impel."

Skye Alexander

Planets In Signs

1469 Morstein Road
West Chester, Pennsylvania 19380 USA

Planets in Signs
by Skye Alexander

International Standard Book Number: 0-914918-79-6
Library of Congress Catalog Card Number: 87-63416

Edited by Marah Ren
Cover design by Bob Boeberitz
Published by Whitford Press
a division of Schiffer Publishing Ltd.
1469 Morstein Road
West Chester, Pennsylvania 19380

Manufactured in the United States of America

This book may be purchased from the publisher.
Please include $2.00 postage
Try your bookstore first.

For my friend and mentor, Hugh William Lockhart, who introduced me to the fascinating study of astrology, and for Izmir and Aynsley, whose companionship brightens my life.

Acknowledgments

My special thanks to those who have helped make this book possible: Peter Schiffer, my publisher, for his support and encouragement; Marah Ren, my editor and friend, for her enthusiasm, wisdom and critical ability; Carol Coles, for her friendship, help and sense of humor when they were most needed; and Frank Molinski, who started the *Planets* series.

Contents

Chapter One

Getting Started

How to Use This Book

The first step is to have your birth chart drawn up. Either you can consult a practicing astrologer, or you can write to one of the many mail-order computerized chart companies (see Sources at the end of this chapter). You'll need to know the date, time and place of your birth in order to have an accurate chart done. If you don't know your time of birth, you may be able to secure this information by writing to the hospital where you were born. Or, you might find it was recorded at the Department of Vital Statistics in the state where you were born.

If you are unable to learn the time of your birth, don't despair. You still can use this book easily. You will need to consult an *ephemeris,* a collection of tables showing the positions of the Sun, Moon and planets by sign and degree on each day of each month of each year. (Recommended *ephemerides*— plural of ephemeris—are listed at the end of this chapter.) In the ephemeris, locate the table which corresponds to the year and month of your birth. You will see several columns of figures, each column headed by the name or *glyph* (symbol) of a planet. Find your birth date in the left-most column, then place a straightedge across the table underneath the line of figures that corresponds to your birthdate. (See following diagram.)[1]

SEPTEMBER 1947

Day	Sid. T.	Sun	Moon	Merc.	Venus	Mars	Jup.	Saturn	Uranus	Nept.	Pluto	N.Node
1	10:39:14	8Vi12 4	17Pi27	11Vi26	7Vi38	12Cn 1	20Sc54	15Le49	25Ge45	9Li22	13Le45	27Ta15
2	10:43:11	9 10 7	29 59	13 19	8 52	12 39	21 2	15 56	25 47	9 24	13 46	27 12
3	10:47: 7	10 8 13	12Ar41	15 10	10 7	13 17	21 10	16 3	25 48	9 26	13 48	27 9
4	10:51: 3	11 6 19	25 34	17 1	11 21	13 54	21 18	16 11	25 50	9 28	13 49	27 6
5	10:55: 0	12 4 28	8Ta39	18 50	12 36	14 32	21 26	16 18	25 51	9 30	13 51	27 3
6	10:58:57	13 2 39	21 57	20 39	13 50	15 9	21 34	16 25	25 53	9 32	13 53	26 59
7	11: 2:53	14 0 52	5Ge30	22 26	15 5	15 47	21 42	16 32	25 54	9 34	13 54	26 56
8	11: 6:50	14 59 7	19 20	24 12	16 19	16 24	21 51	16 39	25 55	9 36	13 56	26 53
9	11:10:47	15 57 24	3Cn26	25 56	17 34	17 1	22 0	16 47	25 57	9 38	13 57	26 50
10	11:14:43	16 55 44	17 49	27 40	18 48	17 38	22 8	16 54	25 58	9 40	13 59	26 47
11	11:18:39	17 54 5	2Le25	29 22	20 3	18 16	22 17	17 1	25 59	9 42	14 1	26 44
12	11:22:36	18 52 28	17 10	1Li 4	21 17	18 52	22 26	17 8	26 0	9 44	14 2	26 40
13	11:26:32	19 50 54	1Vi56	2 44	22 32	19 29	22 35	17 15	26 1	9 46	14 4	26 37
14	11:30:29	20 49 21	16 36	4 23	23 47	20 6	22 44	17 21	26 2	9 49	14 5	26 34
15	11:34:25	21 47 50	1Li 2	6 1	25 1	20 43	22 53	17 28	26 3	9 51	14 7	26 31
16	11:38:22	22 46 21	15 7	7 38	26 16	21 19	23 3	17 35	26 4	9 53	14 8	26 28
17	11:42:19	23 44 54	28 47	9 14	27 31	21 56	23 12	17 42	26 4	9 55	14 10	26 25
18	11:46:15	24 43 28	12Sc 1	10 48	28 45	22 32	23 22	17 49	26 5	9 57	14 11	26 21
19	11:50:12	25 42 4	24 51	12 22	0Li 0	23 8	23 32	17 55	26 6	9 59	14 12	26 18
20	11:54: 8	26 40 42	7Sg20	13 55	1 15	23 44	23 41	18 2	26 7	10 1	14 14	26 15
21	11:58: 5	27 39 22	19 31	15 27	2 29	24 20	23 51	18 8	26 7	10 4	14 15	26 12
22	12: 2: 1	28 38 4	1Cp31	16 58	3 44	24 56	24 1	18 15	26 8	10 6	14 17	26 9
23	12: 5:58	29 36 47	13 23	18 27	4 59	25 32	24 11	18 21	26 8	10 8	14 18	26 5
24	12: 9:55	0Li35 31	25 14	19 56	6 13	26 7	24 22	18 28	26 9	10 10	14 19	26 2
25	12:13:51	1 34 18	7Aq 8	21 24	7 28	26 43	24 32	18 34	26 9	10 12	14 21	25 59
26	12:17:48	2 33 6	19 9	22 51	8 43	27 18	24 42	18 40	26 9	10 15	14 22	25 56
27	12:21:44	3 31 56	1Pi19	24 16	9 58	27 54	24 53	18 47	26 10	10 17	14 23	25 53
28	12:25:41	4 30 48	13 42	25 41	11 12	28 29	25 3	18 53	26 10	10 19	14 25	25 50
29	12:29:37	5 29 42	26 18	27 5	12 27	29 4	25 14	18 59	26 10	10 21	14 26	25 46
30	12:33:34	6 28 38	9Ar 7	28 27	13 42	29 39	25 25	19 5	26 10	10 24	14 27	25 43

9/23 Sun in Lib. 21:29 9/8 3rd Qt. 3:57 9/14 New 19:28 9/22 1st Qt. 5:42 9/30 Full 6:41

At the top of each column, usually sandwiched between numbers, you also will see either the name or the glyph of an astrological sign. This is the sign in which the planet at the head of that column was positioned on that particular day. You'll notice, too, that sometimes the signs change frequently as you proceed down the column—particularly in the case of the Moon. This is because the faster-moving bodies travel through the signs at a rapid rate, while the slower-moving, outer planets take years to complete their passages. In each column, look at the sign which most immediately precedes the date of your birth to determine which sign that planet was in when you were born.

For example, let's say you were born on September 8, 1947. In the above diagram the sign Virgo (Vi) appears at the top of the column for the Sun, and does not change until September 24. Thus, the Sun was in the sign of Virgo on the eighth of September. Now look at the column for the Moon. Notice that the sign which most immediately precedes September 8 is Gemini (Ge); the Moon moved into Gemini on September 7 and remained in this sign until September 9.

You'll also notice that there are two additional columns, one headed "Sid. T." and one headed "N. Node." Some ephemerides show other columns, as well; however, we will not be considering the information which relates to these columns in this book. If you decide to continue studying astrology you'll want to learn about these things as well.

The numbers which appear in the ephemeris columns indicate the degrees and minutes of the sign in which the planet was positioned. Each sign contains thirty degrees, and each degree is made up of sixty minutes. (In this case, "minutes" refers to a portion of a degree and is not the same thing as a minute of time.)

If you find that the numbers which correspond to the Moon on the date of your birth fall at the beginning or end of a sign, it may be that your Moon is actually in either the preceding or following sign, rather than the sign which is recorded for your birthdate. This is because the planetary positions shown in this ephemeris are calculated for noon in Greenwich, England—which is approximately 7:00 A.M. EST in New York City.

For example, if you were born in New York at 1:00 A.M. Eastern Standard Time, and you are looking at an ephemeris which lists the Moon as being at

1 degree 24 minutes of Taurus on your birthday at noon in Greenwich, your Moon would be in Aries, not Taurus. The Moon was in the early degrees of Taurus at approximately 7:00 A.M. Eastern Standard Time in New York (noon in Greenwich) and since the Moon moves through a sign at a rate of roughly half a degree per hour, at the time of your birth the Moon would not yet have reached the sign Taurus. Some ephemerides are calculated at midnight Greenwich Mean Time, and if you are using one of these, remember that the same type of time adjustment must be made for your place of birth. The other planets move more slowly through the signs, so you aren't likely to encounter this problem with them.

When you know into which signs your planets fall, you can look up in this book the entries that describe your planetary placements. There is a chapter for each planet, and a section within each chapter for each sign.

The Signs

Our zodiac is composed of twelve signs. In order, these are Aries, Taurus, Gemini, Cancer, Leo, Virgo, Libra, Scorpio, Sagittarius, Capricorn, Aquarius and Pisces. Until the Gregorian calendar was adapted in the sixteenth century in England (the eighteenth century in the United States), the new year began when the Sun entered the sign Aries and ended when the Sun completed its passage through Pisces. Astrologers still think of astrological "years" or cycles as beginning with Aries, the first sign of the zodiac, and ending with Pisces.

Each of the signs has a symbol or glyph associated with it. Each sign also has a planetary "ruler," that is, one of the planets is said to rule each sign, which means, very simply, that the planet and the sign have similar energies and vibrations. (To the ancients, the planets were viewed as divinities, each having dominion over or "ruling" certain things on Earth.) When a planet is positioned in the signs it rules, it is able to express its energies most easily and fully. Following is a table which shows the twelve signs, their glyphs, their ruling planets and the glyphs for the planets.

Sign	Glyph	Ruling Planet	Glyph
Aries	♈	Mars	♂
Taurus	♉	Venus (Earth?)	♀
Gemini	♊	Mercury	☿
Cancer	♋	Moon	☽
Leo	♌	Sun	☉
Virgo	♍	Mercury (Chiron?)	☿
Libra	♎	Venus	♀
Scorpio	♏	Pluto	♇
Sagittarius	♐	Jupiter	♃
Capricorn	♑	Saturn	♄
Aquarius	♒	Uranus	♅
Pisces	♓	Neptune	♆

Before the outer planets (Uranus, Neptune and Pluto) were discovered, astrologers attributed rulership of the signs Aquarius, Pisces and Scorpio to Saturn, Jupiter and Mars respectively. Consequently, you may see these associations made in some astrology books, particularly older ones. You'll notice that Venus and Mercury rule more than one sign each, and that in parentheses I've suggested possible alternate rulers for Taurus and Virgo. Perhaps if we find other planets in our solar system some day, we will have to make further adjustments in our rulership assignments.

Note

1. *World Ephemeris for the 20th Century at Noon,* (Rockport, MA: Para Research, Inc., 1983).

Sources

World Ephemeris for the 20th Century, Noon or Midnight editions, Para Research, Inc., Rockport, MA, 1983.

The American Ephemeris for the 20th Century, Noon or Midnight editions, by Neil F. Michelsen, ACS Publications, Inc., San Diego, CA, 1980.

Astral Research, 83 Eastern Ave., Gloucester, MA 01930.

Astro Computing Services, Box 16430, San Diego, Ca 92116-0430.

Astrolabe, Box 28, Orleans, MA 02653.

Chapter Two

Astrological Families

The twelve astrological signs can be broken down into "families" known as the elements (or triplicities) and the modalities (or quadruplicities). The signs are grouped according to similarities in the ways they express themselves. However, as is true in other kinds of families, each sign is individual and unique in itself even though it shares some characteristics with its family members.

Each sign belongs to one element and one modality. Below is a table which shows how the twelve signs are grouped, according to element and mode.

	Fire	Earth	Air	Water
Cardinal	Aries	Capricorn	Libra	Cancer
Fixed	Leo	Taurus	Aquarius	Scorpio
Mutable	Sagittarius	Virgo	Gemini	Pisces

The Four Elements

The elements, or triplicities, are fire, earth, air and water. Together these four elements make up our world, and references to them abound in metaphysical literature and mythology. In Tarot, they appear as the four suits: wands, pentacles, swords and cups respectively. They also relate to the four "humours" which, in Medieval Europe, were thought to have influenced human temperament: choleric, phlegmatic, sanguine and melancholic. In Jungian psychology, they correspond to the four character types: intuitive, sensation, thinking and feeling.

The four elements may be divided further into two groups of two. Fire and air are considered "masculine" in the sense that they express themselves in an outer-directed, assertive and active manner. Together they correspond to the Chinese concept of *yang* and the Greek *Apollonian* personality types. Earth and water are thought of as "feminine" in that their energies are inner-directed, passive and receptive. Collectively, these two elements fit the Chinese *yin* and the Greek *Dionysian* energy divisions.

The element of fire contains the signs Aries, Leo and Sagittarius. The earth element is made up of Taurus, Virgo and Capricorn. Air consists of the signs Gemini, Libra and Aquarius, and water includes Cancer, Scorpio and Pisces.

All astrological birth charts contain these four elements somewhere within their twelve houses. Many charts, however, feature a number of planets in one or another of the elements and thus are weighted in a particular elemental direction. Some charts have no planets at all in one of the elements; others show a preponderance—perhaps five or six—of the ten planets in a single element. Such a preponderance usually produces a person who tends to function only in one way, in accordance with the element that is represented so strongly in his/her birth chart. Someone who has no planets positioned in one of the elements generally lacks true understanding of the energy represented by that element.

Fire

In her book, *The Crystal Tree,* Kelynda describes fire as "the spirit: the life force that drives all things to grow, flower, reproduce, and die."[1] Stephen Arroyo calls fire "a universal radiant energy . . . which through its light brings color into the world."[2] Rob Hand describes it as "the energy of spirit (operating) within the universe by energizing and transforming."[3] The fire element can best be understood if you relate it to the Sun. The Sun's energy—heat and light—"feed" Earth's inhabitants in both obvious and subtle ways. Without the Sun, life on Earth would be impossible. The Sun is the heart of our solar system and the planets, moons and asteroids revolve around it, attracted to its energy field.

Fire Dominance

Fire people—those whose birth charts are dominated by planets in the fire signs Aries, Leo and Sagittarius—project a radiant, vitalizing energy so that they almost seem to glow with warmth and exuberance. Like the Sun, you beam your energy onto everyone within range, invigorating, inspiring and activating others through sheer force of will. Your enthusiasm and *joie de vivre* are contagious and you light a spark in people who are more lethargic. Though you have the ability to stimulate and encourage others to action, your relentless zest and zeal quickly exhaust those who are more retiring or sensitive.

Good-natured, fun-loving and optimistic, you are always ready with a joke, a smile, a word of encouragement, a game of backyard ball or a round of drinks. Everybody's friend, you are generous with your time, energy and money. Though to some extent, your magnanimity is calculated to win friends and influence people, you genuinely enjoy making people happy and place greater value on good times and pleasurable experiences than on possessions.

Your internal flame never goes out and you have the energy to keep going long after everyone else is exhausted. For example, basketball star Kareem Abdul-Jabbar, who continues to play professionally although he is over forty, has five planets in fire signs. You never seem to relax or grow tired, and usually burn the candle at both ends. Because your natural vitality is so strong, you may abuse your health by keeping long hours, eating poorly, smoking cigarettes and overindulging in alcohol and/or drugs, believing that you are invincible. And, you seem to get away with it. If you notice your body at all, you see it only as a vehicle for getting you where you want to go and not really as a part of your Self: You are not your body, but your spirit.

Like the Sun, you view yourself as the center of your own personal Universe. In your psychological self-centeredness, you believe that everyone and everything revolves around you, and exists for (or because of) you. In the words of Marc Edmund Jones, the fire personality "is ultimately oblivious to things outside his own private reality . . . (and) is definitely unaware, most of the time, that anything other than himself is alive on its own account . . . He feels himself to be all there is of life."[4] Bruno Hauptman, convicted killer of the Lindbergh baby, and Nazi leader Heinrich Himmler are two extreme examples of this callous disregard for the rights and feelings of others; both had six planets in fire signs.

Because you are so self-absorbed, you have very little understanding of others and don't place much value on their abilities. You may not even notice other people's strengths and talents, and as a result aren't able to make use of them. You are a poor manager and don't know how to delegate authority; instead, you try to do everything yourself. Consequently, you frequently overextend yourself or botch things because you can't admit you don't know how to do something. You are able to accomplish more than most people and often can be quite creative as well as energetic in figuring out ways to get things done. However, when you can't solve a problem yourself you are totally stumped since it would never even occur to you to ask someone else for help. According to Jones, the fire person "is able to uncover magnificent resources in himself, but when blocked he is baffled most thoroughly because there is no other greater source to which he can turn."[5]

Your ignorance of others also can leave you vulnerable to those who are more surreptitious and conniving. Childlike in your straightforward honesty and directness, you don't understand deviousness or subtlety. You believe everyone is an open book like yourself and thus tend to be quite gullible and naive.

You possess an indomitable spirit and an irrepressible belief in yourself. This tremendous self-confidence allows you to attempt incredible feats of daring—in battle, sports or business—since you can't imagine failing at anything. Your positive attitude often brings you success, if for no other reason than that you refuse to take no for an answer. Your courage is legendary, but you may not consider yourself brave since you rarely see the potential danger in a situation. Instead, you see the challenge: The mountain exists to be climbed, and the thought of falling off never enters your head. However, in your brash and blustering certainty you rarely take time to plan and often miss obvious pitfalls, so that when you fail you fail abysmally. You don't dwell on past mistakes, though, and quickly pick up the pieces, ready to push ahead toward your next adventure.

A natural leader, you encourage others to believe in you and follow your example. As a team captain, military leader, politician or corporate head, you are capable of inspiring (or pushing) your associates to surpass themselves and reach new heights. The charts of Winston Churchill, former prime minister of Britain, and guru Ram Dass (Richard Alpert) both feature a predominance of fire signs.

Because you see yourself as the source of all things, and don't look to others for inspiration and answers, you are highly independent and individualistic. Actor Marlon Brando, who has five fire signs in his birth chart, is a good example. You also are creative and inventive. Not only are you unwilling to play by society's rules, you may not even realize such rules exist. As a result, you do things your own way and often discover new, better avenues that more cautious and practical people were afraid to try. However, you tend to disregard the rights of others in your headlong pursuit and often "steamroll" over those who are less forceful.

Although you don't realize it, you do need the attention and acknowledgment of others, but not necessarily their approval. Constantly playing to your audience, whether entertaining or antagonizing them, you want desperately to get a response from others, to see that your presence and actions are noticed. Nothing hurts you more than being ignored.

Your only gear is high and you charge ahead in a whirlwind of activity. Sitting still makes you anxious and irritable, and you have to be on the move all the time. In your haste, however, you are sometimes reckless and tend to be accident prone. Also, you often miss some of the finer things in life because you don't know how to slow down to appreciate them. In order for you to notice something, it has to be bigger than life, dramatic and powerful enough to distract you from yourself.

You love life fervently and strive to partake of all the glamor, excitement and pleasure it has to offer. "Nothing in moderation" might be your motto. You seem to enjoy yourself more than other people and never lose your youthful optimism or your sense of humor. You believe the world is your oyster, and even if it isn't, you'll never notice.

A strongly-placed Saturn (aspecting several personal planets or positioned in the first house) will make you more pragmatic, persevering and restrained.

Fire Weakness

People who have no planets, or perhaps only one outer planet, in the fire signs tend to lack the passion for life that those whose charts are dominated by this element possess. This is not to say that you don't enjoy life, but rather that you don't throw yourself headlong into the pursuit of pleasure, thrills or glory. Your pleasures are likely to be of a more subtle, sensitive or sedentary nature: a walk in the park, a good book, fine wine or a friend's company. You don't feel a need to live life in the fast lane and are content with smaller, less dramatic achievements, less rigorous adventures and a quieter, gentler pace.

Peace and quiet may appeal to you, and you might be something of a recluse. The chart of Indian guru and mystic, Meher Baba, who spent thirteen years in silence and meditation, shows no planets in fire signs. Less extroverted than fire-dominated people, you look inward for stimulation and may be more active mentally than physically. Writers Anaïs Nin, Elizabeth B. Browning and Henry Miller are three examples.

Rather than charging ahead blindly, chasing dragons, windmills or Olympic gold, you proceed cautiously toward your goals, testing the waters before you jump in. You lack the fire person's daredevil courage (and foolhardiness) and are well aware of the risks involved in any venture. Your fear of taking chances may cause you to miss out on opportunities, or to buckle when the going gets tough. Intimidated by stiff competition, you may let your timidity interfere with your ability to get ahead professionally. You underestimate your capabilities and often end up assisting others whose talents are less than your own but whose drive and desire are greater. You don't enjoy having the spotlight on you, and tend to be modest and retiring.

In your personal life, you are less likely than the fire-dominated person to make an immediate impression on others. Because you sometimes lack self-confidence, you are inclined to let other people make the first moves. With qualities such as competence, consideration for others, loyalty, responsibility, intelligence and sensitivity, rather than surface charm or bravado, you gain the admiration and affection of friends. Respectful of others' space, you never force yourself on them and your companionship "wears well."

Your energy level and vitality are rather low, and you need more rest than other people. You also have to take better care of your health than those who have a preponderance of fire signs in their charts, and your body complains loudly when you treat it badly. Though you might enjoy sports, you don't have the energy, enthusiasm or competitive spirit necessary to achieve great heights. In extreme cases, you may detest any kind of physical exercise and avoid it altogether.

You are inclined to take life too seriously, and at times need to learn to lighten up and laugh at your mistakes and others'. You may lack a sense of humor and often see the dark side of a situation rather than the positive one.

Some individuals whose charts are weak in the fire element choose to overcompensate by pursuing typically fire-type activities. You have to work harder than those whose charts are dominated by fire signs, but you can achieve much through your effort and determination to overcome your "weakness." Tennis champion Alice Marble is one such example.

A strongly-placed Mars (one which is in the first house or aspecting several personal planets, for instance) will help off-set some of the characteristics of a fire-weak birth chart, and provide a greater degree of vitality, optimism and assertiveness.

Earth

The element of earth can be understood best when related to our own planet. This element represents all that is physical, material, tactile, permanent, stable and quantifiable. It is the awareness that comes through the physical senses. Marc Edmund Jones describes it as the "substance of all things."[6] Stephen Arroyo calls it being "attuned to the world of 'forms' " and having an "innate understanding of how the material world functions."[7] Kelynda defines the earth element as "the embodiment . . . of thought, feeling, and energy."[8]

Earth Dominance

Individuals whose birth charts contain many planets in the earth signs (Taurus, Virgo and Capricorn) have a natural and direct relationship with life here on Earth, and are, perhaps, the most at home of all people on this planet. You approach life in a practical, physical way and need to be able to touch, taste, see, hear, smell and measure something in order to comprehend it. Dreams, ideals, concepts and philosophies don't hold much meaning for you; you're more interested in that which can be held in your hand or tabulated in your bank book.

Your concern for the physical world and the mundane aspects of existence makes you the ultimate realist. You are the one who gets things done in the workplace, who builds the homes and office complexes in your community and who creates the structures, traditions and laws by which people order their lives. It is important to you that everything be clearly defined, organized, regulated and carried out according to a plan, and you want to see your efforts reflected in some material way. You aren't satisfied with conceptualizing a building, for example, you want to see it built.

Hard-working and persevering, you have the skills and attitude necessary to succeed in the business world. Entrepreneur Helena Rubenstein, known for her shrewdness and effort, is a good example of earth-sign dominance; her chart features six planets in the earth element. Another example is the hard-working and dedicated French scientist and professor Louis Pasteur, who developed the process of pasteurization; his chart contained seven planets in earth signs.

A pragmatist, you rarely take chances—with your money, time, emotions or other resources—and though your gains may be less rapid and dramatic than those of more adventurous types, they also are steadier and more permanent. You are the person who invests in blue chip stocks and real estate, rather than brainstorms or fly-by-night schemes. You believe in establishing firm foundations and building gradually upon them, with an eye toward endurance, like the little pig who built his house of bricks.

Your personal relationships are handled in much the same way. Friendships are often developed out of business associations or for practical reasons. You might be accused of maintaining "contacts" rather than true friendships, or of manufacturing relationships that serve some material purpose. It's likely that you associate primarily with others who come from the same social stratum as you do, but this isn't only for reasons of snobbery; you feel most comfortable with people who are like you and from whom you know what to expect. You don't like surprises and want interactions of all kinds to proceed according to a prescribed set of rules. Though your true friendships may be few, they are usually longstanding and firm, based on trust and loyalty. You can always be depended upon to aid a friend in need, especially when it comes to finding him/her a job, helping him/her paint the house or offering advice on tax shelters. Not the type to go out drinking with the boys, you prefer having a quiet dinner with one or two close associates.

You enjoy sensory pleasures of all kinds, since you perceive the world and relate to it through your physical senses. A good meal, fine clothing made of luxurious fabrics, an elegant home filled with beautiful furnishings please you greatly.

You want to surround yourself with nice things, and your possessions satisfy both your love of sensory gratification and your need to see the material results of your efforts.

Sex, too, is extremely important to you, for it is through physical contact that you best relate to other people. You have a natural understanding of sexual pleasure and may project a powerful sensuality, though you are rarely "kinky" or lewd. Actress Raquel Welch, known for her great physical beauty, and actor Sean Connery, who exudes dignity and class as well as sex appeal, both have earth-dominated birth charts.

Although physical and sensual experience is key to your existence, you are not particularly energetic and may have little or no interest in athletics, exercise or other such physical activity. Your strength and endurance may be great, but your metabolism tends to be rather sluggish; this, in connection with your love of good food can cause you to have trouble keeping your weight down.

Dependability, diligence and a pragmatic, no-nonsense approach to life are your greatest strengths. Lack of imagination, dullness, rigid conservativism, extreme materialism and blind adherence to rules and conventions are your potential faults. A strongly-placed Mars or Jupiter (aspecting several personal planets or positioned in the first house, for instance) will help counteract some of the ponderousness of an earth-dominated birth chart and make you more adventurous, active and outgoing.

Earth Weakness

People who have no earth signs in their birth charts, or perhaps only one outer planet in this element, are not at home on this planet. Often you seem to be lost in space, in a world of fantasy or illusion, rather than having your feet on the ground, and others may consider you "flaky." The day-to-day realities of earthly life don't interest you much, and you forget to pay bills, keep appointments, take care of your body or go to work. Such mundane things just aren't very important to you.

You may project an image of childlike innocence and naïveté in your inability to handle simple everyday problems, and might become dependent on other more practical types to take care of you. Actress Marilyn Monroe, for instance, had no planets in earth signs. Or, you may seem reckless, irresponsible and impractical, heedless of your own finite physical existence. Zelda Fitzgerald (wife of writer F. Scott Fitzgerald) who lived "life in the fast lane," is a good example of the earth-weak individual.

Perhaps you neglect your earthly responsibilities, focusing instead on intellectual or artistic pursuits, or philosophical/religious abstractions. Material pleasures and wealth hold no meaning for you; your satisfactions are of a transcendental sort, and not to be found in this world. French painter Paul Gauguin, for example, who abandoned his family and a successful business and went to Tahiti to paint, had no planets in earth signs. Neither did Indian religious leader Ramakrishna.

A strongly-placed Saturn (one that aspects several personal planets or is positioned in the first house, for instance) can help counteract the "spaciness" of an earth-weak birth chart, and make you more stable, disciplined and practical.

Air

Stephen Arroyo describes air as "the world of archetypal ideas behind the veil of the physical world."[9] Liz Greene calls air the "human element, the quality which has enabled man to create societies, rules for living together, codes of ethics, writing, learning."[10]

A good way to understand the air element is to relate it to the wind. Like the wind, you cannot see or easily hold and contain spoken words or thoughts. They are intangibles, without physical form or substance. The wind is always in motion, restlessly blowing over the face of the Earth, scattering bits and pieces of the physical world before it. It picks up seeds from one place and carries them to another where they take root and grow.

So it is with the air element. Ideas are spread from person to person, place to place via the medium of words (spoken and written). Concepts and philosophies are carried through the air—we even refer to radio and TV transmissions as "airwaves"—spread like seeds on the wind to people and places far away, to germinate and grow and inspire more ideas.

Air Dominance

People who have a majority of planets in the air signs (Gemini, Libra and Aquarius) emphasize thinking, language and communication. You relate to the world in terms of intellectual constructs, and you use verbal skills to interact with others. Harvard professor and former U. S. Secretary of State Henry Kissinger, known for his negotiating abilities and his keen intellect, is a good example; he has his Sun, Moon and three planets in air signs. Ideas and concepts are of primary importance to you, and probably you are more concerned with the theory than with its application. In the extreme, you might be an impractical dreamer, always thinking but never doing.

Your energy is directed into mental activity and your mind is rarely still, so that it can be difficult for you to meditate, relax or even sleep. Nervous and high-strung, you may neglect your body and live in your head. You carry on an internal running dialogue with yourself. Every experience and feeling is translated into words so it can be examined, logically and reasonably; you must make "sense" of something before you can integrate it into your understanding. According to Liz Greene, the air-dominated person "must have explanations and names for the things which come into his field of awareness. They need not be tangible, but they must be explainable."[11]

Whether or not you are intelligent yourself you respect intelligence and verbal adeptness. You enjoy sharing ideas with others and might spend a great deal of time in activities that require some form of communication. Quite loquacious, you aren't always a good listener. Your interest in communication of all kinds could lead you to pursue a career in sales, writing, teaching, lecturing, telecommunications, computers or any field that requires exchanging information. For example, writers Lord Byron, William Butler Yeats, Sir Arthur Conan Doyle and T. S. Eliot all had air-dominated charts.

Even your leisure time is likely to involve mental or language skills rather than physical activity. Reading, word games, crossword puzzles, talking on the phone, writing letters, playing cards and visiting with friends probably appeal to you more than sports, sex, dancing or going out to dinner (unless you also have several planets in fire or earth signs). You're the type who actually reads the articles in *Playboy.*

Rational and logical, you analyze situations fully, thinking them through and planning carefully before you act. Consequently, you are less likely to make foolish mistakes than people with fire-dominated charts. However, your tendency to ponder, contemplate and vacillate can result in lost opportunities because you fail to seize the moment and take chances. You're still at the drawing board while someone more daring markets your idea.

Air is the least personal and self-absorbed of the four elements. It is also the most detached and unemotional. Rob Hand writes that the air-sign person "is more inclined to abstractions that have little to do with the individual" and is "primarily concerned with a reality external to the self."[12] Therefore, you can be dispassionate, objective and fair-minded, and are capable of seeing another person's point of view as well as your own.

People-oriented, you are highly social and enjoy the company of others. You like to curl up with a good book, of course, but you are most content when interacting with congenial companions and wouldn't be happy if you had to spend much of your time alone. You are comfortable in casual friendships or groups; however, you have trouble in close, one-to-one relationships that require intimacy and emotional involvement. Because you are so dispassionate and impersonal, it is hard for you to relate to a partner in a deep, personal, emotional way unless you also have planets in water signs.

You function well in a busy, active work environment where you must deal with many different people, and a career that allows you plenty of contact with the public probably would suit you best. Your interests are many and varied. Most likely, you've pursued a number of vocations and also may have several avocations or hobbies as well. A lifelong student, you enjoy learning and might take continuing education courses, attend lectures or read to improve your knowledge of everything from astrology to zoology. However, you lack perseverance (unless Saturn is strong in your chart or you have several planets in Taurus, Capricorn or Scorpio) and tend to scatter your energies, so that you rarely become proficient in any area.

Air Weakness

People who have no planets in air signs, or perhaps only one of the outer planets, don't emphasize intellectual or mental activity in their lives. This doesn't mean you aren't intelligent, only that you don't place much value on the world of ideas. "Improving your mind" is not very important to you and the last time you read a book that wasn't assigned or job-related was when your plane was five hours late. However, you may feel threatened or intimidated by people who do stress intelligence and "book learning." George Wallace, the former governor of Alabama and presidential candidate who railed against northern "pointy-headed intellectuals," has no planets in air signs.

Your vocabulary may be rather limited and you probably hate writing letters, term papers or reports. Verbal adroitness isn't your strong suit and you might be better at communicating emotionally, physically or psychically than with words. Because you don't express yourself eloquently, people sometimes underestimate your intelligence. You may have been a poor student when you were a child, and as an adult you aren't interested in learning something unless there is an immediate and tangible reason for doing so. You aren't likely to pursue knowledge for its own sake; you want to be able to apply what you know.

You have trouble remaining detached and objective, and it is hard for you to understand viewpoints that differ from your own. Once you've made up your mind you don't change it easily. You won't "waste time" contemplating abstractions, philosophical or religious theories, political ideologies or social issues unless they directly affect you. Because you lack the ability to examine and evaluate issues you can tend to be narrow-minded, bigoted or at least very conservative in your beliefs.

However, you may feel insecure or inadequate about your air-sign weakness and overcompensate by working hard to develop your vocabulary and communication skills, as if to prove to yourself that you can do it. As a result, you might accomplish greater intellectual feats than people whose charts do contain planets in air signs. Erudite writer, editor and television talk show host William F. Buckley, for example, has a chart that is devoid of air-sign planets. French writer Guy de Maupassant had only one outer planet in air. Neither of these air-weak individuals was ever at a loss for words!

A strong Mercury (one that is well-placed in your chart by sign or house position, or favorably aspected) will enhance a chart that is weak in the air element.

Water

In dream analysis water often is seen as a symbol of the emotions: A dream about being submerged in water suggests that you are immersed in your emotions; a dream about a turbulent sea indicates that your emotional life is chaotic; etc. In an astrological sense, water also is connected with emotion. To understand the water element, think of the ocean: mysterious, unpredictable and constantly changing. The source and supporter of all life, its vast hidden depths are complex and rich with variety. So it is with the emotions, and the element of water.

Water also relates to the deepest, unconscious, hidden, "primitive" part of ourselves, that which does not behave in a logical or orderly fashion, and which we sometimes wish didn't exist. When repressed, however, this secret and powerful force becomes like the caged minotaur, a monster dwelling in a labyrinthine underworld. "The element of water, astrologically, is the most enigmatic of all the elements . . . furthest from the rational realm which we are pleased to call human thought," says Liz Greene.[13] Water operates at an internal, instinctual level that is intuitive instead of rational, and is emotional rather than mental. In our sophisticated society, the emotional realm often is denigrated and denied.

Water Dominance

People whose birth charts contain a preponderance of planets in the water signs (Cancer, Scorpio and Pisces) approach life and understand it through their emotions. Your feelings are extremely sensitive, easily engaged and easily hurt. A beautiful sunset, a sad song or a harsh word can trigger a strong response in you. At times you are overwhelmed by the profusion of emotions you feel and may erect all sorts of defensive barriers to protect yourself from pain. Some water-dominated people suffer from depression and may attempt to block their feelings with alcohol or drugs. German writer Hermann Hesse, for example, whose Sun, Moon and three planets were in water signs, struggled with depression, suicidal tendencies, hypochondria and alcoholism. This intense sensitivity, however, also allows you to experience the heights of emotional bliss as well as the depths of despair.

Rather than intellectualizing about something, you respond to it according to how it feels. If it feels right, you go with it. Your "gut" responses are usually correct; trust your hunches and don't let your head get in the way. Your keen intuition lets you "know" things that can't be comprehended logically, and you often appear to be psychic. This is because you can tap into the underlying emotions of other people and sense what they are feeling, what is going on inside them regardless of what they say or do. Noted American psychic Edgar Cayce, for example, had his Sun and three planets in water signs.

Close emotional relationships are absolutely essential to your happiness. Superficial interactions don't satisfy you; you want to merge your feeling nature with someone else's. Romantic, sentimental and affectionate, you are only truly alive when you can love and be loved.

Once you've established an intimate bond with someone, you almost feel that you and the other person are one being and you can no longer separate your needs, desires and feelings from his/hers. You become so intensely involved in the lives of your loved ones that you can't see them as individual and independent entities. As a result, you tend to be "smothering" toward your children, possessive of your partners, overbearing and interfering with your friends and associates. You simply can't "live and let live."

You communicate best in non-verbal ways, emotionally, psychically or through such forms as art, dance, music, poetry and photography. Your sensitivity allows you to see and feel colors, rhythms and tones more vividly than other people do. The birth charts of Renaissance artist Michelangelo, poet Dylan Thomas, trumpet player Miles Davis, and singers Billie Holiday and Muddy Waters (whose name even reflects this element) all are dominated by water signs. You are more at home in these abstract realms of images and symbols than in the more linear and defined world of words. The language you speak is universal and eternal, conveyed and comprehended at an unconscious level.

Your heart definitely rules your head. Because you are dominated by your emotions, you have trouble making rational decisions. Highly impractical and impressionable, you sometimes use bad judgment in business dealings or invest unwisely because you can't be objective and evaluate situations impersonally. You also tend to change your mind frequently according to how you feel at any given moment, and may reverse your decisions from day to day, seemingly without cause. You are strongly attached to your views and opinions—whether or not they seem reasonable or sensible to others—and no one can change your way of seeing things with facts or a logical argument.

Water Weakness

People who don't have any planets in water signs, or perhaps only one outer planet, lack emotional intensity. This is not to say you have no feelings. However, your emotions are not so easily engaged, nor do they run so deep as those of water-dominated people. You don't tend to form close relationships with others and even your lovers are more likely to be friends or sexual partners than true intimates. You never make a deep feeling connection with anyone and may feel smothered or threatened by the emotional demands of others.

Unlike water-dominated individuals, you recover from emotional bumps and scrapes without suffering lasting scars. At best, you take the good times with the bad and don't let disappointments get you down. At worst, you can be rather callous and cold, detached and unfeeling toward others. Bank robber Bonnie Parker and labor leader James Hoffa, for example, each had only one outer planet in water.

Depending on which element is strongest in your chart, you might channel your energy into intellectual studies, your career or physical activity instead of relationships. The birth chart of French mathematician and philosopher René Descartes, for example, contains no water-sign planets; that of American adventurer Davy Crockett features only Uranus in Cancer. Since Western society often connects strong emotions with weakness, people whose charts are weak in this element—especially men—may not see their lack as particularly problematic.

A dominant Moon (one that is in favorable aspect to the personal planets or prominently placed in the chart) can help offset a water-weak birth chart and make you more emotional.

The Four Modalities

The modalities, or quadruplicities, show the manner or mode by which you go about doing things. The four modalities are known as cardinal, fixed and mutable, and each group contains four of the zodiacal signs. The cardinal signs are those which would fall on the angles of a natural chart: Aries, Cancer, Libra and Capricorn. The fixed signs include those which would occupy the succedent houses of a natural chart: Taurus, Leo, Scorpio and Aquarius. The mutable signs, Gemini, Virgo, Sagittarius and Pisces, are positioned on the cadent houses of a natural chart.

Some birth charts show a preponderance of planets positioned in one of these four modalities; other charts lack or are weak in one of them. The way in which your birth planets are arranged, according to modality, affects your behavior, attitudes and perception.

Cardinal

Rob Hand associates the cardinal signs with "the impetus to create."[14] These four signs share a desire to create something, to have some sort of impact that can be felt, seen or experienced. Aries—the first sign of the zodiac, the sign that begins the astrological new year—desires creation of life in all its myriad forms. Cancer seeks to create children, a home and family. Libra strives to create relationships. Capricorn's creations are career-related.

The cardinal signs are called active because they initiate or act to bring their desires to fruition. Their actions may be obviously assertive, as is the case with Aries, or apparently passive, as is the case with Cancer. However, all four signs are devoted to achieving their goals—toward creating their special objectives—by using whatever methods are available to them. In a sense, cardinal people are the ones who call the shots, influencing, stimulating or maneuvering others, rather than reacting to the actions of others. It may seem that Libra and Cancer are somewhat malleable and easily affected by other people, but even though their manner is more gentle and subtle than that of Aries, they are no less eager or energetic in the pursuit of their desires.

Cardinal Dominance

People who have many planets in the cardinal signs (Aries, Cancer, Libra and Capricorn) are likely to be ambitious and industrious when it comes to going after the thing they most want. Whether it's fame, money, security, love or pleasure you're seeking, you put all your energy and effort into achieving your goals. Not willing to sit idly by, waiting for someone else to offer it to you, you strive to obtain it for yourself.

Cardinal Weakness

Those of you who have no planets in the cardinal signs, or perhaps only one of the outer planets, can lack initiative and drive. Rather than pursuing your desires actively and eagerly, you sometimes look to others to satisfy them for you. Or, you may sit around waiting for a lucky break instead of making your own luck. If you have many planets in fixed signs, you may be better at developing and refining what the cardinal-sign person has started than you are at initiating something of your own. If you have many planets in mutable signs, you are likely to scatter your energies in so many directions that you don't achieve much in any one area.

Fixed

The fixed signs (Taurus, Leo, Scorpio and Aquarius) solidify and carry out what the cardinal signs begin. Fixed signs might be thought of as the construction crew that builds what the architect (cardinal signs) designed. With unwavering determination, the fixed signs get things done, holding true and firm to their course.

Fixed Dominance

What you lack in daring you make up for in perseverance. Once you start something you don't quit until you've achieved your goal. Steady, stable and enduring, you have the ability to make commitments and stick with them—whether those commitments are to another person, a job or an idea. Your great strengths are loyalty, dependability, constancy, trustworthiness and devotion.

You run the risk, however, of becoming so attached to your desires that you can't see their flaws or make changes when necessary. "Fixed" can mean "stuck." You tend to become set in your ways and can be terribly stubborn. You'd rather dig in your heels and fight than compromise. It can be hard for you to see another's viewpoint or to make adjustments for other people in your life. Rigid and intransigent, you don't know how to roll with the punches or adapt to changing situations.

Fixed Weakness

People who lack planets or perhaps have only one outer planet positioned in fixed signs tend to be better at starting things than finishing them. You don't have the determination to achieve your goals or follow through with your promises. Either you become bored with something soon after beginning it, or you take on so much that you don't have the energy or focus to accomplish anything. You may have trouble sticking with one thing for long, and might change jobs, lovers or religious philosophies every time something new peaks your interest.

Mutable

The mutable signs (Gemini, Virgo, Sagittarius and Pisces) are noted for their flexibility, their ability to adjust to situations and their tendency to change their colors like chameleons when necessary. They take what the cardinal signs have designed and the fixed signs have built and adapt it so that it can be assimilated into the environment. As situations change, the mutable signs alter what has been designed and built so that it can continue to operate effectively.

Mutable Dominance

Those of you who have many planets in the mutable signs may be so changeable that it's almost impossible to pin you down. Always going in several directions at once, you have trouble focusing your actions, thoughts or feelings on any one thing. As a result, you are inclined to scatter your energies and fail to accomplish your goals, unless other stabilizing factors (such as a strong Saturn) are also part of your total chart makeup.

You lack inner structure and form, and your identity may not be very well-established. Consequently, you can seem somewhat amorphous and undefined, even to yourself. Easily influenced by others, you might find it difficult to decide what you really want or what you truly feel, and you are likely to be swayed by public opinion, fashionable trends or the desires of people you admire.

Mutable Weakness

If you have no planets in mutable signs, or perhaps only one outer planet, you are likely to have trouble making changes in your life. You are wary of trying new things and prefer to stay with what you know to be safe. As a result, you can end up stuck in a rut. Change may seem threatening to you. You just don't know how to adjust your attitudes and behavior to evolving conditions in your world, or to the needs and desires of others. Your inflexibility isn't necessarily due to stubbornness or ego, but stems instead from a desire to maintain order and stability in your life.

Notes

1. Kelynda, *The Crystal Tree* (West Chester, PA: Whitford Press, 1987), p. 100.
2. Stephen Arroyo, *Astrology, Psychology, & the Four Elements* (Davis, CA: CRCS Publications, 1978), p. 95.
3. Robert Hand, *Horoscope Symbols* (Rockport, MA: Para Research, Inc., 1981), p. 185.
4. Marc Edmund Jones, *Astrology: How and Why It Works* (Baltimore, MD: Penguin Books, 1971), p. 137.
5. Jones, p. 138.
6. Jones, p. 145.
7. Arroyo, p. 99.
8. Kelynda, p. 101.
9. Arroyo, p. 96.
10. Liz Greene, *Star Signs for Lovers* (New York: Day Books/Stein and Day, 1980), p. 294.
11. Greene, p. 295.
12. Hand, p. 188.
13. Greene, p. 383.
14. Hand, p. 196.

Chapter Three

The Sun

The Sun is the center of our solar system, around which all the other heavenly bodies revolve. Without the Sun, life as we know it could not exist. In astrology, the Sun also plays a vital role. For most people, it is the "center" of the birth chart, the most powerful and important of the astrological bodies. Consequently, its influence is felt and demonstrated in nearly every area of your life.

The Sun describes you as an individual entity, pure, distinct and unaffected by others or your environment. Liz Greene says it "symbolizes the urge to be yourself."[1] Stephen Arroyo connects it to your "sense of individuality and self-identity."[2] You could think of it as the indicator of your "true colors," your essential self, the "you" you are striving to be in this lifetime. It is the side you show to the world, the part of yourself that you probably like best and the way you want others to see you.

The Sun represents your *yang* side, that part of you which is outer-directed, conscious, active, energized. If you are psychologically-oriented, you might want to relate the Sun to your conscious or aware side, and the Moon to the subconscious or unconscious. If you believe in reincarnation, you may see the Sun as signifying your present life, while the Moon represents the past. In Eastern terms, the Sun could be thought of as the embodiment of *dharma,* the role or "assignment sheet" you've chosen for this lifetime, and the Moon might be associated with *karma,* or what you've carried over from previous existences into your current one.

The sign in which the Sun is placed colors or shapes the way you play this role. When someone asks you what your sign is, he or she usually is referring to the sign in which the Sun was positioned at the time of your birth: your Sun-sign. It takes the Sun approximately 365 days to travel through all twelve signs of the zodiac, and it remains in each sign for about thirty days.

Of course, the Sun doesn't actually move through these signs. However, as the Earth orbits around the Sun, it *appears* from our vantage point on Earth as though it is the Sun that is moving. Each of us is the center of our own personal Universe. And since we are concerned with how the heavenly bodies influence life on Earth, rather than the other way around, we speak of the Sun as traveling through the signs of the zodiac—because that is how it looks to us here.

Some astrologers interpret the Sun in the birth chart as an indicator of your father, and often its sign position and aspects do show your perception of your father. Siblings are likely to describe the same father differently in accordance with their Sun placements.

The Sun is the natural ruler of Leo, the fifth sign of the zodiac. Aspects between the Sun and other planets in your chart, its house position and your level of development also will be important in the Sun's interpretation.

Sun in Aries

The Sun enters Aries at the spring equinox and remains in this sign from about March 21 to April 20, though it varies slightly from year to year. Aries is the sign of new beginnings. While the Sun is in Aries, the Earth awakens from her long winter's sleep and in many parts of the northern hemisphere, new life begins to sprout after a period of barren cold. Sap flows in the trees, and the energy and vitality of the "new year" starts to rise in all of us.

People who have their Suns in Aries are energetic, active, assertive and direct. You approach life eagerly and aggressively, and there is nothing subtle in your method, manner or motivation. Your only "gear" is high, your only direction is forward. Baseball great Pete "Charlie Hustle" Rose is a good example of Sun in Aries. You know what you want and go after it fervently, rarely taking no for an answer and often succeeding through sheer energy and force of will.

You are enthusiastic and curious, and each day offers you new challenges—if it doesn't, you'll create some! You can't stand to have life go along smoothly, and you like to keep things stirred up. Activity, conflict and crisis nourish you, and you are at your best under pressure, when you must think and act quickly. You are always testing yourself, trying to jump over the next hurdle or to beat the next opponent. You need to keep defining yourself *against* something or someone else, to prove to yourself that you exist and have impact on your environment.

Athletics offer a clear-cut set of challenges and opponents against which you can pit yourself, and you probably have some athletic ability or at least an interest in sports. Sports also provide an outlet for your abundant energy.

Challenges in the business world can be just as invigorating and satisfying for you. You have an entrepreneurial nature, and are willing to take chances and risks that scare away more cautious people. Financier J. P. Morgan and *Playboy* magazine's former publisher Hugh Hefner are two good examples of Sun in Aries.

Your pioneering spirit is strong and you long to go where no one has gone before, to break new ground and do the impossible. Wilbur Wright, who introduced the world to flying, had his Sun in Aries. Always rushing in where angels fear to tread, you approach every endeavor with the same head-long, reckless, indefatigable abandon, and you either succeed gloriously or fail dismally. Failure doesn't discourage you, though, for you have a naïve and irrepressible self-confidence that lets you go on believing in your ultimate success, regardless of the odds. Since you never look back and don't learn from your mistakes, however, you are likely to make the same ones again and again.

Your attention span is that of a young child and you become bored easily. You are much better at starting things than finishing them, for you lose interest once the initial excitement has faded and routine, day-to-day operations are in place. Therefore, you probably begin lots of projects, jobs, relationships, etc., but rarely see them through to maturity. Goals that can be achieved quickly are better choices for you than ones that require years of planning and development.

In your chest beats the heart of an adventurer, and you are both courageous and daring. You want to keep the adrenalin rushing through your veins at all times. Although you never back down from a fight, you don't know how to walk away from one with dignity either. In fact, you are often the instigator. Aggressive and feisty, long on nerve and short on tact, you enjoy a good argument or even a fist fight now and again to clear the air. In a dangerous situation, anyone would like to have you on his/her side.

Strongly individualistic, you have trouble compromising or working as part of a team or group. You need to be free and independent to do things your own way, regardless of how iconoclastic or outrageous your methods may seem to others. Although you are usually quite self-sufficient, when you run into a problem you can't solve yourself, you don't know where to turn. Since you basically are unaware and unappreciative of others' strengths, you aren't able to benefit from their knowledge and experience.

A rebel at heart, you tend to see society as your adversary and thwart authority at every turn. The birth chart of Thomas Jefferson, American patriot, president and author of the Declaration of Independence, features Sun in Aries. So do those of radical scientist/psychologist Wilhelm Reich, bank robber Clyde Barrow, feminist, activist and editor of *Ms.* magazine Gloria Steinem, and outspoken former U. S. First Lady Betty Ford.

Your self-centeredness makes relationships difficult, for you can't seem to see another's point of view or to adjust your behavior to accommodate someone else's needs. Your sex drive is strong, but when it comes to tenderness and affection you fall short. You are inclined to think of your partners as conquests rather than lovers, and sex with you resembles hard rock music: fast, rough, adolescent and without much variation in mood, style or tempo.

Though you can be abrasive and annoying at times—sports caster Howard Cosell, for example, has his Sun in Aries—you possess an endearing, childlike quality that makes people enjoy being around you. Your enthusiasm is infectious and your unabashed, up-front, uncomplicated manner never leaves any doubts about your motivations or intentions. You can be irresponsible and careless at times, but you are also honest, fun-loving and willing to stand up for what your believe. Your greatest failings usually are the result of your impatience, haste and self-centeredness. Your greatest strengths are your optimism, courage, drive and vitality.

Sun in Taurus

The Sun is in Taurus from about April 21 to May 20, though it can vary slightly from year to year. During this period of fertility and fecundity, crops are planted, flowers bloom in profusion, birds and animals give birth to young and the human heart turns to matters of love.

For people who have Sun in Taurus, love relationships are of primary importance. You don't like being alone and will settle for a partnership that is less than ideal rather than do without. Once you've set your sights on someone you pursue him/her doggedly, undaunted by delays, obstacles or rejection. After you've bagged your game, you hold on tightly and are extremely possessive of your partners. Aquarians, Geminis and Sagittarians may feel suffocated by your love, but Cancers and Capricorns might appreciate your constant and uncomplicated devotion.

Your intense interest in sex is a powerful impetus to forming relationships. Sex is usually foremost in your mind and it's one of your greatest pleasures. Psychoanalyst Sigmund Freud, for example, had his Sun in Taurus. For you, sex is a natural bodily function, a primary need, and your approach to it is down-to-earth, uninhibited and unabashed. However, your strong sex drive and preoccupation with satisfying your physical desires can cause you to be rather indiscriminate and indulgent, and sometimes any warm body will do.

Good-natured and easy-going, you are an amiable and loyal companion. You are patient and slow to anger, and tend to take life as it comes. However, when pushed too far you can be a stubborn and formidable opponent.

To the people you love, you are attentive, affectionate, loyal, devoted and generous. You enjoy doing things for your loved ones and giving them gifts. However, your "gifts" often have strings attached and you are inclined to try to buy love or to make others feel obligated to you. You also may expect lovers to lavish material bounty upon you, and your less materialistic friends might think you are a bit mercenary.

Indulgent and luxury-loving, you relish creature comforts and appreciate beautiful things: clothing, jewelry, furniture, art, good food and drink. You derive great pleasure from your possessions, and are usually in debt because you can't say no to yourself.

You probably have good taste in clothing and furnishings, and could succeed in a career in fashion or interior design. Or, your affinity with nature might incline you toward horticulture or landscape architecture. Frederick Law Olmstead, creator of the beautiful chain of Boston parks known as the Emerald Necklace, had his Sun in Taurus. The original "Earth Mother," you love plants, have two green thumbs and can make just about anything grow. In everything you do you need to see the physical results of your labors. You aren't very assertive, innovative or especially hard-working, however; thus, you'd probably be better off working for someone else or in a partnership, rather than striking out on your own.

Because Taurus rules the throat, you may have musical ability and a fine singing voice. David Byrne, Barbra Streisand and Perry Como, for example, have their Suns in Taurus.

Cooking is another area in which you excel, and many people with Taurean Suns are employed in the culinary fields. Chef James Beard is one good example. Whether or not you decide to put your talents to work for you professionally, you probably like to bake and cook for yourself, your friends and family. And you certainly enjoy sitting down to a good meal! As a result, you may always be at least a few pounds overweight. Your slow metabolism and lack of interest in exercise can compound the problem, and you might find yourself waging a lifelong battle with the scales. But then, who'd take a skinny chef seriously?

Unwilling to take chances or risk lowering your standard of living, you'll stay with an unsatisfying job or relationship for years rather than make a switch. You are truly a creature of habit and always prefer something familiar to an unknown. You are likely to view your career and relationships as investments, and once you've put a great deal of time and effort into something you are loathe to cut your losses and move on. Consequently, you have a tendency to get stuck in a rut.

Because you are reluctant to try anything new and are anything but adventurous, you can become a bit dull and overly-conservative. Others sometimes underestimate your intelligence because you aren't especially interested in mental pursuits or witty conversation (unless your Mercury is in Gemini). Your concerns are with the material, tactile world and its tangible realities, and you don't place much value in abstractions. In fact, you might have trouble even getting your mind around some philosophical or metaphysical concepts. You need to guard against being narrow-minded and dismissing out-of-hand anything with which you aren't already familiar, or that you can't see, touch, smell or taste.

Your greatest strengths are your constancy, your sweet and loving temperament and your appreciation of all things beautiful. Your greatest failings result from your indulgence, stubbornness, laziness and greed.

Sun in Gemini

The Sun is in Gemini from about May 21 to June 20, though it varies slightly from year to year. Gemini is connected with learning, mental activity, verbal and written communication. The school year is completed while the Sun is in Gemini and students take final exams to test what they've learned during the term. In the United States, the publishing and bookselling industries hold their national convention each year during this period.

For people with Sun in Gemini, communication is of utmost importance. You are fond of talking, writing, reading—anything that involves the written or spoken word. As a result, you may pursue a profession or avocation which involves some form of communication, such as writing, teaching, public speaking, advertising, sales, data processing, talking on the phone or telecommunications. Many writers have their Suns in Gemini; William Butler Yeats, Alexander Pushkin, Joyce Carol Oates, Walt Whitman, Dashiell Hammett, Sir Arthur Conan Doyle, William Styron, Lillian Hellman, Ralph Waldo Emerson, Anne Frank, Ian Fleming, Bob Dylan, Thomas Mann, Allen Ginsberg and Thomas Hardy are only a few examples.

Mentally-oriented, you enjoy discussing ideas with others and respect intelligence. For you, knowledge is power. The written word has great appeal for you and you are probably an avid reader. Former U. S. President John F. Kennedy, who had his Sun in Gemini, often gave books as gifts to visiting dignitaries. You also are eager to acquire as much information as possible and want to share what you know with everyone you meet.

A life-long student, you never tire of learning new things and might enjoy attending adult education classes, taking mail-order courses and going to lectures. Your tendency, however, is to collect facts and tidbits of data without integrating them into the larger picture, so that you possess lots of information but no true knowledge. You gather so many disassociated bits and pieces, facts and figures, that you frequently mix them up, confusing words, events and people in the style of Mrs. Malaprop.

Your interests are many and diverse; almost anything will attract your attention for a brief time. However, you don't have the perseverance to stick with one thing for long. One week you're fascinated with scuba diving, the next it's Tarot, then stamp collecting, weaving, oil painting, etc. Truly the jack of all trades, master of none, you are eager to try everything but rarely become proficient at anything.

Insatiably curious, you want to know and experience as much as possible. You have trouble limiting yourself to one job, one relationship, one residence or even one book at a time, and usually have several things going on simultaneously. You might switch jobs on a regular basis, or have a primary occupation and one or more avocations. You may engage in a series of brief relationships or several concurrent ones; at the very least, you are something of a flirt and never stop looking around even if you don't act on your fantasies. You can watch TV, cook dinner, hem a skirt and do a crossword puzzle while you talk on the phone. You're afraid you might miss out on something more interesting if you devote yourself to a single pursuit or activity. At times, you can seem a bit schizophrenic, and may have trouble getting the divergent sides of your personality to work together harmoniously. You also tend to scatter your energies and spread yourself too thin.

A consummate shopper, you love to get a bargain and pride yourself on never paying full price. You know the price of everything, but the value of nothing, and would rather buy a dozen inexpensive items of poor quality than a single good one. You aren't a big tipper and usually ask for separate checks when you go out to lunch.

Extremely friendly, you enjoy companionship and probably have plenty of friends and associates. Usually you are cheerful and good-natured, and are always available for a movie, a card game, a party or a good chat. You don't like being alone or still and keep busy doing things, running from place to place or socializing—anything to avoid looking at yourself deeply. Not at all introspective or reflective, you don't understand your own motivations or those of others, and can be rather shallow and naïve.

Gemini rules the hands, and consequently, you might be quite dexterous. Perhaps you are skilled at drawing, woodworking, playing a musical instrument, typing, sewing or some other handcraft. Trumpet player Miles Davis, pianist and songwriter Cole Porter, painter Paul Gauguin and architect Frank Lloyd Wright are a few good Gemini-Sun examples.

Sun in Cancer

The Sun enters Cancer at the summer solstice. It remains in this sign from about June 21 to July 22, though this varies slightly from year to year.

People who have their Suns in Cancer are highly sensitive and emotional. Because you are emotionally tuned in to the moods and feelings of others, you are quite intuitive and sometimes seem to be psychic. You may choose to express your sensitivity by being caring and compassionate toward others, or through some artistic medium. If, however, you believe that sensitivity is a sign of weakness, you might try instead to hide behind a mask of bravado, and some men who have their Suns in Cancer affect a macho attitude as an overcompensation. For example, author Ernest Hemingway, who went to great lengths in his behavior and writing to portray himself as a "man's man," had his Sun in Cancer.

You place great importance on the home and family. Actor and comedian Bill Cosby, known for his best-selling book *Fatherhood* and his television role as a father, has his Sun in Cancer. So do newspaper columnists and sisters Ann Landers and Abigail Van Buren, who have offered advice to families for decades. Your family is at the center of your life, and whether or not your experiences with family members are positive, your ties to them are strong. Your family provides you with a sense of security and belonging. It is hard for you to see yourself as an independent entity, for your role within the family structure is integral to your self-image and usually overshadows your sense of individuality. Even as an adult, you may have difficulty breaking away from your parents and their expectations, or living a lifestyle which is different than theirs.

The sign Cancer also is associated with mother and motherhood, and both men and women with this Sun sign are strongly attached to their mothers. At their best, men tend to be caring, respectful, protective and devoted to their mothers; at worst they are neurotically dependent "mamas' boys," who never untie the apron strings and expect all women to be substitute mothers. Women see their roles as mothers as all-important, and often think of themselves as mothers first, people second. For example, former U. S. First Lady Nancy Reagan has her Sun in Cancer, and husband Ronald refers to her as "Mommy." Whether your feelings toward your own mother are fond and loving, or hostile and resentful, you probably have trouble severing the umbilical cord.

You love children and if you don't have any offspring of your own, you are probably an adoring aunt/uncle, godparent, teacher, or work with children in some way. Mother Francesca Cabrini, who founded orphanages and missions and was dedicated to helping children in need, had her Sun in Cancer. So do television personalities Captain Kangaroo and Art Linkletter, whose shows were centered on children.

You respect the image of the traditional, nuclear family and see it as a microcosm of society. You consider your friends, co-workers, neighbors and fellow citizens as part of your extended family.

Alternative lifestyles and attitudes are threatening to you. You believe that someone is either with you or against you. The United States, for example, which insists on dividing the world up into American-allied nations and Soviet-allied nations, has its Sun in Cancer. To those whom you define as being "in your camp," you are protective and supportive. However, anyone who is too "different" is potentially dangerous and must be cast out of the group. Differences might destroy the structures and securities you've established so carefully.

You are affectionate and generous toward those you love and enjoy doing things for them. You especially like cooking for your family and friends, and are fond of having people come to your home for dinner, particularly on holidays. The "Jewish Mother" cliché fits you perfectly. A warm and gracious host, you make guests feel welcome and no one goes away from your home hungry. You might choose to use your talent for cooking professionally, as a chef, baker, restaurateur or in another area of food service. Your hospitality also could make you the ideal innkeeper.

Hard-working and ambitious, you are the perfect employee, for you are loyal, dedicated, respectful of authority and rarely question company policy. As a boss, you are supportive and protective, almost maternal, toward employees who agree with you, but intolerant of anyone you view as contradictory. You tend to surround yourself with "yes-men" who reinforce your decisions. Always a bit unsure of yourself, you try to insulate yourself from those who question your actions or motives.

Conservative and traditional in your personal and political beliefs, you are not very open-minded or tolerant of new or progressive ideas or methods. You only feel safe and comfortable with things that are established, tried-and-true. You fear taking chances and cling to the past, only making changes when you are forced to do so.

Money is very important to you, not for what it can buy (as is the case with Taurus) or because it frees you to do what you want (as is true of Sagittarius), but because it gives you a sense of security and status. At your core, you feel dependent, even defenseless. You seem to be at the mercy of your ever-changing and powerful emotions. Consequently, you attempt to find security, stability and protection in external things and amassing large reservoirs of cash, stocks and real estate make you feel more secure. Or, you may work for a large, stable company that provides you much-needed job security as well as a sense of being part of a larger family. You also tend to look to your family and/or partner for security.

Sun in Leo

The Sun is in Leo from about July 23 to August 22, though this varies slightly from year to year. Among other things, Leo is the sign of entertainment, leisure and play, and in many countries, the peak vacation period occurs while the Sun is in Leo.

People who have the Sun in Leo are generally good-natured, enthusiastic, confident and gregarious. You are an amiable and well-liked companion, popular with men and women, young and old alike. Your favorite role, however, is that of the lover and you can be amorous and ardent. Actually, you are in love with being in love, with being the center of your beloved's attention and with the excitement and drama of love's first blush.

Leo is the sign of self-expression, and you seek to express yourself with flair in all you do. Highly creative, you may choose some artistic form through which to express yourself. Maxfield Parrish, Henry Moore, Marcel Duchamp and

Andy Warhol are only a few artists whose charts feature Sun in Leo. At the very least, you love beauty and don't hesitate to adorn yourself and your home with fine (and often showy) clothing, furnishings and artwork. Fashion designers Coco Chanel and Yves Saint Laurent are two good examples of Sun in Leo.

Or, you may consider your children to be expressions of your creativity. Most likely, you enjoy children, especially their vitality and *joie de vivre.* At best, you are an inspiration to your sons and daughters, a loving benefactor and protector; at worst, you can be a petty despot and treat your children as your subjects and slaves.

Though you have a high opinion of yourself, you need others to reinforce your ego and to serve as your admirers and followers. In short, you need an audience. It is important for you to be the focus of everyone's attention and you will do just about anything to keep the spotlight on yourself. Rock stars Mick Jagger and Peter Townsend, and TV evangelist Jerry Falwell, for example, have their Suns in Leo. This desire to be at center stage might lead you to a career in the theatre. Actors Dustin Hoffman, Robert De Niro, Robert Mitchum, Robert Redford and Arnold Schwarzenegger and actresses Lucille Ball, Clara Bow, Shelley Winters, Maureen O'Hara and Mae West are some examples of Sun in Leo. Whether or not you pursue acting professionally, however, you have a natural talent for drama and theatrics which you likely employ in all areas of your life. With your powerful persona, regal bearing and lack of modesty, you make your presence known in any crowd.

You see your "role" in life as that of the leader. You possess natural leadership ability and project such confidence and authority that you inspire others to follow you unquestioningly. MVP and Cy Young Award-winning pitchers Vita Blue of the Oakland Athletics and Roger Clemens of the Boston Red Sox, who led their teams to the World Series, have their Suns in Leo. So do basketball greats Wilt Chamberlain and Magic Johnson.

However, you feel you should automatically be granted power, as if by Divine right, and might not be willing to work your way to the top. Though you are ambitious you can be lazy, and only want to work at jobs that offer you prestige, glamor, power or a good time, where you can exhibit your "star" quality and garner the attention and respect of others.

You long to be "king," to have absolute authority and the total devotion and adoration of all. French Emperor Napoleon Bonaparte and Italian dictator Benito Mussolini, for instance, had their Suns in Leo. So does Cuban leader Fidel Castro. Though you'd prefer to be a benevolent monarch, you can be ruthless and cruel to those who don't show you the respect you feel you deserve. You can't bear insubordination or anything that injures your enormous but rather fragile ego.

Your greatest gift is your ability to inspire others, whether on the battlefiel d, the playing field or the stage. Your greatest failings, however, result from your exaggerated sense of self-importance and prideful arrogance.

Sun in Virgo

The Sun is in Virgo from about August 23 throught September 22, though it can vary slightly from year to year. Work and study are connected with this sign; while the Sun is in Virgo students go back to school after the summer holiday and Labor Day is celebrated in the United States.

People who have their Suns in Virgo are usually hard-working, conscientious, meticulous and well-organized. You pride yourself on your efficiency and your dedication to duty, and you can always be depended on to get the job done. What you lack in creativity you make up for with effort. You express yourself in practical ways and want to see the results of your work. Modest and unpretentious, you consider yourself and "ordinary guy" and identify with the common people rather than the elite. Former U.S. President Lyndon Johnson, for example, had his Sun in Virgo.

Methodical and analytical, you have an eye for detail that could serve you well in careers that require precision and accuracy, such as accounting, tailoring, watchmaking, dentistry, drafting, microbiology, engraving or finish carpentry. For instance, Dr. Walter Koch, mathematician and developer of the Koch system of astrological house division, had his Sun in Virgo. You patiently and diligently work to hone you skills, always striving for perfection. Golfer Arnold Palmer and conductor Leonard Bernstein are two examples of people with Sun in Virgo who have painstakingly developed their skills to a high degree of excellence.

However, you need to guard against carrying you perfectionism to extremes. Your focus on individual details often causes you to miss the larger picture. The expression "can't see the forest for the trees" certainly describes you.

You expect yourself and everyone around you to be perfect, but because your expectations are impossibly high, you set yourself up for disappointment. Your outlook is often rather negative, and you can be overly critical and "picky," finding fault with things that others don't even notice.

You see you "role" in life as serving others, and frequently prefer to remain in the background, in a support position, rather than grabbing the spotlight. Timid, shy and self-effacing, you tend to undervalue yourself and, as a result, often allow yourself to be taken advantage of by others. You rarely seek rewards or recognition for what you do. When others take you for granted, however, you become bitter, complaining and resentful, yet you still might not stand up for yourself.

Exceptionally neat and orderly, you can be a bit neurotic about cleanliness. You may wash your hands every fifteen minutes, brush your teeth after every cup of herb tea and wouldn't think of wearing the same shirt twice without washing it. Your desk is the epitome of organization, your checkbook is always balanced, and unless your Moon is in Pisces, Scorpio or Aquarius, your home probably looks a bit like an operating room.

Also fastidious about your health, you worry excessively about germs, take your vitamins and are fussy about what you eat. Sensitive, nervous and not particularly vital or energetic, you might experience a variety of stress-related illnesses. When you're upset, you are more likely than other people to suffer from problems with the digestive system. Your interest in health and nutrition might lead you to pursue a career in a medical or dietary field — which also would satisfy your desire to serve and help others. Mother Teresa, who is known for her selfless work with the world's sick and starving, has her Sun in Virgo. So did nurse and activist Margaret Sangar, who founded America's first birth control clinic.

Sun in Libra

The Sun enters Libra at the fall equinox, and remains in this sign from about September 23 to October 22, though it can vary slightly from year to year.

Libra is the sign of balance and harmony, and you see your "role" in life as that of the peacemaker. Mahatma Gandhi, who stressed peaceful rebellion in

India's struggle for independence from Britain, is a good example of Sun in Libra. English Quaker and founder of Pennsylvania, William Penn, also had Sun in Libra. So vital are peace and tranquility to you that the least sign of discord upsets you. You can't bear anger, hostility or conflict of any kind, nor can you stand to have anyone mad at you. You strive for peace at any cost, and often fail to speak your mind for fear of starting an argument or alienating someone. Always ready to compromise in order to keep the peace, you may let others take advantage of you or back down when you should take a stand. As a result, you sometimes seem wishy-washy or unreliable.

You are the one called in to mediate family disputes or on-the-job squabbles. Because you can see both sides of any issue and remain a detached and impartial judge, you are well-suited to this task and may even put this skill to work for you professionally. Former U. S. President Jimmy Carter, who negotiated a peace settlement between warring Middle Eastern powers, has his Sun in Libra.

Your ability to see merit in all sides of any issue, however, causes you to have difficulty making decisions about even simple things in life, such as which movie to see or what to have for dinner. When faced with larger decisions, you might vacillate indefinitely.

Tactful, refined, diplomatic and socially adept, you are concerned with saying and doing the "right things." You want to make a good impression and to have everyone like you. Your personal appearance is neat and attractive, your manners are impeccable, and you value such things as etiquette and social graces as ways to set you apart from the *hoi polloi.* You share Virgo's love of cleanliness and order, and want everything to be "nice" at all times. The grande dame of etiquette, Emily Post, had her Sun in Libra.

Because you are intent on maintaining balance and harmony at all times, you shun strong emotion of any kind. Emotions are too unpredictable, messy and even dangerous, and you prefer to remain detached. Although you are superficially pleasant and friendly, you can be a bit bloodless. Your dispassionate nature, however, allows you to see things in a detached, rational manner, and you might be a master strategist. Dwight D. Eisenhower, who had his Sun in Libra, was noted for this when he was a general. At the very least, you are good at laying plans, organizing people and objectively analyzing situations.

Your love of balance and harmony incline you to appreciate music, art and all beautiful things. Even if you don't have any special talent yourself, you probably enjoy most art forms and might be a patron of the arts. You have good taste, though you tend to be overly traditional and not very imaginative.

Libra also is the sign of relationships, and relationships of all kinds are important to you. Unless you are involved in a partnership you don't quite feel whole, and you'll settle for a relationship that is less than ideal just to have someone around. You think of yourself as half a couple instead of as an individual, and will hold on to an unsatisfactory marriage for decades rather than have to face yourself alone. Always willing to put your partner's needs and desires ahead of your own, you may have trouble even deciding what you really want, since you are so intent on trying to figure out what your partner wants.

You take great joy in your partner's happiness, and bask in the reflected glory of his/her successes. Supportive and dedicated to helping your mate achieve his/her goals, you may be content with being thought of only as your partner's "other half." Or, you may achieve success or recognition through your partner. Eleanor Roosevelt, wife of Franklin D. Roosevelt, and Farah Diba Pahlavi, wife of the former Shah of Iran, are two such examples of Sun in Libra.

Although you invest much time and energy in relationships, you don't invest much feeling or passion. Formalized partnerships appeal to you more than torrid love affairs, and you'd really like to return to the days of courtly romance, chivalry and idealized love. John Lennon, for example, who had his Sun in Libra, wrote dozens of idealized love songs. For you, love exists more in the head than in the heart.

Sun in Scorpio

The Sun is in Scorpio from about October 23 to November 22, though it can vary slightly from year to year. In many parts of the northern hemisphere, this is a time of death: the trees have lost their leaves, hibernating animals crawl into their burrows for the winter and birds depart for more hospitable regions. The sign Scorpio is associated with death, decay and transformation.

People who have Sun in Scorpio usually experience lives filled with dramatic, even traumatic changes, and encounter situations which transform them in some way. It seems that old parts of you are continually dying and new parts are being born, so that your life is never static.

You also have the ability to strongly affect others, even to change their lives, and you see your "role" as that of the transformer. Perhaps you are a therapist who helps people uncover and work through their deep-seated problems. You might be a teacher who awakens hidden talents in your students, a councilor who rehabilitates substance abusers, or a rapist who terrorizes victims. Regardless of the form your influence takes, you transform everyone you know in some way. You have a powerful, almost magnetic persona, and though you may not say much it's impossible not to be aware of your presence.

As a child, you probably experienced some deep, emotional "crisis," a loss of some kind which made you feel you were alone in the world, with no one but yourself on whom to rely. Sometimes this crisis is an obvious and extreme one, such as the death of a parent, the loss of your home, a serious illness or a violent incident. In other cases, it may be more subtle and internal, such as coming to the realization that your parents will never love you the way you want them to. As a result, you withdraw into yourself, becoming skeptical and self-reliant at a very early age.

When you were a child, you insisted on doing everything for yourself and were quite content to spend time alone, entertaining and teaching yourself. As an adult, you are self-protective and suspicious of others, hiding your thoughts and feelings behind an almost impenetrable wall. Very few people earn your trust, fewer still gain access into your private world and no one will ever know you completely.

Although you reveal little about yourself, you want to know everything about everyone else. You are eager to find out what makes others tick, and delve into the secrets and hidden agendas of friends, family members and business associates. By understanding their underlying motivations and desires, you can manipulate them for your own advantage, or at least anticipate their moves to protect yourself. You'd be a good psychiatrist or private investigator, for you understand human nature— especially the dark side of life—better than anyone. Russian novelist Fyodor Dostoyevsky, for instance, had his Sun in Scorpio. So does movie director Martin Scorcese, whose films often depict life's dark underbelly.

You approach everything with intensity and passion; nothing is done half-heartedly. An extremist, you throw yourself heart, mind and soul into any undertaking. Former U. S. Attorney General Robert Kennedy, for instance, had his Sun in Scorpio. In your career, you can accomplish more than most people. Your perseverance and your ability to focus your energies toward a goal can take you to the top of your field. However, you also run the risk of becoming a workaholic.

No one takes relationships more seriously than you. Though Scorpio has a reputation for being intensely sexual, what you truly desire is an intense emotional connection. You want to merge with your partner in every way. Only rarely do you give your affection to another, and you expect your mate's total devotion and fidelity. Highly emotional, you know how deeply you can be hurt and are reluctant to leave yourself open to potential pain. When you do fall in love, however, you immerse yourself completely in the relationship. You see your partner as an extension of yourself and can be extremely possessive and jealous. If betrayed, you find it impossible to forgive and forget, and may become vengeful, vindictive, even violent.

You have uncanny intuition, keen perception and make instantaneous emotional connections with other people. You seem to see into their unconscious minds and thus appear to be psychic. This natural psychic ability coupled with your desire to discover the inner workings of the Universe may lead you to become interested in the occult arts. Dr. Israel Regardie, who revealed the secrets of the Golden Dawn, had his Sun in Scorpio. However, you need to guard against developing your powers for the purpose of manipulating others or the forces of nature.

Power and control issues are likely to arise frequently in your life. Perhaps you experienced your father (or your dominant parent) as being authoritarian, domineering, even cruel. You may have trouble with authority figures and employers who attempt to overpower, control or manipulate you. It is important to realize that you, too, desire power and total control, and are inclined to try to dominate others. The former Shah of Iran, Mohammed Reza Pahlavi, for instance, had his Sun in Scorpio. The Soviet Union is another example of the Sun in Scorpio. Stubborn and willful, you want your own way and are reluctant to compromise or answer to someone else for your behavior. And, you can be ruthless in pursuit of your desires or goals.

Your greatest gift is your power to destroy old, worn-out structures and give birth to new ones. Your greatest failings usually result from your extremism and your intense desire for power and domination.

Sun in Sagittarius

The Sun is in Sagittarius from about November 22 through December 21, though it can vary slightly from year to year. In many countries, this is a month of holiday festivities, of indulgence, celebrating, socializing and feasting. It is also a period of generosity, filled with the spirit of giving, when budgets are stretched to buy Christmas and Hanukkah presents. The sign Sagittarius is associated with pleasurable social activity, good cheer, expansiveness and excess.

People who have their Suns in Sagittarius are generally jovial, friendly, fun-loving souls who know how to have a good time and never take life too seriously. Optimistic and future-oriented, you don't let problems or disappointments get you down for long. You quickly put failures behind you and immediately start planning your next great adventure or million-dollar scheme. Never satisfied with just getting by, you want to do things on a grand scale, to make it big and live life to the fullest.

Your glibness, self-confidence and positive attitude make you the quintessential salesperson, and you could sell running shoes to a cheetah. However, you lack the organization and perseverance to see projects through to completion, and are much better at starting things than completing them. You tend to overestimate yourself and often promise more than you can deliver. Consequently, you might earn yourself a reputation for being unreliable. You rarely get anyplace or finish anything on time and are usually over budget. Somehow, though, things work out in the end—Lady Luck seems to smile on you—and despite your irresponsibility and rather cavalier attitude, it's hard to stay mad at you for long.

Your quick wit and ready humor make you a much-loved companion, and you lift the spirits of everyone around you. Comedians Woody Allen, Richard Pryor, Harpo Marx, Dick Van Dyke, Bette Midler and cartoonist Charles Schulz all have their Suns in Sagittarius. You tie together the mundane and the cosmic in unexpected ways, and help us laugh at ourselves and the world around us.

You have a vivid imagination and may seek to enhance the monotony of daily life with fantasy. Walt Disney, for example, had his Sun in Sagittarius. So did artist Paul Klee, writer Mark Twain, and the author of *Gulliver's Travels,* Jonathan Swift. However, you sometimes try to avoid reality through escapism, and may be unwilling to assume responsibilities such as earning a living, paying your bills, committing to a relationship or taking care of your children.

Expanding your horizons in every possible way is your primary goal in life. You are eager to learn everything you can, preferably through personal experience. You want to see the world, meet interesting people and try everything once. You like to listen to radio talk shows, watch television programs about exotic places and read *National Geographic.* Your boundless curiosity (which sometimes borders on voyeurism) could lead you to a career in journalism.

You see your "role" in life as that of the teacher, bringing knowledge to all. John Harvard, founder of Harvard University, had his Sun in Sagittarius. Facts and figures, however, don't interest you much; you're in search of knowledge on a broader scale and enjoy discussing abstract concepts and universal truths. You may be a student of religion, metaphysics, psychology, philosophy or mythology.

You love to share your knowledge with others and can talk endlessly about your ideas and worldviews. Overly zealous at times, you are inclined to proselytize and can be something of an evangelist for your beliefs, without much tolerance for differing opinions. Spain's former head of state Francisco Franco, for example, had a Sagittarian Sun, and some astrologers believe that Spain itself, home of the infamous Spanish Inquisition, also has the Sun in Sagittarius.

You probably enjoy music, particularly jazz or music that is rather grandiose and inspiring. Beethoven, Ira Gershwin, Arthur Fiedler, Frank Sinatra, Dave Brubeck, John Mayall, Andy Williams, Jim Morrison, Jimi Hendrix, Lou Rawls, Ramsey Clark, Randy Newman and Dick Clark are a few examples of Sun in Sagittarius.

Sagittarius rules the legs, and you might enjoy sports such as running, bicycling, skiing, soccer or basketball. For example, Boston Celtics star Larry Bird has his Sun in Sagittarius. You are an enthusiastic sports fan, but may not ever become proficient in any sport yourself. You prefer to watch and bet on the games, with a beer and hot dog in hand, rather than exert the energy and effort required to play. If something isn't fun you don't want to do it, and you tend to be rather lazy and indulgent.

You are at your best when you're making others laugh and encouraging them to expand their lives, minds and experience. At your worst, you carry your happy-go-lucky, no-strings-attached attitude to extremes, and become a reckless, irresponsible and aimless wanderer.

Sun in Capricorn

The Sun enters Capricorn at the winter solstice. It remains in this sign from about December 21 through January 20, though this can vary slightly from year to year. During this time, many parts of the northern hemisphere are cold and barren. The previous month of Sagittarian revelry is over, and the bills from holiday splurging are coming due. Capricorn, then, is associated with harshness, stark reality and responsibility.

People who have their Suns in Capricorn are usually serious, hard-working, cautious and pragmatic. You may have had to assume adult responsibilities or go to work at an early age, and as a child you always seemed much older and more mature than your years. Your childhood may not have been particularly enjoyable, and perhaps you couldn't wait to grow up. Peers may have thought you were dull or uptight, and even as an adult you sometimes find it hard to relax and have fun. However, you age well, become more comfortable with yourself after turning forty, and seem to get younger as you grow older.

Conservative with your time, money and other resources, your philosophy might be "waste not, want not." You don't like to do things spontaneously or without adequate planning, and want your life to be carefully ordered and clearly defined. You also are likely to be conservative in your political and social attitudes. Traditional values and structures that have survived the test of time appeal to you most; you don't trust people, ideas or products that haven't "proved" themselves yet. U. S. Senator Barry Goldwater is a good example of Sun in Capricorn.

The quintessential career person, you take your job very seriously and are never one to shirk work or duty. Louis Pasteur, who gave us the process of pasteurization, missionary Albert Schweitzer, U. S. statesman and author Ben Franklin, and Clara Barton, founder of the Red Cross, had their Suns in Capricorn. You tend to be something of a workaholic. Ambitious and diligent, you climb your way to the top of the corporate ladder with slow, steady steps. Writer Horatio Alger, for instance, had his Sun in Capricorn. You probably won't set the world on fire and you make your own luck. Your success is based on competence, common sense and perseverance, and employers, employees and clients know they can depend on you.

Though you enjoy being in a position of power, you aren't fond of the limelight and prefer to run things from behind the scenes. You also may be ruthless, unscrupulous or unconcerned about those you step on as you move upward, adopting an attitude of "the ends justify the means." Former U. S. President Richard Nixon, FBI Chief J. Edgar Hoover, Chinese Chairman Mao Tse Tung and Russian leader Joseph Stalin are some examples of Sun in Capricorn.

Your public image is very important to you and you see your "role" as the pillar of society. You are the loyal, conscientious and reliable good citizen, the backbone of your family and community, the person who gets things done and holds it all together. Practical and predictable, you support the status quo and rarely go against majority opinion or community standards.

You tend to show your best face to the public. In private, you are less adept. You are quite shy and sensitive, though you try to hide it behind a gruff exterior. As a result, you feel more comfortable with the ordered, detached relationships of the business world than with more personal ones that can be unpredictable and emotionally demanding. Unless your Moon is in a water sign, you might feel awkward and unsure of yourself in intimate situations. Your love relationships can seem more like business partnerships or practical arrangements, and you probably subscribe to traditional attitudes when it comes to male/female roles. Though highly sensual and sexual, you aren't the "playboy" type and take your relationships seriously. You also can be something of a moralist, and tend to conceal your lasciviousness behind a refined, well-controlled, even prim exterior. TV evangelist Jim Bakker, for instance, has his Sun in Capricorn.

Your greatest gift is the structure, order and stability you provide, particularly in the public and professional spheres. Your greatest failings usually result from your coldness, rigidity and fear of change.

Sun in Aquarius

The Sun is in Aquarius from about January 21 to February 19, though this can vary slightly from year to year.

People with Sun in Aquarius are usually independent, unconventional, outspoken and fair-minded. You see your "role" in life as the rebel, the person who rejects bogus authority and outworn traditions and ushers in the new order. American revolutionary Thomas Paine, for example, had his Sun in Aquarius. So have outspoken political radicals Angela Davis and Vanessa Redgrave. However, you sometimes lack perspective in your battle with the establishment. At times, you simply provoke confrontations to see what impact you have on others, and you enjoy antagonizing people who are in positions of authority. Tennis star John McEnroe is one such example of Sun in Aquarius. You like to take chances, to keep things stirred up and relish a good argument now and again. However, you may become the rebel without a cause. Actor James Dean, for instance, had his Sun in Aquarius.

Always ahead of your time, you are seen by others as a bit different or unusual—an image you encourage. You like to shock people and shake up institutions that have become too rigid. You have the ability to bring a breath of fresh air into stale, stagnant environments. Jackie Robinson, the first black to play professional baseball, is a good example of Sun in Aquarius. So are French painter Edouard Manet and composer/musician Wolfgang Mozart, whose work broke with the accepted standards of their times.

Equality, freedom and fairness are important issues for you. You believe all people are created equal and should have the same rights and opportunities. You are willing to stand up and fight for the rights of others as well as your own, often without regard for your own safety or advantage. Former U. S. President Abraham Lincoln, who is most remembered for ending slavery, had his Sun in Aquarius. Other good examples are writers Germaine Greer, Betty Freidan, Gertrude Stein and Virginia Woolf. Most likely, you are socially and politically progressive, and are concerned with humanitarian issues. American statesman Adlai Stevenson, who had his Sun in Aquarius, is a good example. Though you are interested in the well-being of others, your interest is an abstract, ideological concept and does not stem from empathy or true feeling. Unless you also have several water signs in your chart you can be quite detached and impersonal.

Inventive and ingenious, you eagerly seek out new ways to do things and may excel in scientific or electronic fields, aerospace technology, computer science, astronomy or astrology. Inventors Thomas Edison and Nikola Tesla, for example, both had Sun in Aquarius. Generally you can be found on the cutting edge of technology and scientific or "new age" thought. Always looking to the future, you run the risk of losing touch with the present and not learning from the past.

Friendly and sociable, you probably have an extensive and diverse collection of friends and associates, and your friends are very important to you. You are not status conscious; you choose your companions for their ideas and enjoy the company of others of like mind. Intellectually oriented (though not necessarily intelligent), you are happiest in the world of ideas. You love to share what you know with others and become bored easily with people who don't provide grist for your mental mill. Although at times you can be a bit abrasive and tactless, you are usually good-natured, enthusiastic, off-beat and willing to try almost anything—qualities which gain you popularity among your peers. You are most comfortable in group situations and might belong to numerous organizations, clubs, professional or social groups.

However, you may have some trouble in intimate, personal relationships since your feelings don't run very deep and you tend to be quite detached. Close emotional relationships also can threaten your independence. You insist on remaining "free" to do your own thing, and to engage in relationships with whomever you please. Unless your Venus and/or Moon are in more emotional, possessive signs (such as Scorpio, Cancer or Taurus) you may decide to remain single or insist on an "open marriage."

At your best, you are the one who fights for liberty and justice for one and all. At your worst, you are the freedom monger who seeks change for the sake of change, without offering a better alternative to replace the structures you've destroyed.

Sun in Pisces

The Sun is in Pisces from about February 20 through March 20, though this can vary slightly from year to year.

People who have their Suns in Pisces are usually sensitive, shy, introverted, emotional and compassionate. Peace-loving, kind-hearted and passive, you recoil from all forms of violence, coarseness and aggression. Christianity, for instance, with its emphasis on peace and love, often is considered to be a Piscean religion. Your gentle spirit is easily bruised and you need regular periods of quiet isolation, to rest, meditate or simply restore your inner balance.

You see your "role" as the savior/martyr, and frequently help others at your own expense. Because Pisces is a non-personal sign, more concerned with the universal than the individual, you rarely consider yourself first. In fact, you may neglect yourself altogether, either through sacrificing yourself for an ideal, another person or God, through religious asceticism, or through ignoring your health and your body's needs. For this reason, Pisces sometimes is called the sign of self-undoing. At times, it may seem that you follow the most harmful or unproductive course, or get involved with people who aren't good for you. Your ego isn't very strong and you may lack self-esteem and confidence. Consequently, your attitudes and behavior are sometimes self-destructive.

You are more concerned with others' well-being than your own, and want to save people from themselves. Sympathetic to the plight of the world's unfortunates, you'd like to bring home every stray animal and helpless soul you meet. You are easily taken in by a hard-luck story and often leave yourself open to being used. Tender-hearted and non-judgmental, you are always there with a shoulder to cry on and a cup of herb tea for a friend in need. Friend and stranger alike tell you their problems and you not only commiserate with them, you actually feel their pain. Your sympathetic and supportive nature is a soothing balm for those in need. However, you have to guard against letting others influence you too strongly or take advantage of you.

Your caring nature and concern for the welfare of others may lead you to a career in social services, psychology, nursing, nutrition, veterinary medicine or religion. Nutritionist and author Adelle Davis had her Sun in Pisces. Ralph Nader and Massachusetts Senator Edward Kennedy, staunch advocates of human rights, also have Sun in Pisces.

Your sensitivity to others allows you to tune into their unconscious sides, and you often seem to know what they are thinking or feeling. As a result of your keen intuition and your fascination with the spiritual realm, you may become interested in the psychic or mystical arts. Prophet Edgar Cayce and witch Sybil Leek, both recognized psychics, and occultist Rudolf Steiner are good examples of Sun in Pisces.

Most likely, you have an artistic sensibility and may possess musical, poetic or other artistic talents. The birth chart of Renaissance artist Michelangelo, for example, features Sun in Pisces. So do the charts of painters Winslow Homer and Pierre Renoir, writers Anaïs Nin, Henry Wadsworth Longfellow, John Steinbeck and Elizabeth Browning, singers George Harrison, Nat King Cole, and Liza Minnelli, film maker Bernardo Bertolucci and composers Frédéric Chopin, Antonio Vivaldi and Maurice Ravel. At the very least, you probably appreciate art and music, and are sensitive to color, tone and rhythm.

Overly idealistic, you sometimes find it hard to live in the physical world and deal with the harsh realities of earthly existence. The non-physical realms may be more real to you than the physical one, and you rarely seem to have both feet on the ground. You might forget to pay bills, keep appointments or put gas in the car. Your unwillingness to deal with practical issues might cause you to become dependent on others to take care of you physically and/or financially. At times you appear "spacey" or unfocused, lost in daydreams and fantasies. This can be the source of great imagination and creativity—author Dr. Seuss, creator of fanciful children's books, is a good example of Sun in Pisces—but it also can be dangerous if carried too far. You have a tendency to retreat into your own fantasy world in order to avoid responsibilities, painful experiences or other difficult "real-life" situations. In the extreme, you may escape through alcohol, drugs, insanity or religious isolation.

Your greatest gifts are your compassion and your all-encompassing love for the least as well as the greatest of God's creatures. Your greatest failings usually result from refusing to face facts and learn the lessons of earthly existence.

Notes

1. Liz Greene, *Star Signs for Lovers* (New York: Day Books/Stein and Day Publishers, 1981), p. 40.

2. Stephen Arroyo, *Astrology, Psychology and the Four Elements* (Davis, CA: CRCS Publications, 1975), p. 77.

Chapter Four

The Moon

The Moon represents your *yin* side, the part which is inner-directed, passive, receptive, reflective, responsive. It is associated with the emotions, intuition and the feeling nature. The sign in which the Moon is placed shows the "color" of your emotions. The Moon also indicates the manner in which you respond to stimuli, how you sense or intuit things unconsciously without filtering them through your rational mind.

Throughout history, cultures have regarded the Moon as a symbol of fertility. Along with Cancer, its sign of rulership, the Moon represents "mother" and all things connected with motherhood. Its placement in your chart is indicative of your relationship with your mother and your feelings about her. In a family of several children, each will view the same mother differently, in accordance with his/her Moon sign. What "feeds" or nurtures you and how you provide nurturing—to your own children, your friends, or other members of the human race—are also shown by your Moon.

Mother is your first connection with the physical world; thus the Moon describes your early years and your past in general. It reveals deeply-ingrained, habitual patterns and responses that reside below the level of consciousness. Under stress or when you are tired or ill, you revert back to instinctive Moon behavior, for this is what comes most naturally to you.

The home—both that in which you were raised and that which you establish for yourself in adulthood—is the Moon's domain. How you feel about your childhood home, as well as where you choose to live as an adult, with whom, what you do in your home, even how you furnish it are all shown by the position of your natal Moon. The home also provides security and protection. Thus your Moon describes your needs for security and protection and how you go about satisfying those needs. It reveals how you behave when you are unguarded and vulnerable as well as what makes you feel comfortable and relaxed.

Your Moon also shows innate talents, abilities or "gifts," and what comes naturally and easily to you. But because these are rooted in the past, you may not value them so highly as the ones associated with your Sun or Ascendant sign. You may repress your Moon-side or look at it askance, as the "black sheep" of your astrological chart.

In all relationships, especially those of a close, personal nature, the Moon is extremely important. As the seat of your emotions, it is involved in all interpersonal interactions which engage your feelings. First impressions are generally Moon responses to others. Deep, emotional bonds between people are often Moon connections. The relationship between two individuals' Moons is a good indicator of whether they feel tense or comfortable in each other's company, and compatible Moons often create a positive link that can be beneficial in day-to-day living or working situations.

Because the Moon embodies one of the female archetypal energies, women generally find it easier to relate to than men do. Some women demonstrate their Moon-sign characteristics more obviously than their Sun-sign ones. Men, on the other hand, are more likely to repress their Moon sides or to project them on to the women in their lives. Or, they may express their Moon natures only to people they trust or with whom they feel comfortable—family members, close friends, lovers.

The Moon travels through all twelve zodiacal signs every twenty-eight days. Its house position in the birth chart, the aspects between the Moon and other planets, as well as your level of development also will be important in interpreting the Moon.

Moon in Aries

Regardless of your age, you're still a child at heart. Playful, fun-loving, enthusiastic and rather naïve, each day is new to you and full of adventures. You have an irrepressible *joie de vivre* and people like you in spite of themselves, and might describe you as a bit of a scoundrel. Writer Mark Twain, for example, had his Moon in Aries.

However, you also can behave like a spoiled brat at times. Argumentative and assertive, you are known for your emotional outbursts and your quick temper. Your anger is usually short-lived, though, and once you've aired it you're ready to get on with the business at hand. You could engage in a no-holds-barred fist fight then go out for a drink with your opponent when it's all over.

Fiercely competitive, you like nothing better than a good challenge with a worthy opponent. Most likely, you have natural athletic ability and are happiest when on the playing field. Tennis star Martina Navratilova, for example, has her Moon in Aries. Even if you aren't MVP material, you probably possess boundless energy and vitality, enjoy a game of backyard softball with your "jock" friends and wouldn't miss the Superbowl to have dinner with the President.

However, you tend to see everyone as a potential opponent and every interpersonal interaction as a contest. Your relationships sometimes resemble boxing matches—figuratively or literally. Intensely individualistic, it's almost impossible for you to see another's point of view. Nor are you willing to compromise on most issues, and diplomacy is a foreign word to you. Brusque, abrasive and often tactless, you rarely hold your tongue and can hurt other people's feelings without realizing it. If you're involved with someone who also relishes an occasional shouting match (an Arien or Aquarian, for example) you'll probably be best buddies, though you'll never convince your neighbors of it. You aren't likely to stay with a partner who won't stand up to you, however. Strongly sexual but not sensual, you approach love and relationships with gusto, but fall short when it comes to romance and affection.

You live in the here-and-now; you never look back and rarely more than a few weeks ahead. As a result, you don't learn from your mistakes. You also have a great deal of trouble making plans or laying the groundwork for future projects. In truth, you don't want things to be too carefully worked out in advance; it's the unexpected that makes life exciting.

You never learned to play by the rules, and might be considered something of a renegade. Isadora Duncan, for example, had Moon in Aries and was a maverick in the world of dance and in her personal life. Your successes in life come from taking chances, or as Tom Wolfe put it in his book *The Right Stuff,* "pushing the outside of the envelope." You are both courageous and reckless. As a result, you tend to be accident prone, for you never look before you leap.

There may have been lots of turmoil, competition or aggressiveness, even violence in your family when you were young and heated arguments were frequent. Or, perhaps you were raised in an athletic or military family. Because Aries represents one of the archetypal male energies, your parents probably encouraged traditional male values and behavior rather than female ones. Your mother may have been the dominant parent and somewhat masculine; at least she was strong, independent, feisty and assertive.

You adore children, partially because you've never entirely grown up yourself. You especially enjoy playing with them, but can be a bit rough at times. When it comes to discipline, however, you are a little lax. (You're not very good at disciplining yourself, either.) You also tend to be irresponsible, and may not be very good about such things as making child support payments, helping with homework or being there when your kids need you.

Women with this Moon placement are anything but "feminine" in the traditional sense. Strong-willed and assertive, you rarely back down from a contest and don't believe there's anything a man can do that you can't do better. More comfortable with men than with women, you probably have many male friends who think of you as "one of the guys." Some men project their Arien-Moon sides on to the women in their lives and are attracted to independent, brash, outspoken, dynamic and/or athletic women.

Moon in Taurus

Easy-going, even-tempered and good-natured, you are a pleasant companion and a devoted friend. It takes a lot to make you mad; you're a lover, not a fighter. You don't waste a lot of emotional energy worrying over trifles or engaging in life's intrigues and melodramas.

Your needs and desires are simple, down-to-earth and of a practical, physical nature. Sensual and strongly sexual, your enjoyment of sex is direct and unabashed, and you have an innate understanding of what makes people feel good. You are nurtured by all kinds of physical contact, and are especially fond of hugs and back rubs. With friends and lovers you can be quite demonstrative, and even like to touch casual acquaintances and total strangers when you talk to them.

No lover of yours will ever feel starved for affection, though s/he might feel smothered at times by your possessiveness. You understand the world in terms of material goods and ownership, and tend to forget that people are not possessions. Generous with those you care about, you need to guard against trying to buy love. Not above being "bought" yourself, you might be of the opinion that it's just as easy to fall in love with a rich wo/man as a poor one, and the road to your heart may lead through Tiffany's. You tend to measure someone by what s/he owns and are inclined to look only at a partner's physical appearance and portfolio; thus, you can be quite superficial in your choice of mates.

Your fondness for wealth and your innate understanding of the material world might result in natural business sense or a gift for making money. Chrysler's Lee Iacocca is a good example of Moon in Taurus.

You need stability, predictability and a sense of permanence in your life. You don't make changes easily, aren't interested in anything new or "different," and are anything but spontaneous. Once you settle in—to a job, a home or a relationship—you want to stay put, forever. Consequently, you are a loyal and steadfast partner. However, you are also terribly stubborn. Like a large, slow-moving oil tanker, it's almost impossible to turn you around (mentally, physically or emotionally) once you've set your course.

This characteristic may show up in your socio/political attitudes, too. You are inclined to be cautious, conservative and concerned with material, practical day-to-day issues. The birth charts of former U. S. President Ronald Reagan, political theorist Karl Marx, and theologian John Calvin show Taurean Moons.

You love your creature comforts and appreciate beautiful clothing, jewelry, furniture, art, good wine and food. Extremely indulgent, especially when it comes to sensory pleasures, you hate to deny yourself anything and are usually in debt. Your possessions also give you a sense of self-worth and stability.

You have innate good taste; your home seems to be waiting for *House Beautiful's* photographers and your wardrobe is right out of *Vogue* magazine. Your "good taste" usually includes fine food and drink, and if you aren't a gourmet chef, you at least enjoy cooking and eating well. Your motto might be "eat, drink and be merry." And since you're not fond of exercise, you have a tendency to put on weight.

Most likely, you possess some artistic ability and good color sense. Your natural talents probably lean toward sculpture, interior decorating, theatre set design, pottery, or other art forms that involve three dimensional objects and the use of physical space.

The home in which you were raised was probably stable, materially secure and relatively placid (unless Mars, Uranus or Pluto is in hard aspect to your Moon). Intellectual stimulation may have been minimal, but your physical needs were always taken care of (unless the Moon and Saturn are in hard aspect). Your parents might have emphasized material things; either they were financially well-off, or were eager to appear so. Your mother, in particular, (or your nurturing parent) was probably affectionate, attentive to your needs and dependable. She also may have been a good cook and was dedicated to making the home as pleasurable as possible. However, you might have felt a bit limited or smothered by your mother, and she probably tried to keep you tied tightly to her apron strings.

With your own children, you also are loving, affectionate and overly protective. You can't imagine your children as independent entities, and might even think of them as your possessions. You want them to have the best of everything, lavish them with gifts and probably spoil them shamelessly.

Women usually respond to this energy easily and openly. Men sometimes project it on to the women in their lives, and may be attracted to women who are affectionate, domestic, earthy, strongly sexual and sensual.

Moon in Gemini

You are generally easy-going and good-natured, and rarely stay angry or unhappy for long. Friendly, gregarious and sociable, you probably have a large circle of friends, lovers and acquaintances. You enjoy parties and get-togethers of all sorts, and will find any excuse to socialize. When you can't visit with friends or family members in person, you call them on the phone or write them long, chatty letters.

All types of communication interest you, and you are never at a loss for words. You probably enjoy reading, writing, languages, word games, and of course, talking. Many people with this Moon placement have natural writing ability; the birth charts of Nathaniel Hawthorne, Henry David Thoreau, Franz Kafka and Saul Bellow all feature Gemini Moons.

You are always eager to meet new people and want to experience as many different kinds of relationships as possible. As a result, you find it almost impossible to remain faithful to one partner for long. You might miss out on something! Quantity is more important than quality to you, and you are inclined to be fickle. You'd prefer to have two (or more) partners simultaneously—if you can keep them from finding out about each other.

Emotionally shallow, you don't tend to form strong attachments or get deeply involved with anyone. Though you may marry or maintain long-term relationships, you never become really intimate with your partner(s). Unless you also have water signs prominent in your chart, it's almost as though you think your emotions rather than feel them. You aren't very introspective and don't examine life below the surface. Consequently, you tend to misinterpret other people's needs, motives and desires. Unless you have Scorpio or Capricorn energies prominent in your chart, you can be quite naïve and are easily duped.

Freedom is important to you and you don't want to be restricted by emotional demands. Jealousy and possessiveness have no place in your relationships, and if a partner becomes too clingy or serious, you might start looking around for someone new.

Infinitely curious, you want to know something about everything. A life-long student, you enjoy taking classes, reading, going to museums, attending lectures, socializing with people who can teach you new things, and sharing what you know with others. Ideas nourish you, and your mind never stops buzzing. Your interests are many and varied, and you'll try just about anything once. However, you have trouble sticking with anything for long and don't usually become proficient in any area. Nervous and high-strung, you are rarely still and tend to flit from one thing to another like a butterfly sampling flowers.

At an early age, you displayed your cleverness and your ability to learn quickly. You probably impressed your parents, who encouraged you to develop your mind. Perhaps your parents, or at least your mother (or nurturing parent), were intellectuals and valued mental ability. Your earliest recollections might be of your mother reading you stories or teaching you the alphabet. Your parents may have sent you to good schools and praised your mental acuity, but neglected to nurture your feeling side.

You strive to teach your own children all you can, and try to instill in them your love of knowledge. Though you enjoy talking with them, taking them places and playing games with them (non-physical ones), you aren't very comfortable showing them affection. Any sort of physical closeness can seem cloying, and your children may not get enough hugs and kisses from you.

Your physical home isn't terribly important to you and you may never choose to own property; you don't want to be tied down or be responsible for maintaining it. Probably you change residences more often than most people. Other than books, you don't tend to acquire many possessions and your home may seem rather stark and uncomfortable to those whose nesting instincts are stronger.

Because the Moon is an embodiment of female energy, women usually respond to it more easily than men do. Women with this Moon placement are likely to demonstrate their Gemini characteristics readily; men sometimes project this part of themselves on to the women in their lives and are attracted to women who are friendly, communicative, intelligent, high-strung and somewhat superficial.

Moon in Cancer

You are highly emotional and very sensitive. From day to day, your emotional state fluctuates noticeably, and you might discover that the Moon's changing phases affect you significantly. Unless many of your planets are in air and/or earth signs, you may "wear your heart on your sleeve."

Inclined to let your heart rule your head, you can have trouble making rational, detached decisions. Actually, your intuition is quite keen and you'd be wise to trust it. You have the ability to tune in to what other people are feeling and are quite psychic.

Security is of primary importance to you, but often you feel your life has no inherent stability. Thus you may attempt to find security in external things: family, country, money, your home, traditions. Your family provides a sense of belonging, as does your country on a larger scale. Your home offers protection from the dangers of the outside world. Because you fear being dependent, you can be overly concerned with having money, and believe wealth will bring the security you desire. Or, you may look to your partner to take care of you.

At the center of your universe is your family, and your children are your pride and joy. Naturally maternal and nurturing, you adore all children, not only your own, and are a strong supporter of the traditional, nuclear family. Dr. Benjamin Spock, whose books helped raise an entire generation of "baby boom" children, has Moon in Cancer.

The emotional attachments you form are strong and binding. You cling tightly to other people and it is almost impossible for you to separate your own needs from theirs. This is especially true in the case of your partner and/or children. This Moon position symbolizes the archetypal mother, but your tendency is to be a "smother" to those you love. You are willing to devote yourself entirely to your loved ones, but your love is not unconditional. You never want your children to grow up. With partners, you can be every bit as possessive and jealous as someone who has Moon in Scorpio. Even friends and employees are seen as part of your extended family, and you expect their complete loyalty and dedication.

Because you feel vulnerable and defenseless, you sometimes imagine threats to your security that are not real. A difference of opinion or lifestyle can seem downright dangerous to you. For this reason, you find it hard to tolerate individuality and diversity—in your family, workplace, city or country—and tend to view others as either being with you or against you.

Both the Moon and Cancer are associated with the mother and your mother is very important to you. Regardless of your age, it is unlikely that you've severed the umbilical cord. Your tie to her can be either positive or negative; even if you were orphaned at an early age, the loss of your mother is a significant, underlying dynamic in your life. If you live near your mother, you probably see her frequently; if career or other demands take you far from home, you undoubtedly miss her greatly.

Your own role as a parent is very important to you and you are protective, nurturing and devoted to your children. However, you may have trouble seeing your children as individuals, and need to guard against thinking of them as extensions of yourself. You also worry too much about your children and can be overly protective of them.

Providing nourishment to others is one of your fortes; you are probably a good cook, or at least enjoy cooking. The "Jewish Mother" cliché certainly describes you, and you demonstrate your love for family and friends by feeding them. You enjoy having family and friends over for dinner, and no one goes away from your home hungry. You also like to eat and appreciate fine food. However, you must guard against a tendency to use food as a substitute for emotional nourishment, and try not to overeat when what you really want is love and attention.

Going out on the town doesn't appeal to you much; you'd rather stay home with your family or partner, and prefer that others come to visit you. You especially like to celebrate holidays in your home. Your home is important to you, and you want to own the nicest one possible. Your home serves many functions for you: security, status, stability, a place where those you love can gather. Because permanence and family traditions are important to you, you'd probably like to continue living in or near your childhood home even as an adult, if possible.

Since Cancer and the Moon embody one of the female energies, women usually respond to it more easily and express it in a more obvious manner than men do. Women with this placement enjoy being mothers and homemakers, and are comfortable in traditional female roles (unless they also have Aquarius or Aries prominently figuring in their charts). They show their emotions openly and are able to empathize with others' feelings.

Men with this Moon position may project this energy on to the women in their lives, and might seek mates who provide them with the maternal nurturing and emotional support they desire. You may attempt to find a substitute mother in your partner. Like the woman with this placement, you are a devoted and protective parent, but are less likely to reveal your feelings. Frequently, the man with Moon in Cancer attempts to satisfy his needs for security by working with a large, established company where he can feel he is part of a bigger family.

Moon in Leo

Self-confident, cheerful and optimistic, your outlook on life (at least your own life) is generally sunny and not much dampens your spirits for long. You always assume that things will work out for the best, and usually they do. You have a knack for attracting people and circumstances into your life that will benefit you. A natural leader, others follow you because you project an aura of knowing what you're doing. British statesman Benjamin Disraeli, for example, had his Moon in Leo.

For you, love certainly makes the world go 'round, and in relationships, you are romantic, affectionate, generous and enthusiastic. You love the idea of being in love. Being the center of a lover's attention feeds your sizeable ego, and you like nothing better. Flattery will win you over every time, and you are rather naïve when it comes to affairs of the heart. A wily partner could separate you from everything you own, simply by doting on you and keeping you entertained.

Self-centered and rather vain, you believe everyone is as fond of you as you are of yourself. You probably flirt with everyone you meet, but it's because you thrive on constant attention, not because you are inherently fickle. Once committed to a relationship, you are generally a loyal and devoted partner. You desperately need to be loved and approved of, and nothing hurts you more than being unappreciated—unless it's being humiliated in public. The one offense you can't forgive is someone stepping on your pride.

You have an innate sense of the dramatic and always do things with a flair. A natural showman, you can be quite entertaining and are often the life of the party. Circus leader P. T. Barnum and colorful band leader/singer Cab Calloway are two good examples of Moon in Leo. Perhaps you dress in an exotic, flamboyant manner, or in the height of style. Perhaps you are a talented actor or entertainer, always ready to perform for an audience. However, you need to be careful of being loud or showy simply to get attention.

Your natural abilities probably include some sort of artistic talent, and you are quite creative. In addition, your self-confidence allows you to keep on believing in yourself, regardless of what others think—a necessity in fields like art or the theatre.

Quite likely you use your creativity to make your home a showplace. You may have a gift for interior design and are good with color, though your taste is never subtle and can tend toward garishness. Your home is your castle, and you want to live like a king/queen. As a result, you are inclined to overextend yourself financially to impress others with your house and lifestyle. You enjoy entertaining at home and are a generous and gracious host/hostess.

When you were young, your mother (or nurturing parent) probably showered you with attention and reinforced your efforts so that you grew up believing you could do anything. If you displayed talent early, s/he may have enrolled you in acting or dance classes, or arranged for you to take art lessons. Though you were a bit spoiled, you were nonetheless a loving and good-natured child and perhaps the family favorite. You learned quickly that you could get almost anything you wanted without much effort. As an adult, you expect things to continue being easy and can be quite lazy.

You adore children, and especially enjoy playing with them and entertaining them with your antics and theatrics. A loving, devoted and affectionate parent, you are inclined to spoil your children. However, they never doubt that you love them and you aren't the type to put a business trip ahead of your son or daughter's Little League game. The one thing you demand, however, is respect and you won't tolerate insubordination or disobedience. Consequently, you might earn yourself a reputation in the family as a benevolent dictator.

Women with this Moon position are usually affectionate, strong-willed, self-centered and excessively concerned with their appearances. Men sometimes project this side of themselves on to the women in their lives, and may be attracted to women who are dramatic, creative, vivacious, glamorous, even a bit gaudy.

Moon in Virgo

You are not unemotional, but it is difficult for you to express what you feel. Consequently, others might consider you cold, detached, perhaps a little prudish and stuffy. Actually, you are quite sensitive and your feelings are easily hurt. To hide your vulnerability, however, you try to give the impression of being aloof and coolly professional—even in situations that call for warmth and openness.

Overly critical of yourself (and others), you assume that people will judge you harshly and find you lacking. Whether or not it's true, you probably feel that people don't like you, and may even believe there's not much about you to like. So to avoid the pain and disappointment of rejection, you keep your emotions under wraps and can be quite stingy about sharing them.

Even when your feelings are engaged, your shyness makes it hard for you to be demonstrative with your affections. Instead you express caring by doing things for the people you love: cleaning, mending, repairing a leaky faucet or running errands, for example. You want to make yourself indispensable to your loved ones so they won't be able to get along without you.

You have trouble accepting praise for what you do and perform your tasks so efficiently and modestly that others—especially your family members—don't always notice how much you do for them. This can cause you to become resentful, and you may feel you are unappreciated. When this happens, you are inclined to become irritable and complaining. You need to realize that because you tend to take on more than your share and don't stand up for yourself, you make it easy for people to take advantage of you. Be careful of falling into the role of martyr, especially with your family members. Because you feel guilty when you refuse to do something for someone else, you may allow your children, parents and/or partner to turn you into their servant.

In truth, you enjoy serving others and derive a sense of satisfaction from being able to help someone else. You are concerned about the welfare of all, particularly those who are most vulnerable or helpless. Senator Edward Kennedy, a staunch supporter of social programs, is a good example of Moon in Virgo. You are at your best when you are taking care of the sick or needy, and are willing to do even menial chores that most people find distasteful. Hard-working and conscientious, you never shy away from responsibility. Your kindness is not limited to humans, and you are probably an animal lover. Many people with this Moon position put their compassion, practicality and efficiency to work in the healing fields or social services.

As a child, you were probably the one who tried to "fix" whatever was wrong in your family. If you grew up in a dysfunctional family, you tried to make things right. If your family was poor, you may have begun working at a young age to contribute your share. If you were the oldest, you may have taken on adult responsibilities or extra chores to help out. As an adult, you're still the one family members call on for assistance, whether it's picking the kids up after school or caring for an elderly parent.

This Moon position usually indicates deep-seated feelings of inadequacy and lack of self-esteem. Perhaps when you were a child, your parents were overly-critical of you or expected you to be perfect. If you feel you haven't lived up to their expectations, you might not be satisfied with yourself or your accomplishments. You may view your mother (or your nurturing parent) as being particularly fault-finding and fussy. You also are quite critical of her yourself.

With your own children, you can be rather picky. Extremely neat and orderly yourself, you may find their messiness irritating. Though you probably don't care if your home is lavish or beautifully decorated, you want it to be clean and organized, and others (including your family members) might think you're a bit neurotic about it.

Most likely, you are interested in health and nutrition, and are very particular about your diet and your family's. For example, Frances Moore Lappé, author of the best-selling natural food cookbook *Diet for a Small Planet* has her Moon in Virgo. Some people with this Moon placement are susceptible to allergies and digestive problems, and must be careful about what they eat. Others are fussy eaters.

Your cautious, meticulous and methodical nature enable you to excel at tasks that require neatness, precision and attention to detail. You have a natural aptitude for order and organization that can be utilized in such areas as accounting/bookkeeping, tailoring, woodworking, drafting, needlepoint, model building, dentistry or working with precision instruments.

Because the Moon is the embodiment of one of the archetypal female energies, women tend to express its characteristics more easily than men do. Thus, women may readily display their Virgoan qualities, while men sometimes project these characteristics on to the women in their lives. Or, they might attract women who are modest, efficient, helpful, meticulous and/or perfectionists. Men with this Moon position also can be quite critical of the women in their lives, and of women in general.

Moon in Libra

Balance, harmony and domestic tranquility are important to you. Unless you have several other planets in water signs, your emotions are rather shallow and controlled. You don't experience intense feeling yourself and might even be offended by any strong display of emotion in others. Somehow this seems undignified to you. Though you may be romantic, you are almost courtly in your relationships; you behave according to protocol and your affection seems to be ruled more by your head than your heart.

Even-tempered, congenial, sociable and well-mannered, you are well-liked and probably have many friends and associates. In social situations you are at your best, and while you aren't the "life of the party" you are always a pleasant, thoughtful, tactful and good-natured companion.

You go out of your way to be nice to everyone, and can't stand to have anyone mad at you. Arguments, animosity or confrontations of any kind disturb you deeply. You'll do almost anything to avoid a fight. Peace-loving and diplomatic, your friends and family members probably look to you to solve disputes and negotiate compromises. Former U. S. Secretary of State Henry Kissinger, who is recognized for his skills as a negotiator, has Moon in Libra.

Too willing to compromise, you frequently allow others to take advantage of you, or you sacrifice your own wishes for someone else's. Often you're so busy trying to figure out what someone else desires that you can't decide what you want yourself. You can always see both sides of any issue and weigh decisions endlessly before making up your mind. As a result, you usually have trouble being decisive, assertive or standing up for yourself, particularly with family members and partners.

Relationships are important to you and you don't like being alone. You'll devote much time and energy to pursuing and maintaining relationships of all kinds, and are a devoted, faithful and attentive partner. Not inclined to play the field, you want one stable, reliable, congenial companion with whom you can go to concerts, the art museum, nice restaurants and civilized parties with other intelligent, refined people. For you, passionate, whirlwind love affairs are exhausting, frightening and just a little bit unseemly.

You are concerned with what others think and with doing what is correct or proper. Therefore, you are quite conventional in your social and romantic relationships and usually prefer marriage to living with a lover.

Because you don't like disagreements and because you want to maintain stability and constancy in your emotional life, you don't express dissatisfactions you may have with your relationships until the situation is terminal. You might walk away from a twenty-year marriage leaving your partner in a quandary; s/he didn't know you were unhappy since you never even had an argument! For this reason, you may be accused of being unfeeling, even cruel.

Most likely, you have some natural artistic or musical talent. Musicians Frédéric Chopin, Nat King Cole, Benny Goodman, Quincy Jones, and painter Edouard Manet are a few artists with Moon in Libra. At the very least, you appreciate art, music and the finer things in life, and might be a patron of the arts. Your home is probably tastefully, if somewhat conservatively decorated, and you want to surround yourself with as much beauty as possible. You also can be fanatical about cleanliness and neatness. If you have children, you are always picking up after them or are upset by their messiness.

Unless your Moon is in hard aspect to Mars, Uranus or Pluto, your childhood home was probably stable, orderly, harmonious, civilized, perhaps aesthetically-pleasing, where seldom was heard a discouraging word. Your mother may have been the "perfect lady" for whom nice manners, a pleasing personality and good standing in the community were all-important.

Because both the Moon and Libra are astrological representatives of archetypal female energies, this placement is usually easier for women than for men to express. Women with this Moon position are usually gentle, peace-loving, sociable, thoughtful, artistic, ultra-feminine and very concerned with their looks. They can be quite vain and devote much time, energy and money to beauty treatments, clothing and other physical adornments. Actress Zsa Zsa Gabor, for example, has Moon in Libra. Men also tend to be fashion-conscious, or at least excessively neat and clean. Some with this Moon position project these characteristics on to the women in their lives, and seek partners who are beautiful, kindly, refined, artistically-oriented and even-tempered.

Moon in Scorpio

You are extremely emotional and highly sensitive, though you hide it from others. Aware of how deeply you can be hurt, you refuse to share your feelings with someone until you are certain your affection will be reciprocated. You are almost pathologically secretive and never reveal yourself entirely, and no one knows very much about what really goes on inside you.

Intensely passionate (about all things, but especially relationships), you probably are considered highly sexual. You exude a powerful and almost mesmerizing sensuality. Actress Elizabeth Taylor, for example, has Moon in Scorpio. However, your passion is never merely physical. With your lovers, you want nothing less than total merger—emotional, spiritual and physical—and while you may settle for sexual merger when that's all you can get, casual sex doesn't satisfy you.

When you become involved with someone, you throw yourself completely into the relationship and actually feel that you and your partner are one entity. Therefore, if the relationship ends, you are devastated; it's as though you'd lost a piece of yourself.

This is also the reason behind your infamous jealousy and possessiveness, for you can't conceive of your partner as an independent individual. Power struggles and issues of control often arise in your relationships. Because your inner, emotional life can be chaotic and overwhelming, you feel a strong need to be in control of the people and situations in your external life. At times, you are domineering, authoritarian or manipulative toward your partners.

When you feel you've been betrayed, you can be vindictive and ruthless in seeking revenge. You are not an adversary to be taken lightly, for once you've made your mind up nothing stops you from achieving your goal. A genius when it comes to understanding human motivations and weaknesses, you always know intuitively what your adversary's greatest fears and vulnerabilities are and readily take advantage of them. Film maker Alfred Hitchcock, who had Moon in Scorpio, used this uncanny talent in creating his masterful suspense thrillers.

You are intrigued by what lies beneath the surface, and your desire to understand the innermost workings of people, governments, the Universe can result in an interest in psychology, espionage or the occult. Your keen perception, insight and intuition make you appear to be psychic—and perhaps you are. For example, the birth charts of sixteenth-century metaphysician and seer Nostradamus, and contemporary British occultist/writer Colin Wilson feature Moon in Scorpio.

You are an extremist in all you do, and you never pursue anything (or anyone) half-heartedly. Once you begin something—a job, a sport, a diet, and especially a relationship—you can be obsessive about it. If the situation turns out to be detrimental to your well-being, you still refuse to give it up and can become self-destructive in your obsession.

Your childhood and early home life were probably difficult, fraught with intense, emotional outbursts, intrigue, manipulation, domination, even cruelty. Your mother (or your nurturing parent) may have been authoritarian and repressive, never allowing you much freedom or individuality. The threat of violence may have been there, even if it was never acted upon. Or, you might have been threatened instead with alienation, isolation and loss of parental love if you didn't obey. Though your mother may have loved you very much, she had trouble expressing it. Or, she might have manipulated you with subtle (or not so subtle) sexual suggestiveness. Regardless of whether you feel positively or negatively about your mother, you are strongly attached to her and her influence continues long into your adulthood.

The hidden demons, the subterranean emotional turmoil, the unspoken fears and hostilities that were never brought out into the open were, perhaps, the hardest thing for you to deal with when you were young. As a child, you knew things weren't right in your family, but you couldn't talk about it. There was probably some deep, dark family secret—alcoholism, violence, insanity, sexual abuse, criminal activity, or something less dramatic—that was kept hidden.

Though you probably love your own children deeply, you may have trouble showing it, because you guard your emotions so closely. Often you find yourself behaving badly toward them even though you don't mean to, especially when they've made you worry about their safety. Intensely protective and possessive of them, you can't bear the thought of losing them. As a result, you can sometimes become overbearing, controlling and smothering.

Women with this Moon placement usually find it easier than men do to express their Scorpionic characteristics. Men sometimes project this part of themselves on to the women in their lives. As a result, you may attract women who are strongly emotional, sensual, passionate, willful and powerful. Or, you may be terrified of women because you see them as devouring, controlling, manipulative, sinister or deceitful.

Moon in Sagittarius

You are good-natured, fun-loving, optimistic and sociable. With your easy-going manner, wit and sense of humor you attract many friends and acquaintances, and are rarely without companions. You don't like to be alone and surround yourself with people and activity whenever possible.

Though your circle of friends and associates may be large and diverse, you have difficulty forming close, emotional bonds. Even with your partner and family members you are not really intimate. Family ties are rather loose and you may either live some distance from your parents, siblings and/or children, or spend much time traveling, working or engaged in activities that keep you away from home.

Perhaps you have an avid interest in sports. Although your love of the game may be sincere, it's important to realize that you also might be using this to escape from reality and to avoid anything more than superficial interaction with others. Many people with this position do have natural athletic ability, but even if you aren't particularly good at playing any game, you are probably an "armchair athlete" and enjoy watching sports. You're not adverse to placing a bet now and again, especially on the horses.

Your love relationships probably are romantic friendships rather than deep emotional commitments. You can be affectionate and enthusiastic, but your emotions are somewhat shallow and you probably are happiest with a partner who will play, socialize and go places with you. One of your deepest, most fundamental needs is to be free and unfettered, and intimacy is a bit frightening to you. As soon as you start to care about someone you begin to feel trapped. When this happens, you usually end the relationship or simply keep your emotional distance. Obviously, this can cause problems if you are involved with someone who is more serious and intense emotionally, such as a Scorpio- or Cancer-Moon individual.

You are always eager to expand your horizons—through personal experience or vicariously through the experiences of others. You enjoy learning from others and sharing ideas and adventures with them. Afraid of missing something, you are reluctant to limit yourself in your relationships. All sorts of people intrigue you and you may have trouble remaining monogamous. Italian adventurer and renowned lover, Casanova, is a good example of Moon in Sagittarius.

Optimistic and idealistic, you can always see the silver lining inside every cloud and believe things will turn out for the best. The future may seem dismal for others, but you never doubt that your own will be bright. Though you can be something of a "Pollyanna," your positive attitude and belief in yourself often bring you good fortune. You have a way of attracting people who can help you in life, and because you focus on success rather than failure, you are ready to take advantage of opportunities that come your way. Consequently, you seem to be naturally lucky. Notorious gangster and crime boss "Lucky" Luciano, for instance, had his Sun, Moon, Mercury and Mars in Sagittarius.
Even when you fail, you don't give up, and bounce back from defeats easily. However, because you never look back, you rarely learn from your mistakes.

You also have a tendency to scatter your energies, and to fail to finish what you start. Your intentions are good, but you need to be careful of promising more than you can deliver. Your inclination to think big and to overestimate yourself can lead you to go too far out on a limb and end up disappointing others. As a result, you can earn yourself a reputation for being unreliable.

You probably love to travel. Pilot and adventurer Charles Lindbergh, for example, had Moon in Sagittarius. If you aren't able to travel, you probably long to see the world and try to satisfy your desire through reading and watching TV/movies about faraway places. When you were a child, you may have moved frequently, lived abroad or traveled extensively. As an adult, you may be reluctant to buy a home of your own or to spend money furnishing it, since you don't believe that you're going to stay in one place long. Physical possessions would only tie you down.

This planetary position truly represents the rolling stone that gathers no moss. You are happiest and at your best when you are on the go, and are actually nurtured by movement. Driving appeals to you, too, but you tend to drive too fast and take too many chances on the road. If chained to a desk, or forced to stay indoors performing the same task day after day you'll be miserable. Scientist and psychoanalyst Wilhelm Reich had Moon in Sagittarius. When imprisoned, his spirit was crushed and he died.

You need physical outlets for your restlessness and energy. Running, skiing, dancing and bike-riding in particular might appeal to you. Prima ballerina Dame Margot Fonteyn, for example, has Moon in Sagittarius. Exercise can also help you keep your weight down, since you have a tendency to overindulge in food and drink.

Your mother (or your nurturing parent) was probably quite lenient with you when you were a child and encouraged you to be independent and adventurous. Perhaps she also inspired you to seek knowledge and experience wherever you could find it. As a result, you are eager to expand your understanding of the world in which you live, and might pursue philosophy, psychology, religion or metaphysics to broaden your perspective. Quite likely, you want your own children to be free to experience life to its fullest and encourage them to learn and explore everything they can. You see yourself more as a friend to your children than as an authority figure, and enjoy playing with them. When it comes to discipline, however, you can be a little lax. You might be a bit irresponsible about some of your other responsibilities to them, too, such as providing material support or being there when they need you. If Saturn stressfully aspects your Moon, you may see your children as inhibiting your freedom.

Women with this Moon placement are usually cheerful, sociable, perhaps a bit "scattered," with many diverse interests and activities filling their lives. Men with Moon in Sagittarius might seek partners who fulfill this side of them, and be attracted to women who are fun-loving, friendly, optimistic, athletic and/or philosophical. However, you have a tendency to be too idealistic about your partners and may spend most of your time searching for the perfect lover rather than settling down with any one of them.

Moon in Capricorn

Expressing your emotions is difficult for you, and others may view you as cold, rigid or unfeeling. It's also hard for you to relax and let go. All work and no play, you can seem terribly serious and even depressing at times. You fear you will be rejected if your show someone how you really feel about him/her and thus are cautious and defensive, keeping your emotions carefully under wraps.

Underlying your practical, "in-control" persona is an insecure, sensitive and very shy side.

In relationships with others, you are loyal, devoted and dependable. However, you aren't very demonstrative. If you tell your partner you love him/her on your wedding day, you don't feel you need to say it again until your Golden Wedding Anniversary. You show your caring for someone else by doing practical, physical things for him/her, by coming home dutifully every night, or by providing financial support.

Hard-working, practical and conscious of your responsibilities to others, you build carefully for the future and make certain that whatever you build—a house, a relationship, a business or a country—has a solid foundation. U. S. founding fathers George Washington and John Quincy Adams, for example, had their Moons in Capricorn.

However, you often do things for others out of a sense of duty rather than because it's what you truly want to do, and this can leave you feeling put upon or resentful. For example, if your marriage is not working out you may "stick it out" anyway because you feel you've made a commitment or because you have responsibilities to the children. You don't expect life to be easy or happy, and accept hardship as a necessary evil. Unwilling to make many changes in your life once you've settled into a routine, you are more likely than most people to endure an unsatisfactory job, home life or relationship long after you should have ended it. And, because you are both secretive and self-reliant, you aren't the type to seek outside help from a therapist or marriage counselor.

At an early age, you found it necessary to become independent and take care of yourself. Mature beyond your years, as a child you seemed to be a miniature adult. Probably you couldn't wait to grow up and may have assumed adult responsibilities when you were still quite young. Perhaps your family was poor and you had to go to work to help put food on the table. Or, if you were the oldest in a large family, you became a substitute parent to your younger siblings. Possibly your mother (or the nurturing parent) died when you were still a child or was absent for some reason, and you took on her role and duties.

In some way, your early home life was hard or barren. Even if your physical environment wasn't bleak, your emotional one certainly was. Quite likely, your mother (or the nurturing parent) was unavailable to you when you needed her.

Either she was physically absent because she was working, dead, ill or your parents were separated, or she was simply an unexpressive, restrained, serious person. You may describe your mother as severe, unloving, distant or very strict. But she also was dependable, conscious of her responsibilities to you, hard-working and efficient at managing the household. Perhaps she was the family breadwinner and also the disciplinarian. If she was a professional person, you might be proud of her career successes even if you feel you suffered emotional deprivation as a result.

With your own children, you are likely to be strict and demanding. You want them to grow up to be self-sufficient, responsible adults and don't believe that being lenient would be doing them any favors. Though you may love them deeply, it's hard for you to show your feelings for them, to be affectionate, tender, playful or even openly encouraging. You might long to be more expressive and emotional, but are rather cut off from your feeling side and don't know where to begin.

Security and stability are very important to you. You might try to achieve this by making lots of money, establishing yourself as a pillar of your community or marrying someone who will take care of you. Your physical home also is a symbol of security, but even if it is expensive, prestigious or historically significant it probably isn't very comfortable or inviting. Your tastes tend toward the traditional and you might choose to live in an older house or furnish it with antique pieces. It's also possible that due to Capricorn's conservative, practical nature, you may live in relative austerity, eschewing all "luxuries" and making do with only the bare essentials.

Both men and women with this Moon placement hold rather conventional, traditionally-oriented attitudes about male/female roles and are inclined to glorify the past. A good example of this tendency is American artist Norman Rockwell, whose birth chart contains Moon in Capricorn. Men often seek partners who will stay at home and manage their domestic/family lives. Women may marry men who have sound portfolios, stable jobs and good reputations, who will take care of them physically and financially—even though these women are more than capable of taking care of themselves!

Moon in Aquarius

Emotionally, you can be quite unpredictable, excitable, even explosive. Given to temper tantrums and sudden outbursts, you express your feelings with uncensored candor. You are most upset by social injustices and inequities, and might be more passionate about causes than people. Although your anger is easily aroused, it doesn't last long; once you've vented it you see no reason to hold a grudge and may behave as if nothing had happened. You can't understand why others might be hurt by your harsh words.

In truth, you enjoy a good confrontation now and again, and don't really want things to go too smoothly. Tense and high-strung, you like to keep the emotional pot boiling and don't want your home life or relationships to become routine or predictable. For you, boredom is the deathblow to a relationship. If you are involved with someone who has Moon in Aries or Aquarius, you might fight a lot but still get along famously. However, you are likely to trample or bully people whose Moons are in more gentle or emotional signs. Stubborn, brusque and willful, you can be insensitive to the feelings of others.

Though your emotions are easily engaged and displayed with great force, they aren't very deep. With those who love you, you sometimes seem detached and aloof, and it's difficult to be truly intimate with you. Intimacy and emotional closeness smack of possessiveness to you. You demand freedom to come and go as you please, to associate with whomever you choose, and anyone who doesn't like it isn't worth your time anyway.

Although you may change lovers frequently or have several simultaneously, you are intensely loyal to your friends. Friendship, in fact, is far more important to you than romantic love, and you probably have many friends and associates. Casual companions and relationships that don't make too many demands on your emotions are more comfortable for you. Above all, you expect honesty, equality and fairness in all your relationships.

Your childhood home was probably chaotic, constantly changing and/or unstable in some way. Perhaps you moved frequently. Your parents may have fought a great deal, or split up when you were still young. Most likely, there was something unusual about your upbringing and/or your parents.

Your mother (or nurturing parent) might have been avant garde, unconventional, or in some way different from her contemporaries. Though she probably encouraged you to develop your intellect and become independent as soon as possible, she wasn't very nurturing or supportive of you. Possibly she found parenting too restrictive, and resented being tied down with children when there were so many other exciting things to do. She may not have been there when you needed her, and had trouble showing affection, sympathy and compassion.

You want to be a friend to your own children rather than an authority figure. When they are very young, you can be quite impatient with them. You don't like their dependency, and want them to hurry and grow up so they won't make so many demands on you and you can have more freedom. As a result, you may "push them out of the nest" too soon. Unless you have several planets in Taurus, Leo, Cancer or Pisces, you aren't very affectionate with them and prefer reading them bedtime stories to rocking them to sleep. Unless Capricorn or Scorpio is prominent in your chart, you probably aren't much of a disciplinarian and your kids might be a bit rebellious and wild.

Because of your deep concern for humankind, you might want to initiate programs to protect and feed the world's homeless orphans and take care of all who are in need. Even if you have no biological children, you may feel as though you are "mother" to many. Mary Baker Eddy, founder of the Christian Science Church, had no children of her own, but considered herself a mother to all her followers; her Moon was in Aquarius.

Your physical home isn't very important to you (unless you have Cancer or Taurus prominent in your chart). You may change residences frequently or have an unconventional living arrangement, such as sharing a house with an odd assortment of other people. Some might describe your lifestyle as "bohemian." At the very least, your house is probably decorated in an eclectic, ultra-modern or off-beat fashion, and housekeeping isn't your most obvious talent.

Both men and women with this Moon placement revel in being "different" and will go out of their way to shock the more conventional members of their families. Men with Moon in Aquarius enjoy women who are strong-willed, independent, unusual and intelligent. Women are not particularly maternal and usually aren't happy in traditional roles or relationships that aren't "equal."

Moon in Pisces

Your emotions are like the ocean: deep, mysterious, rich with life and constantly changing. You are reluctant, however, to reveal this vast and complex inner side of yourself to even your closest friends and family. Your feelings are easily engaged and easily hurt, so to protect yourself you hide your vulnerability behind a veil of secrecy.

Like a chameleon, you take on the color of your environment, at least in an emotional sense. For this reason, it is important for you to spend as much time as possible with congenial people in harmonious surroundings. You have a tendency toward depression and morbidity, therefore cheerful, upbeat companions can stimulate more positive feelings in you. Meditation also can help you to center yourself and develop inner tranquility.

Highly sensitive, you connect with others on an unconscious, emotional level. You actually feel what they feel. This produces a sympathetic and compassionate nature. You cannot bear to see anything hurt and identify with all the world's weak and helpless creatures. In an effort to help allieviate the suffering of others, you may become involved in humanitarian causes or social programs.

You appear psychic since you seem to "know" things without being able to explain how. This extrasensory ability can be developed to a high degree, but you must be careful because you are also very impressionable and lack discrimination.

You expect yourself to be perfect and are unforgiving of your own shortcomings. In your heart-of-hearts, you feel unworthy and it is easy for you to become a martyr. Pisces is sometimes called the sign of self-undoing and you are all too willing to sacrifice your best interests for someone else, especially for lovers and family members.

You have a vivid imagination and are highly sensitive to color, sound and rhythm. Many people with Piscean Moons possess artistic talent. Artists Michelangelo, Leonardo da Vinci, Paul Cézanne and Paul Klee all had Moon in Pisces. In particular, you might be drawn to painting, photography, poetry, music, and film making or screen acting. Your ability probably revealed itself at an early age and you seem to express it almost effortlessly. However, you can be lazy about developing your talents. You prefer to dream about the symphonies you'll write or the films you'll make one day rather than working to bring your dreams to fruition.

Somewhat shy and reclusive, you like being alone some of the time. For the artist, this is absolutely necessary. It is also important for spiritual development, and many people with Moon in Pisces are involved in religious pursuits of some sort. Be careful, though, that your retreat into solitude is not an excuse for escaping the demands and harsh realities of the "real" world.

Your home is a refuge from the stress of the outer world, a place where you can recharge yourself with peace and quiet. You don't really enjoy entertaining at home, and when you do, prefer to see one or two close friends at a time rather than giving large parties. A lover of beauty, you might collect art and other things that appeal to your keen sense of aesthetics. You are less concerned with neatness, however, and your home may be in constant disarray. Some Pisces-Moon people feel that acquiring earthly possessions is materialistic and spurn creature comforts to live in monkish austerity.

There was probably some instability in your childhood home: an absent or alcoholic parent, poverty, mental illness or perhaps parents who were not emotionally supportive of you. You may have felt helpless or defenseless, alone, even fearful. As a result, you grew up with a sense of insecurity that still exists, deeply-rooted, in adulthood. Perhaps your mother (or the nurturing parent) was weak, ineffectual or ill. Perhaps she was absent in your life, physically or emotionally unavailable when you needed her.

The forgiving nature of Pisces, however, will let you apologize for your mother's ineptness, and regardless of the facts, you probably believe she was a kind and loving parent—even a saint. In some cases, this can be true, for Pisces is also the sign of the saint. Indeed, your mother may have been a kindly, compassionate individual who was always raising money to help the poor, or doing charity work, or caring for others in some way—while neglecting her own children.

With your own children, you are usually too lenient. Though generous and loving, you sometimes fail to provide them with the structure and discipline they need. You also tend to worry too much about them and can be overly protective.

Your "mothering" is not limited to your own family. You want to nurture and protect everyone in need: stray animals, homeless street people, starving refugees in third world countries. People with problems seek you out and you always offer a shoulder to cry on. Easy prey for the unscrupulous, you need to discriminate between those who genuinely need your help and those who are taking advantage of you. You also must learn not to feel guilty if you refuse to help someone.

This is especially true in close personal relationships. Sympathetic to those who have problems, you believe your love can cure them. The expression "love is blind" can be applied to you. Romantic and overly-idealistic, you have difficulty seeing your partners as they really are. You prefer to view them in the light of your fantasies, as your fairy princesses or knights in shining armor, and you constantly seek the perfect lover.

It is usually easier for women with this Moon placement to express Piscean characteristics. Men who don't connect with the energy in themselves might be drawn to women who are gentle, submissive, compassionate, idealistic, artistic and/or spiritually-inclined.

Chapter Five

Mercury

In ancient Roman mythology, Mercury was the messenger of the gods. In astrology, Mercury's role is much the same: it serves as "messenger" between human beings. The planet of communication, Mercury is associated with all forms of intellectual and verbal exchange—speaking, writing, conscious thinking—as well as the vehicles used for conveying communications: telephones, letters, books, perhaps even computers. It does not represent the mind *in toto,* however; the unconscious sector comes under the Moon's domain.

Mercury is the fact-gatherer of the zodiac. It is concerned with collecting information and relaying it. It does not, however, discriminate or evaluate what it gathers, so that it is attracted equally to mental treasures and trash.

This cosmic messenger also is associated with short trips, but not long journeys, and the methods of transportation you use to make these trips: cars, subways, buses, etc. Thus, Mercury's placement in your chart will show how you feel and go about traveling in and around your immediate environment (your community and near vicinity).

Mercury rules the hands, and its chart position can indicate how you use your hands. It also suggests your degree of manual dexterity or clumsiness.

In the birth chart, Mercury signifies your intellectual functioning, but is not an indicator of your intelligence. How you think, learn, process ideas and express yourself using language skills are all related to Mercury's placement in your chart. This planet also shows how you feel about your mental abilities, how easy intellectual pursuits are for you, how you go about developing your mental capacities and how much (or little) you value intelligence in yourself and others.

Mercury can never be more than 28 degrees away from the Sun, which means your Mercury will be positioned in the same astrological sign as your Sun, or in one of the adjacent signs. A fleet traveler, Mercury completes its orbit around the Sun in about eighty-eight days. However, due to periods of retrogradation (when a planet *appears* to be moving backward in the sky), it takes Mercury approximately a year to traverse all twelve signs of the zodiac.

If your Mercury is in the same sign as your Sun, you will have an easier time expressing who you are than if Mercury is in a different sign than your Sun. This is because your "mouthpiece" is attuned to the same vibrational frequency as your core identity. If Mercury and the Sun in your chart are in different signs, there is likely to be some divergence in what you *are* and what you *say* you are. This doesn't mean you will be consciously duplicitous, however. Think of Mercury as an interpreter through whom your Sun speaks. If Mercury is fluent in the Sun's "language" (i. e., they are in the same astrological sign), the Sun's message will be communicated clearly and accurately. But if Mercury's fundamental language is different than the Sun's, Mercury will be less facile in translating the Sun's message into words and more apt to mix up some of the meanings. For instance, a person with Sun in Aquarius and Mercury in Capricorn would tend to be more verbally circumspect and/or intellectually conservative than an Aquarian whose Mercury is also in Aquarius.

In order to get a complete picture of how Mercury functions in your birth chart, it is also important to examine its house position and the aspects your other planets make to it. Saturn aspects, for example, will help stabilize even the most restless Mercury; Uranus aspects will help stimulate a sluggish or cautious Mercury's desire for knowledge.

Mercury in Aries

Your mind is active and quick, and you tend to grasp concepts with lightning speed. If an idea or subject interests you, you pursue it with fervor and enthusiasm. However, you have trouble sticking with anything for long and your memory isn't very good. Your mind is always racing from one thought to another and you find it difficult to concentrate. Consequently, you probably weren't an A student even if you are quite bright. Mentally restless and easily bored, you need to be continually challenged intellectually in order to keep you interested.

You especially enjoy exploring new ideas and concepts. You don't believe something just because everyone else does, and you can be something of a renegade thinker. Conventional wisdom and accepted truths don't have much value for you, and you are eager to contest them with original ideas of your own. This is the position of the inventor and the adventurer. Renaissance artist and inventor, Leonardo da Vinci, is a good example of Mercury in Aries. So is American aviation pioneer Wilbur Wright. Because you aren't blinded by rigid attitudes and beliefs, you sometimes come up with brilliant insights and epiphanies. The chart of mathematical genius Albert Einstein, for example, features Mercury in Aries. But in your headlong rush to discover the new you sometimes overlook important bits of information or are careless in your research.

You have a powerful voice and tend to speak loudly and forcefully. This planetary position often signifies the dynamic orator or the irritating loud-mouth. Nazi leader Adolf Hitler, for example, had Mercury in Aries. You love to argue and will debate almost any issue heatedly, even if your purpose is only to exercise your mental muscles. Verbally assertive, even provocative, you get yourself into trouble regularly because you don't know when to hold your tongue or use a bit of tact. You have a real knack for saying the wrong thing at the wrong time. Even when you aren't angry, your tone of voice can be so abrasive that it antagonizes others immediately, and you can be difficult to get along with. Your bark, however, is much worse than your bite, and if your Sun is in Taurus or Pisces, you are probably a pussycat who roars like a lion.

You often espouse unconventional beliefs and aren't afraid to champion an unpopular cause. Actress Shirley MacLaine, for instance, has her Mercury in Aries. Direct and honest (sometimes brutally so), you say what you think. Not deceitful, you believe in laying all your cards on the table so that everyone knows where you stand and what your intentions are. Your purity of intent at times is so innocent and naïve, though, that people who are more conniving or cunning can easily take advantage of you.

Mercury in Aries focuses energy into your hands, giving you great manual strength and/or speed. Guitarist Eric Clapton, for example, has his Mercury in Aries.

Saturn aspects to your Mercury will help discipline your mind and focus your attention so that you can direct your mental energy into productive channels. They also improve your memory so that you are more likely to retain what you learn.

Mercury in Taurus

You are the type who never speaks unless you have something to say. Not one to waste words or engage in frivolous small talk, you appear to be hording words like a miser hordes gold. Others sometimes assume (incorrectly) that you are unsociable or dull-witted. American actor Clint Eastwood, whose screen persona exemplifies the "strong, silent type" is a good example of Mercury in Taurus. In truth, you aren't glib or articulate, and your vocabulary isn't extensive. Unless you also have several planets in more loquacious signs like Gemini, Sagittarius or Aquarius, it's not likely that you'll write the next great American novel. You prefer to communicate in other ways—physically, or through art or music—than with language skills.

This does not mean, however, that you aren't as intelligent as your more verbally adroit friends, only that you don't demonstrate your intelligence with words. Instead, you might be a brilliant painter, dancer or musician. Singers Perry Como and Barbra Streisand, composer/pianist Eric Satie, and dancers Dame Margot Fonteyn and Isadora Duncan are some examples of Mercury in Taurus. You may not have been a very good student, and learning new subjects might have come more slowly to you that to others. Perhaps you never had an opportunity to develop your intelligence fully or to get a good education. As a result, you might feel somewhat inadequate or inferior about your mental capabilities even as an adult. When speaking before a crowd you may become tongue-tied or feel awkward, and when you have to write a report, paper, even a letter you often find yourself at a loss for words. Expressing what you really think and feel can be a struggle for you.

Your memory is good, however, and even though you may not grasp ideas quickly, you retain what you learn. You demonstrate common sense and are able to apply your knowledge in practical ways. In particular, you may have a good head for business and finance. You also are known for your determination, steadiness and reliability. Publisher William Randolph Hearst, for example, had his Mercury in Taurus.

You rarely take chances and usually plan carefully before undertaking any venture. You like things to be clearly defined, down-to-earth and useful and it is difficult for you to grasp abstractions or theoretical constructs. Not an "idea person," you are a doer rather than a thinker—the one who brings the dreamer's visions to fruition. As far as you're concerned, an idea is useless unless it can be applied in some tangible, physical way. Although you aren't going to set the world on fire with an exciting or revolutionary concept, without your persistence and common sense, all those "brainstorms" would never become realities.

Philosophically conservative, you hold onto traditional ideas and beliefs firmly and are not easily swayed or influenced by popular opinion or the attitudes of others. There is a sense of security in concepts that have been around for a while and you don't see why things can't remain the same forever. England's Queen Victoria and former American President James Monroe are good examples of Mercury in Taurus. You want everything to be simple and clear-cut; ambiguity, complexity and "gray areas" baffle you. Once you've made up your mind you aren't likely to change it and can be extremely stubborn. Taurus' symbol is the bull, and the term "bull-headed" certainly applies to you.

If your chart contains aspects between Mercury and Jupiter or Uranus, you'll be more talkative and intellectually expansive, and more eager to pursue knowledge for its own sake.

Mercury in Gemini

Your mind is always active, always seeking. You want to know something about everything and eagerly pursue each new idea that comes along—for a little while, at least. Like a butterfly flitting from flower to flower, you enjoy sampling a bit of everything but rarely stick to anything for very long. There's always something more interesting just over the next hill. One day your passion might be archeology, the next day stock car racing and the next gourmet cooking. You're the sort who'll try anything once, but you haven't the determination or focus to develop any of your many interests and hobbies into a serious avocation or career. In short, you're a dabbler.

You skim the surface, picking up odd bits and pieces of information about a wide variety of subjects, but rarely probe deeply enough into any of them to become truly knowledgeable. Your concern is collecting not evaluating, and you have trouble discriminating or deciding what information is useful and what is drivel. With such a storehouse of random facts and figures, you could be a whiz at crossword puzzles and games like *Trivial Pursuit*. You collect things in the same way, purchasing "bargains" whether you need them or not, and you can be something of a pack rat.

Mentally agile and clever, you learn quickly and joyously; as a child you were probably a favorite with your teachers. In particular, you excelled at languages and all subjects that involve communication skills: typing, computers, literature, creative writing. A lifelong student, you not only want to gather as much information as possible, you wish to share it with others. Thus, you might enjoy being a teacher, especially at elementary levels where you'd have a chance to teach a variety of subjects.

A voracious reader, you enjoy the classics, trashy paperbacks, magazines, and even may peruse the encyclopedia or dictionary on occasion. Most likely you read the great works of literature at some time or other, but missed the deeper significances, and dark, brooding, emotional dramas—by Racine, Dostoyevsky or Joyce, for instance—seem to you much ado about nothing. Philosophy, psychology and metaphysics don't interest you much either, for you have difficulty grasping abstract or theoretical concepts and holistic views. Your worldview is almost childlike in its naïveté and you simply can't comprehend the complexities of human nature or the cosmos.

Your love of the written word may lead you to become a writer yourself. George Orwell, Cole Porter, Bob Dylan, Ian Fleming, Joyce Carol Oates and George Sand are examples of several different kinds of writers whose charts all feature Mercury in Gemini. Unless you have strong Saturn aspects or other stabilizing influences in your chart, however, you'd be better at composing short pieces—newspaper articles, advertising copy or short stories—than full-length books. So many ideas vie for your attention that you are easily distracted from the project at hand, and generally lose interest in your subject almost as soon as you start.

Communication in all its myriad forms is central to your existence. You maintain a large circle of friends, associates and acquaintances with whom you speak frequently and you stay in touch with the ones who live far away via phone or letters. You love to talk (though you aren't always the best listener) and are never at a loss for words. Because you possess at least a smattering of knowledge in many areas, you can find something to say to everyone you meet. You enjoy meeting new people and sharing ideas with them—each individual you encounter teaches you something. Friendly, cheerful and outgoing, you're a good person to have at social gatherings and parties for you keep the guests interacting with each other and the conversation flowing.

Word games, crossword puzzles and card playing are favorite forms of amusement for you. You also enjoy taking classes, attending lectures, visiting museums and historic sites, making short trips, shopping (especially at flea markets and bargain centers), and talking with friends—anything that teaches you something new and/or engages your facile mind briefly without taxing it, allowing you to display your cleverness.

Mercury and Gemini rule the hands, therefore this planetary position signifies a high level of manual dexterity and agility. Perhaps you are skillful at playing a musical instrument, draw well, enjoy handcrafts such as quilting, weaving or basketry, or are accomplished in a sport that requires good hand-eye coordination, like baseball or tennis. American League batting champion Wade Boggs, for example, has his Mercury in Gemini.

Saturn or Pluto aspects to your Mercury will help you to focus your restless and flighty mind, and improve your memory.

Mercury in Cancer

Your mind is focused on internal or personal issues, rather than on the outer world. Something of an introvert, your mental stimulation comes from within, from your emotional core. Thus it is difficult, if not impossible, for you to separate your emotions from your rational thinking processes. Your heart rules your head, and your decisions, opinions and ideas are colored by your feelings and your emotional attachments. You simply cannot step outside your own needs and desires to be objective. You take most things personally and see issues within the context of how they will affect you and/or your family, and you have trouble comprehending the larger picture. Because the source of your beliefs is emotional not rational, you cannot be swayed by a logical argument and no one can change your mind with reason or facts.

Your thoughts are often centered around your home and family. You're the type who monopolizes the conversation with stories about your children's latest accomplishments and talks about your grandchildren to total strangers. For example, Anne Morrow Lindbergh, who wrote about the heart-wrenching experience of having her baby kidnapped and murdered, had her Mercury in Cancer. So does Rose Kennedy, whose claim to fame is being the mother of John, Bobby and Ted. Your interest in the home and family also could lead you to pursue a career in an area such as interior design, real estate, family counseling or pediatrics. Architect Frank Lloyd Wright, who had Mercury in Cancer, communicated his artistic talent by designing homes.

Though you may not be adept with language or the written word, your ability to communicate non-verbally is keen. You seem to "know" what others are thinking and feeling, and with your loved ones and close friends you may have an unspoken rapport that makes you appear psychic. Perhaps you are able to communicate best through a non-verbal medium such as art or music. The birth charts of painters Amadeo Modigliani, Paul Gauguin and Andrew Wyeth, and musicians Igor Stravinski and Van Cliburn, for example, all feature Mercury in Cancer. When you attempt to express yourself in words, however, you often sound confused or nonsensical. No matter how good your ideas are, you have a hard time explaining them to others in a logical, orderly way. As a result, other people sometimes think you are less intelligent than you really are, which can cause you to feel insecure about your own mental abilities.

You are inclined to think a great deal about security issues and attempt to find ways to make yourself feel secure. Sometimes this can translate into seeking wealth and financial stability. You might involve yourself in money matters professionally—as a financial consultant, stockbroker, banker or estate planner—or simply put a lot of mental energy into money issues, investments, real estate, etc. Financial columnist and author Sylvia Porter, for example, has her Mercury in Cancer. Your concern with financial security can make your miserly and tight-fisted at times, though you are likely to be quite generous with your children and family members.

A traditionalist, you hold on tightly to conservative opinions and attitudes. The "old ways" make you feel more secure, and any new or different ideas can seem threatening to you. You want to surround yourself with others who think the way you do, who reinforce your beliefs and give you confidence that you are right in your convictions. People whose opinions conflict with yours are often viewed as subversives or enemies, and ideas that appear to threaten your security are deemed dangerous. Because you take everything so personally, you are likely to interpret differing opinions as attacks or criticisms of you. And because your thinking tends to be insular and narrowly focused on yourself and your immediate environment, you have a great deal of trouble understanding that others simply may march to a different drummer than you do.

Uranus aspects to your Mercury will make you more intellectually progressive, unconventional and fair-minded. Jupiter aspects will increase your sociability and expand your interest in people and cultures beyond your own family/community.

Mercury in Leo

Self-expression is one of your major concerns. It is very important for you to express yourself in a dramatic, colorful way and to be recognized for this. You probably have some creative/artistic talent and enjoy expressing yourself through art forms such as painting, design, music, theatre or dance. Painters Edgar Degas and Marc Chagall, sculptor Alexander Calder, fashion designer Yves St. Laurent, rock musicians Ringo Starr and Mick Jagger, and actor Peter Sellers are several good examples of Mercury in Leo. You may not be especially good with words, but are able to communicate loudly and clearly through visual media.

You enjoy being in the limelight, speaking to crowds of people, sharing your thoughts and visions with the multitudes. Even though your ideas and dreams may be grandiose and unrealistic you believe they are possible, and your self-confidence and charisma are sometimes great enough to enable you to make your ideals realities. The birth charts of former Italian dictator Benito Mussolini and American political radical Jerry Rubin, for example, feature Mercury in Leo.

You can be quite charming, even something of a flatterer when it suits your purposes. You especially love the idea of being in love, of being the lover. The drama of romance appeals to your sense of theatre and at times your "lines" sound like they were taken from an Italian opera. Though your message might be corny, over-blown and heavy-handed, you deliver it with such flair that it usually hits home. For you, love is a game to be enacted on the stage of life, and you relish playing the leading role.

You can be extremely self-centered, and your thoughts are usually focused on yourself and your ideas. It is hard for you to see another's point of view, because in your mind your own opinion is all that counts. That others might not agree with you never even enters your mind. Conversations with you often revolve around your latest accomplishments, projects or activities, and many of your sentences begin with "I." You want very much to appear important in the eyes of others. You may try to impress friends and acquaintances with all the famous people you know and you can be quite a name-dropper.

Even if you are very intelligent you might not have been a good student, partially because you don't value book-learning and partly because you don't really believe that anyone else knows more than you do. Perhaps you attempted to tell your teachers how to teach their subjects and insisted on doing things your own way. You rely solely on your own natural abilities and won't take advice or instruction from others; consequently, you sometimes shortchange yourself and don't develop your skills to their maximum.

Mercury in Virgo

Your mind works in an orderly and organized fashion. Each step of your thinking process is carefully calibrated and predictable; your thoughts work together systematically and logically like the gears of a machine. Though you may not be the most creative of thinkers, you are certainly one of the most practical and efficient. You are the person who operates behind the scenes, figuring out how to make someone else's brainstorm work—the film editor who cuts and splices the director's "masterpiece" until it makes sense, the tailor who takes the designer's sketches and turns them into whole cloth. However, unless you have your Sun in Leo, you probably don't get much credit for your contributions. Shy and timid, you often hold your tongue when you should speak up for yourself, then later complain profusely to friends and co-workers.

You have a good memory and can retain volumes of facts, figures and words. For example, many actors and actresses who must memorize hundreds of lines of dialogue have Mercury in Virgo, among them Dustin Hoffman, Robert de Niro, Anne Bancroft, Lucille Ball, Robert Redford, Lauren Bacall, Greta Garbo and Sean Connery. You learn best though repetition, and by applying what you've learned in some practical way.

Like people who have Mercury in Gemini, you love language and the written word and may have talent as a writer. You are more disciplined, organized and work-oriented than your Mercury-in-Gemini counterparts, however, and thus more capable of completing long projects. The birth charts of authors Herman Melville, Truman Capote, William Faulkner, Mary and Percy Bysshe Shelley, D. H. Lawrence and John Knowles, for example, all feature Mercury in Virgo.

Y ou probably were a dedicated and conscientious student. You enjoy learning and usually prefer to study subjects that can be applied in useful ways—especially ones that will benefit you professionally—rather than art, music, or philosophy. Medicine and other health-related subjects, in particular, might appeal to you. Your interest in health may lead you to give medical advice to everyone you know, and you invest much mental energy in thinking, talking and worrying about your health.

It's hard for you just to take something at face value—you immediately start dissecting it to see what makes it function. In school, you probably loved diagramming sentences and labeling the organs of a frog. As an adult, you might use your keen analytical ability in such fields as accounting, computer programming, medical research, auto repair or book editing. You enjoy trouble-shooting, discovering errors and correcting them, and derive satisfaction from setting things right. You have the patience to search column after column of numbers to find where the books are off, or to examine hundreds of lab samples to determine which bacteria are causing the problem.

A perfectionist, you can be a stickler for detail and exactitude. Your checkbook always balances, you have your car tuned every six months and the letters you write to your mother never have any spelling errors. Since Mercury rules the hands, your perfectionism may be expressed as great manual dexterity, control and precision. Golfer Ben Hogan, artist Aubrey Beardsley, guitarist B. B. King and conductor Leonard Bernstein are some examples of Mercury in Virgo. Your perfectionism can also lead to negativism, pessimism and irritability, however, since nothing can ever meet up to your expectations. You tend to be overly critical and fault-finding with others and yourself.

Cautious and conservative in your ideas and opinions, you are a follower rather than an intellectual leader and rarely initiate any unique or progressive ideas of your own. You are most comfortable with "tried and true" concepts. Philosophy, metaphysics and theology probably don't interest you much—they're a bit too undefined and disorderly. Unless you can "prove" something, you don't believe it, and you can be something of a skeptic. Because you refuse to open yourself up to knowledge that defies quantification in physical terms, you also are inclined to be self-limiting and narrow-minded.

If you have Uranus aspecting your Mercury you'll be more unconventional and inventive in your thinking. If Neptune aspects Mercury in your chart, you'll be less analytical and methodical and more idealistic and creative. Mars aspects will make you more verbally aggressive and outspoken, Jupiter aspects will encourage you to be more optimistic and expansive mentally.

Mercury in Libra

You have the rare ability to see both sides of any issue and to remain detached, impartial and objective. You weigh the strengths and weaknesses in a matter and make judgments based on the facts without letting your feelings get in the way. This tends to make you more fair and equitable than most people, and you could be a good judge, mediator, lawyer, negotiator or umpire. Because you can see the pluses and minuses of everything, however, you have trouble making decisions or sticking with the ones you finally do make. Too often, you let others make up your mind for you or you go along with the crowd because it's easier.

This dispassionate and orderly way of thinking enables you to be an expert strategist. You also have a knack for understanding what your opponent is thinking. As a result, you could be a successful general, chess master or sports team manager. Five-star American General Dwight D. Eisenhower and French General Lafayette, for example, had Mercury in Libra. Or, you could use your logic, planning skills and good judgment in almost any segment of the business world. You are able to evaluate others' talents without feeling threatened by people who are more gifted than you are, and you are especially good at organizing individuals so that they work together as a team.

Always tactful, well-mannered and diplomatic in your speech, you rarely lose your temper and always try to avoid an argument. You may debate issues cleverly, even forcefully, but you never become emotionally involved. Always cool and rational, you can appear bloodless and unfeeling at times. It is this lack of personal involvement, this separation between the heart and the head that allows lawyers to defend heinous criminals and generals to send men into battle knowing they'll be slaughtered.

Libra is concerned with balance and harmony, and loves beauty in all its forms. With Mercury in this sign, you might express your aesthetic appreciation as an artist or a patron of the arts. The birth charts of musicians/composers Johann Strauss, Guiseppe Verdi, John Coltrane and Thelonius Monk, film maker Michelangelo Antonioni, painters Grandma Moses and Robert Indiana, and writers Thomas Wolfe, Agatha Christie, Gore Vidal and Friedrich Nietzsche are some examples of Mercury in Libra.

Libra also is the sign of one-to-one partnerships, thus you tend to think and talk a great deal about relationships, especially those which involve love and romance. You are inclined to idealize romantic attachments and usually think the best of your partner(s). If you are a writer, you may write about love and relationships; if you are a therapist, you may do marriage counseling. Often your thoughts are centered on your partner and you are strongly influenced by him/her and his/her opinions. Since you rarely have firm convictions of your own, you may simply parrot your loved one's ideas or agree in order to avoid arguments.

Your beliefs and attitudes are usually quite traditional and conservative, and you tend to accept the party line rather than diverging in any unique, individual way. This is partially because you don't want to cause friction or seem disagreeable, but also because you are easily convinced by those who have strong opinions and express them forcefully. At best you are open-minded, at worst vacillating and weak-willed.

If Uranus or Mars aspects your Mercury you will be more outspoken, forward-thinking and individualistic. If Neptune aspects Mercury in your chart, you'll be less orderly and rational in your thinking.

Mercury in Scorpio

You are not satisfied with superficial understandings and seek to know the ultimate truths of existence. What goes on behind the scenes, what makes something work, what hidden forces are responsible for exterior conditions—these are the things you want to know. You enjoy probing beneath the surface to uncover the secrets within, whether those secrets are in the human mind, the body, business, government, the Earth or the Universe. As a result, you might be interested in psychology, science, medicine, espionage, geology or the occult. Astrologer Marc Edmund Jones, occultists Israel Regardie and Aleister Crowley and psychiatrist R. D. Laing, for example, had Mercury in Scorpio.

You have an insightful and penetrating mind, and are able to focus your attention deeply, for long periods of time. Infinitely curious, you leave no stone unturned and don't give up until you've found answers to your questions. You ferret out information, analyze it until you understand its essence, then use it for your own purposes. Thus, you could be good at almost any type of research. Your love of intrigue may also manifest as a passion for mystery stories and detective novels.

Often your ideas run counter to the conventions and beliefs of your time. This is because you refuse to accept something until you've proved it for yourself. And, as you examine traditional beliefs, you frequently discover flaws or shortcomings, which leads you to formulate your own theories. Such theories may be revolutionary and have a transformative effect on those they touch. Religious leaders Mohandas Gandhi and Martin Luther, for example, had Mercury in Scorpio and their teachings irrevocably altered the belief structures of masses of people. Jonas Salk, who discovered a vaccine for polio, transformed medicine and the lives of millions of people; his Mercury was in Scorpio, too. So was musician/songwriter John Lennon's; he was responsible for changing the face of popular music.

In order to stand up against strong opposition, one must be firm and determined in one's convictions. Certainly this is true of you. Once you've decided upon something, nothing can make you give it up. You can be incredibly stubborn and emotionally attached to your ideas. And because you've come to your understandings through unique, personal and often unorthodox ways, no one can change your mind with a logical argument. Highly intuitive, you often "know" you're right, even if you can't back up your beliefs with facts.

You express your viewpoints vehemently and convincingly, and enjoy a good argument with a worthy opponent. There is a certain amount of charisma in your verbal delivery and when you speak you project power, authority and intelligence. You intuitively know what others want to hear and are clever at manipulating their emotions as well as the information, so that you can hold an audience in the palm of your hand and win them over to your way of thinking.

You also tend to be direct, blunt, even bitingly sarcastic in your speech. You get straight to the point and don't mince words—and if you step on some toes or offend some sensibilities in the process, so be it. Comedian Groucho Marx, noted for his frank, sometimes rude and often provocative comments, had his Mercury in Scorpio. So did writers Oscar Wilde, Eugene O'Neill and Sylvia Plath. But you also exhibit keen insight and knowledge, especially regarding the nature of the human condition. You truly understand the inner workings of the psyche and the dark side of life, and are fascinated with it. Not only do you have unusual powers of observation, you are also very intuitive, even psychic, and can see to the core of people and situations. Not much gets by you and you are not easily fooled. This intimate knowledge of the hidden recesses of the human mind makes you skeptical, suspicious and pessimistic; you often expect the worst from people.

Venus and/or Jupiter aspects to your Mercury will make you more tactful, optimistic and willing to engage in social amenities.

Mercury in Sagittarius

Tireless in your search for knowledge and wisdom, your goal is to learn and experience everything. Everything interests you, especially subjects that have significance beyond the mundane or which offer universal truths, such as philosophy, psychology and religion. Like Mercury in Scorpio, you are not satisfied with superficial explanations or simple facts and figures; you are seeking total understanding. Your infinite curiosity can cause you to be nosy, even voyeuristic; you want to know everything about everybody.

A lifelong student, nothing is more pleasurable to you than learning. You also enjoy sharing your knowledge with others and can be an inspiring and eloquent teacher. Because you are always contemplating the future and the far horizon, you can seem rather "spacey," forgetful, impractical and disorganized. This is the position of the absent-minded professor.

You have a fantastic imagination and a way with words. A natural storyteller, you can entertain crowds for hours with amusing tales and could turn your talents to writing. Authors Joseph Conrad, J. D. Salinger, Issac Asimov, Louisa May Alcott and Carlos Castaneda are a few examples of Mercury in Sagittarius. Sometimes your imagination can run away with you, however, and you have a tendency to exaggerate. Although you think of this as improving upon the original, such behavior may earn you a reputation as a liar. However, your persuasiveness and entertaining speech could also make you an excellent salesperson.

Your vision is broad and all-encompassing. You are able to comprehend the larger picture and see how all the pieces fit together. Rather than isolating information and taking it at face value, as does Mercury in Gemini, you see it in the context of its entire environment. Thus, you are able to make interesting and even brilliant connections between things that others miss. This is the stuff of which great philosophy and humor are made, and quite likely you are witty, pointedly funny and insightful. Comedians Woody Allen, Harpo Marx, Bette Midler and Jonathan Winters are good examples of Mercury in Sagittarius.

Sociable and very communicative, even loquacious, you'll talk to anyone who'll listen and see every conversation as an opportunity to expand or spread your knowledge. So gregarious are you that you tend to spend a great deal of time socializing with friends, playing games, gambling, or partying. You're really rather lazy and undisciplined mentally. An idealistic dreamer, you talk a lot about what you're going to do tomorrow, but never seem to get around to actually doing it. (However, if your Sun is in Capricorn or Saturn is strongly placed in your chart, you'll be much more focused, persevering and hard-working.)

You are especially interested in seeing, learning about and talking with people from other countries or cultures, and might have a talent for languages. You probably enjoy traveling and like to drive. If you can't actually visit foreign lands, you may be an "armchair traveler" and watch television shows about exotic places and people. Generally, you prefer to get your information from radio, TV, movies or lectures rather than from books.

Even though you are curious about people of different mindsets and cultures, you aren't particularly tolerant of belief systems that diverge radically from your own. You are more interested in spreading your own views and philosophies, and can be something of an evangelist for your opinions. In religious matters in particular, you are inclined to be a bit fanatical, self-justifying, moralistic and proselytizing. South Carolina's Senator Strom Thurmond and TV preacher Jim Bakker, for example, have Mercury in Sagittarius. Unless you have several planets in earth signs, you are more intent on the ideal than the reality, glorifying the spirit while denigrating the flesh.

For the most part, however, you are optimistic and look on the bright side of things. You always have something positive to say, and your enthusiasm inspires and encourages others.

Saturn or Pluto aspects to your Mercury will make you more mentally focused and disciplined.

Mercury in Capricorn

Your mind works in a logical, orderly manner. Each thought follows upon the foundation laid by its predecessor, step-by-step. Before speaking, you carefully examine and edit your words so that what you say is sensible, clear and concise. You rarely say something you don't mean or will be sorry for later. If your Sun is also in Capricorn, you won't be very talkative, speaking only when necessary or when spoken to. You prefer to communicate only with people you know well, and are shy and self-conscious when you have to speak to strangers or before a group. (If your Sun is in Aquarius or Sagittarius, however, you'll be more open, talkative and sociable.)

Mentally practical and down-to-earth, your attention is focused on the here-and-now rather than some distant horizon. Though you may not be very creative or imaginative, you are capable of deep concentration, have a good memory and excel at planning and organization; you get things done while others are still dreaming. Determined and persevering, you are able to focus your thoughts on a single project or idea for long periods of time, and once you put your mind to something you usually accomplish it. You are ambitious, have a good head for business and believe in the work ethic. The birth chart of writer Horatio Alger, for example, features Mercury in Capricorn. Your pragmatic, no-nonsense attitude can help you to succeed in the corporate world or in any field that requires common sense and clear-thinking.

Your ideas and attitudes are generally conservative and traditional, and you are more inclined to look to the past for answers than to try something new or different. Former U. S. Presidents Richard Nixon and Ronald Reagen, Republican Senator Barry Goldwater and writer Ayn Rand are good examples of Mercury in Capricorn. Cautious and skeptical, you often demand "proof" before you'll believe something.

Although you may not learn as quickly and easily as others, you retain what you learn and find ways to apply it. Most likely, you were a good student because you worked hard at your studies and took them seriously. You are most interested in subjects that can be used in some practical way, especially those which will benefit you professionally. Abstract ideas, philosophy, metaphysics or the arts probably don't appeal to you very much; you are more comfortable with facts and figures that you can put to work in the physical world.

Serious and rather pessimistic, you are prone to negative thinking and can be terribly critical of yourself and others. You tend to be a worrier, pensive, contemplative and at times, fearful and morbid, thinking and expecting the worst of people and situations. Former FBI head J. Edgar Hoover, for example, had his Mercury in Capricorn. Such negativity can block you from achieving your goals since you sometimes believe things are worse than they are and give up before you even try.

You are a bit insecure about your mental abilities. Consequently, you work very hard to develop your intellect and want to be respected for your knowledge. Perhaps you believe that others think you are intellectually inferior, and thus you are defensive and rather touchy in this area. In truth, you aren't as witty and quick as your Mercury in Sagittarius or Aquarius counterparts, however, this doesn't mean you aren't as bright as they are. As a child, you may have been stifled intellectually or been denied a good education and opportunities to expand your knowledge. To compensate, you might go back to school as an adult, work doggedly to acquire advanced degrees or go to great lengths to demonstrate your intelligence. Or, you might attempt to prove to others (and yourself) that you don't need a degree or brains to succeed, and strive to become successful and wealthy despite your "deficiency."

If Uranus aspects your Mercury, or if your Sun is in Aquarius, you'll be more progressive, unconventional, quick and abstract in your thinking. If Jupiter or Mars aspects Mercury in your chart, or if your Sun is in Sagittarius, you'll be more outspoken, talkative, optimistic and friendly.

Mercury in Aquarius

Ideas come to you as bursts of insight. Mentally hyperactive, you never stop thinking and have a great deal of trouble slowing down to meditate or rest, for your thoughts are always racing in a dozen different directions and tripping over themselves. You tend to think and speak in fragments, rarely taking time to sort out and organize the profusion of ideas that flash on and off in your head. This is the position of the inventor, the scientist, the person who sees connections that others miss. Benjamin Franklin and Thomas Edison are two good examples of Mercury in Aquarius. You may have trouble, however, bringing your ideas down to earth and applying them in practical ways.

You are always looking to the future and your ideas and attitudes are usually ahead of their time. Others may think you are a little bit crazy, or at least eccentric. Certainly your concepts and beliefs are out-of-the-ordinary and uniquely yours. You take pleasure in being unusual, quirky and avant garde, and enjoy provoking more traditional people with your unconventional attitudes. You have no patience with the "old ways" and little respect for the past. But because you never look back, you fail to learn from history and others' mistakes.

More egalitarian than most people, you judge others according to what they know, not what they own or who they are. You believe in equality and fairness, and are willing to stand up and speak out for what you believe. Civil rights leader Martin Luther King, Jr., feminist writers Betty Friedan, Gertrude Stein and Anaïs Nin, and Massachusetts Senator Edward Kennedy are good examples of Mercury in Aquarius. A humanitarian, you are concerned with the plight of the underdog and "the people," and may be something of a social reformer. However, your interest is purely theoretical and abstract; regardless of what you say about equality for all, you really think that you are just a bit superior and more knowledgeable than everyone else.

You love to rebel against the system, to support causes and ideas that are controversial, revolutionary, unpopular or simply ahead of their time. However, you are an idealist and often forget to take into account the real-life complexities and underlying dynamics that surround the structures and attitudes you are attacking. Outspoken, irreverent and undiplomatic, you might find yourself frequently in trouble with authorities. You hold strongly and stubbornly to your beliefs, regardless of what others think, and will argue your point endlessly. Nothing pleases you more than a good debate. Something of an evangelist for your ideas, you want to convert everyone else to your way of thinking. Your technique is rarely subtle, though, and your abrasive, haughty attitude can put off as many people as it attracts.

Insatiable in your thirst for knowledge, you learn eagerly and easily, and like to impress people with what you know. At times, you come off as a know-it-all. Because you grasp concepts so quickly, you can be impatient with others who need more time to absorb and process information. Your interest in anything new and different, unconventional or controversial might cause you to pursue such fields as computer science, electronics, aerospace, astrology and metaphysics.

Talkative and gregarious, you enjoy sharing ideas with others and probably have numerous friends and/or associates. Although you are quite sociable, you can be rather aloof and cerebral. You like to talk with others but tend to keep conversation focused on generalities, abstractions and impersonal topics, never revealing much about yourself other than your ideals.

A dynamic and colorful speaker, you have the ability to inspire others and to organize groups of people. Often strongly political, you are eager to spread your ideas to the public and might put your intellectual and verbal abilities to work making speeches or writing about socio-political issues such as nuclear disarmament, environmental consciousness and human rights. You are the type who writes to your Congressional representatives and your local newspaper, and you never miss an opportunity to express your views.

Saturn aspects to your Mercury will help focus your thinking and make your ideas more practical. Venus aspects can soften your abrasiveness and increase your diplomacy.

Mercury in Pisces

You rarely pay attention to the here-and-now or the sidewalk in front of you. A dreamer, you are more concerned with your fantasies, your creations or the spiritual world than with remembering to pay your phone bill or studying for an exam. The day-to-day functioning of the mundane world doesn't interest you in the slightest, and sometimes it's hard to determine if you really live here on Earth or are just visiting.

At times it can be difficult talking with you. You drift in and out of conversations and your mind always seems to be preoccupied with something else. Your thoughts are not expressed completely or coherently, and often what you say is so highly personal, muddled or abstracted from reality that others have trouble understanding you. Irish author James Joyce, for example, whose writing tends to be obscure and intensely self-involved, had his Mercury in Pisces.

You probably have a fantastic imagination and are artistically oriented. You see and hear things others don't, and are acutely sensitive to color and sound. Communicating with images or music is easier for you than using language skills; even if you can barely write a coherent sentence you are able to get your point across brilliantly in other ways. The birth charts of musicians/composers Johann Sebastian Bach, Maurice Ravel, Aretha Franklin, Diana Ross, Billie Holiday and Smokey Robinson, painters Auguste Renoir and Vincent Van Gogh, film maker Bernardo Bertolucci and mime Marcel Marceau, for example, all feature Mercury in Pisces. You need to be careful, however, not to let your imagination run away with you. In the extreme, this Mercury placement can signify someone who loses all touch with reality, communicating with spirits, seeing hallucinations or retreating into a fantasy world of his/her own making.

Your keen sensitivity might put you in touch with the unseen realms. Often you "know" what others are thinking or feeling and you are quite psychic, or at least intuitive and perceptive. American psychic Edgar Cayce, for instance, had his Mercury in Pisces. Because you are not so tightly bound to the physical world, it is easier for you than for most people to develop your higher consciousness and connection to the Source. You find solace in meditation, prayer and spiritual thought, and might be interested in religious pursuits. Mystics Ramakrishna and Meher Baba, for example, had Mercury in Pisces.

Your retreat from the harsh demands of the physical world may take the form of escapism, rather than spiritual involvement—Mercury in Pisces tends to be lazy and the spiritual life is demanding and requires much discipline. In some cases, this placement can signify a person who uses alcohol, drugs or other escapist tactics as a way of avoiding responsibilities or facing up to truths about his/her life. Or, you simply may find daily life boring and seek to heighten your experience of it with mind-altering substances instead of working to develop your talents in interesting ways.

Your lack of involvement with the "real world" can cause you to be extremely idealistic and naïve, and you tend to look at life through the proverbial "rose-colored glasses." Gentle, sympathetic and trusting, you usually see the good in everyone and miss the bad. As a result, it is easy to fool you and you can be taken in by unscrupulous people. You are especially susceptible to hard-luck stories. Impressionable and lacking in discrimination, you let others influence you too much and rarely make up your own mind. You can be swayed by any half-baked argument or idea. Often your opinions are based on hazy impressions or romantic notions, and lack substance or logic. Common sense certainly isn't your forte. You need to exercise special care in important business or personal decisions, signing contracts, making investments, etc.

If Saturn aspects your Mercury you'll be more practical, realistic and mentally disciplined. Mars aspects will make you more assertive and individualistic.

Chapter Six

Venus

Venus's position in the birth chart is always within 48 degrees of the Sun's, therefore Venus will never be found more than two signs away from the Sun. Venus completes its journey around the Sun in 225 days, however, due to periods of retrogradation it sometimes takes the planet more than a year to travel through all twelve signs of the zodiac.

In ancient Roman mythology, Venus was the goddess of love, beauty and the arts. (The ancient Greeks knew her as Aphrodite.) In astrology, the planet Venus also is linked with these qualities. Your sense of esthetics, what you consider beautiful, how important art and beauty are to you, even your artistic abilities (or potential) are indicated by the position of Venus in your birth chart. Venus also shows how you are likely to go about making yourself beautiful and attractive, especially to the opposite sex.

However, Venus is best-known for its role in relationships. All one-to-one relationships of a contractual nature are associated with Venus, and its placement in the birth chart shows how you interact with business partners, clients, counselors and advisors (lawyers, therapists, etc.). The planet expresses itself most obviously, though, in love relationships—not brief flings or friendships, but serious, committed partnerships. (Until recently, of course, marriages were essentially business deals arranged between families for practical and/or material purposes.) Venus's position in the birth chart reveals your attitudes toward relationships, what you are seeking in a relationship, what you expect from a partner and what you are willing to give, how you are likely to relate to partners, how you go about attracting a lover, and to some extent how you will behave within the context of a love relationship.

Venus is also the representative of one of the two archetypal female energies: the Hetaera, or woman as lover. (The Moon is the embodiment of the woman as mother.) The astrological glyph for Venus is used widely as a symbol for woman. In a man's chart, Venus also describes the type of woman he finds most attractive, his ideal lover. This may not be the sort of woman he ultimately ends up with, however, for his dream lover isn't always the person best-suited to him or even someone he could stand to be with for any length of time.

In a woman's chart, Venus also indicates her ideal image of herself as a woman, the way she would like to be seen by others (particularly lovers or potential lovers). What she considers "feminine" and how she goes about expressing her own femininity, as well as what qualities she respects in other women will be shown by her Venus placement. In short, Venus's position suggests what makes a woman feel good about herself as a woman.

Of course, it is important to examine Venus's house position and the aspects it makes to other planets in the birth chart in order to get a complete picture of how this energy will be expressed in your life. The seventh house—the sector of the birth chart ruled by Venus—also will reveal much about your relationships and your attitudes toward them.

Venus in Aries

This is a difficult position for Venus. Here, the planet that represents female energy is placed in the most masculine of signs. Consequently, Venus has a hard time expressing its natural characteristics of harmony, union and romantic love in a sign that is individualistic and combative.

In partnerships of all kinds, but especially love relationships, you insist on being the dominant partner and are not willing to compromise very much in order to maintain domestic tranquility. In fact, you don't really want your relationships to be peaceful and harmonious. You prefer to maintain a high level of tension in your relationships, and find conflict and arguments stimulating and exciting. Often you start fights—verbal or even physical ones—with your partner just to see the fireworks. If things stay calm for long, you become bored.

You see love as a contest and partners as opponents to be conquered. It is the chase that intrigues you most, and you are likely to lose interest in someone once s/he succumbs to your advances. The way to keep your attention is to keep you guessing. Always looking for new experiences, new challenges, you tend to be rather promiscuous, or at least to change partners frequently. Actress Elizabeth Taylor, who is better known for her many marriages and divorces than for her acting roles, has her Venus in Aries. Whether male or female, you are usually the aggressor, eagerly pursuing your "quarry" rather than waiting for him/her to make the first move.

Sex is more important to you than affection, and unless you have water signs prominent elsewhere in your chart, you may lack the ability to express tenderness and romance in love relationships. Psychiatrist Sigmund Freud, whose theories centered on sexual issues, had his Venus in Aries.

In itself, this placement of Venus is not an indicator of an artistic sensibility. If you have artistic talent, as a result of other factors in your birth chart, you are likely to be avant garde, even rather provocative in the way you express yourself creatively. You enjoy breaking the rules and antagonizing the staid art world. Your style tends to be highly energetic and forceful, even abrasive or violent. For example, Russian composer Peter Ilych Tchaikovsky, whose music is exciting and original but hardly melodious, had his Venus in Aries.

Women with this planetary placement may reject traditional feminine images and put little value on such things as home, a husband and family. Independent, outspoken and assertive, you refuse to let any man dominate you and insist on being free to do as you wish in matters of love. Feminist Betty Friedan and maverick dancer Isadora Duncan, who had three children by three different lovers and was known for her unconventional attitudes toward adultery and free love, are two good examples of Venus in Aries. You probably aren't "feminine" in a traditional sense, for what makes you feel good about yourself as a woman is being able to do things like a man. You want to show everyone (including yourself) that anything a man can do a woman can do better. Thus, you might express this image of yourself through athletics, by being highly competitive in the business world, or by playing the role of "buddy" to the men in your life. As a child, you probably were a tomboy who beat up your brothers and could out-hit anyone on the local Little League team.

Men with Venus in Aries tend to be out-of-touch with their female sides (unless their Moons are in Cancer, Pisces or Taurus) and have little respect for female values, or even for women in general. German philosopher and misogynist Arthur Schopenhauer, for instance, had his Venus in Aries. Your ideal woman is one who is "one of the guys," who likes to play football with you and your friends on Saturday afternoon and can drink the lot of you under the table afterwards. Emotional, gentle, delicate or sensitive women don't interest you in the least. You want a partner who is strong, feisty and independent, even a little "butch." Thus, you might find women with mesomorphic bodies, athletes and body builders more attractive than those with "hourglass" figures.

Venus in Taurus

With Venus in this earthy, luxury-loving sign, you have a tendency to indulge yourself in all sorts of sensual pleasures. You love good food and wine, beautiful clothing, fine furnishings, good sex, massage—everything that delights the senses. You appreciate the physical world as no other sign can, and experience it in a straight-forward, tactile way. If you can't touch it, taste it, hear it, smell it, you're not satisfied.

Because you so love beautiful things (and want to own as many as possible), you often find yourself in debt. You rarely ask how much something costs and hate to deny yourself anything. You have innate good taste, dress well and decorate your home opulently, proudly displaying your possessions like an athlete showcases trophies. Because of your luxury-loving lifestyle, you might put a prospective partner's financial portfolio first on your list of desirable qualities.

You may express your love of beauty in some artistic way, such as painting or sculpture, music (especially singing, since Taurus rules the throat), dance, architecture, interior or fashion design, landscaping or floral arranging. Artists Leonardo da Vinci and Salvador Dali, musicians/singers Paul McCartney, Eric Clapton, David Byrne, Merle Haggard, Herbie Mann and Bessie Smith, and architects I. M. Pei and Frank Lloyd Wright are a few examples of Venus in Taurus. Most likely, you have an affinity with nature and love plants and flowers. Botanists Luther Burbank and George Washington Carver, whose art form was plant breeding, also had Venus in Taurus.

Love relationships are extremely important to you, so important that you aren't always very discriminating in your choice of partners and often settle for any "warm body." You want constant companionship and aren't willing to give a partner much space. At times, your lover may feel s/he is just another one of your possessions. Faithful and devoted to those you love, you expect total loyalty in return and are terribly jealous and possessive. However, even if the object of your desire doesn't return your love, you keep on showering him/her with affection; once you've set your sights on someone you won't take no for an answer. Often you succeed in wearing down your loved one's resistance with your dogged persistence, but you need to guard against being too cloying and demanding.

You have a strong sex drive and a down-to-earth, natural attitude toward sexual expression; for you, satisfying your sexual desires is just like satisfying any other appetite. You also are affectionate and romantic, and seem to possess an innate understanding of how to please a partner physically.

With those you care about, you are generous to a fault, always buying them gifts, fixing them gourmet meals, taking care of all their physical needs. Nothing makes you happier than caring for your loved ones, and unless you have planets in some of the more individualistic signs like Aries, Leo or Aquarius, you may sacrifice your own best interests for others'.

Women with Venus in Taurus tend to hold traditional views of relationships and a "woman's place" in life. Singer and anti-homosexual activist Anita Bryant, for example, has her Venus in Taurus. You look at a relationship as an investment and expect a good return; there's no reason to waste time on a love affair that won't lead to marriage and security. This planetary placement suggests a degree of dependency, and quite likely you want your partner to support you in high style. The career world doesn't beckon to you as it does your Arien or Aquarian sisters. You are concerned with presenting a conventionally feminine image, and probably spend much time and money on your appearance. However, you don't like exercise much (unless your Sun is in Aries) and can be quite lazy. Thus, you may have a problem keeping your weight down, since you probably like to cook and enjoy rich food.

Men with this planetary position find the Rubenesque woman most appealing. No model-thin, androgynous females for you—you like your women voluptuous, even plump. Nor do you enjoy partners who are independent or assertive. Your feminine ideal is sweet-tempered, sensual, seductive and passive. If she's also a good cook, all the better.

Venus in Gemini

Venus is associated with artistic creations, and Gemini rules communication, therefore, if you have artistic talent you are likely to express it through some form of writing. You love language and the written word, and want to share your thoughts with others. For example, the birth charts of William Shakespeare, Henry David Thoreau, Saul Bellow, Bob Dylan and Cole Porter all feature Venus in Gemini. Or, since Gemini also rules the hands, you might use your hands in some creative manner. Artists Albrecht Dürer, Rembrandt and Maxfield Parrish, and fighter Joe Louis are examples of two very different ways that this combination can be expressed.

Communication is of utmost importance in your relationships. If you can't talk to your partner, no amount of sexual attraction will keep you interested for long. Your lovers must also be your friends. You want a partner with whom you can share ideas, who will teach you new things and expose you to new experiences. Intelligence might be first on your list of desirable qualities in a partner, and you probably find that you learn a great deal from your lovers.

When you are with your partner you never stop talking, and when you're apart, you write long love letters or telephone frequently just to hear his/her voice. You enjoy talking and/or writing about love—your own, or love in general. This is the position of the romance novelist, or the person who carries on a love affair mainly through letters, e. g., Cyrano de Bergerac. You aren't very good about keeping secrets and are inclined to gossip about others' relationships. You also reveal more about your own love life than anyone ever wanted to know. What good is a love affair if you can't tell everyone about it?

Your romantic feelings aren't very deep or intense and others may consider you rather superficial and detached. You bounce back quickly and easily from disappointments in love, eager to move on to new relationships and experiences. What you lack in emotional depth you make up for in variety.

Gemini is a dualistic sign, and you often may have more than one love interest at a time. For example, Brigham Young, who led the Mormon migration to Utah and had seventeen wives, had his Venus in Gemini. So did former President John F. Kennedy, who was known for his philandering as well as his intelligence and oratory ability. Actor and legendary lover Rudolph Valentino and (according to some sources) King Henry VIII of England, who had six wives, are other good examples of Venus in Gemini. In fact, you are happier when you are involved with two (or more) lovers simultaneously, since each of them satisfies different needs and desires in you. You firmly believe that you can't get everything you want from one person, but maybe with two, three or more you'll be able to find total fulfillment. You are perfectly capable of loving several people at the same time and don't understand why your partners can't accept this situation, since you never mean to hurt anyone.

Also, you are afraid of missing out on something if you commit yourself to one mate. The expression, "the grass is greener on the other side of the fence" certainly applies to you. You never stop scanning the horizon for prospective partners and can be an incorrigible flirt. Unless you also have several planets in signs such as Taurus, Cancer, Scorpio or Capricorn, you probably have trouble remaining faithful to one person for long. You can't stand possessiveness and if your partner tries to "clip your wings" you might lie, sneak around or employ other tactics to maintain your freedom. To you, having many different lovers is a form of freedom of expression, a right guaranteed to you in the first amendment to the Constitution.

Women with this planetary position like to think of themselves as being intelligent, articulate, friendly and free-spirited, and want others to see them this way, too. You use your mental and verbal abilities to attract lovers, and consider a good mind to be the mark of femininity. You also value intelligence and well-developed communication skills in other women and look for these qualities in your friends. You have lots of friends and acquaintances, and although they may be quite different in many ways, they all are intellectually stimulating, talkative and hungry for knowledge.

Men with this placement find intelligent women especially attractive. You are not intimidated in the least by a partner who is smarter than you are. You enjoy a woman who can hold up her end of the conversation, and even teach you a few things. Most importantly, you want your lover to be your friend, someone with whom you can share ideas and good times.

Venus in Cancer

Cancer is the sign of the home; therefore, if you have artistic talent you might choose to express it in an area such as interior design, architecture or furniture making. The country in which you live is your home on a larger scale, so perhaps you use your creative abilities in some patriotic manner, or to serve or glorify your homeland. Francis Scott Key who composed the United States' National Anthem, "The Star Spangled Banner," is a good example of Venus in Cancer. So is actor Bob Hope, who is known for entertaining American military troops serving overseas.

In relationships, you are most concerned with security and permanence. It is essential for you to have a close, abiding partnership and a family to provide you with a center of emotional warmth and stability. Quality, not quantity is important to you in love relationships. The emotional bonds you form with a partner are strong and enduring, and the commitments you make in love are forever. Once you are involved in a relationship, infidelity is simply unthinkable. You are extremely possessive and jealous, and couldn't bear to have your mate be unfaithful to you. Other relationships threaten the security the partnership provides for you. Even if your relationship is unhappy you will stay in it for the emotional and/or material security it provides, and nothing could be more devastating to you than to have your partner leave you.
You invest totally in your lover and expect the same sort of unquestioning devotion in return. In fact, you become so enmeshed in the relationship that it's hard for you to distinguish between your partner and yourself; in your mind and heart, the two of you form a single entity and neither exists as an individual. You want to share everything with your partner and feel rejected and left out if s/he has friends or interests that don't include you. If your lover has several planets in Taurus, Cancer or Scorpio this symbiotic existence may work out fine, but someone whose chart is dominated by Arien, Geminian, Sagittarian or Aquarian energies will feel smothered by such closeness.

Within the context of your relationships you are highly emotional, though if your Sun is in Gemini you won't show this emotional side of yourself to anyone other than your lover. In order for you to be content in a partnership you must be able to form a strong feeling connection with your mate. You want to be so entwined that you can intuit each other's needs and desires, and don't even have to speak. Affectionate and demonstrative, you enjoy being physically close to your partner, too, and like to cuddle, hold hands and touch him/her frequently.

You express your love by nurturing your mate: cooking his/her favorite foods, fussing over him/her like the proverbial mother hen. Men and women alike often play a substitute mother role in the relationship, behaving in an overly protective and solicitous manner, calling their loved ones "baby," and thinking of themselves as their mates' caretakers.

Women with this position connect motherhood with femininity. You see a woman's role as that of childbearer and can't imagine why any woman would choose not to have children. You delight in this image, for being someone's mother provides you with a sense of purpose. Your family is the most important part of your life and your reason for living; thus, you may spoil your children and sacrifice everything else for them. You love children—your own and everyone else's—and may devote much time and energy to caring for them. Actress Sally Struthers, who does much to help unfortunate children around the world, is a good example of Venus in Cancer.

Conventional and conservative in your attitudes about women's roles in society, you probably aren't interested in making your mark in the business world. If you have a job outside the home, it's only a sideline—your *real* work is your family. You believe in the concept of the husband as provider and wife as nurturer, and expect your partner to be the one who supports the family monetarily while you take care of the kids and the home. Because you see money as a source of security, you are very concerned with having a mate who can provide for you and your children and buy you the home and creature comforts you desire.

Men with Venus in Cancer are attracted to women who have a maternal, nurturing quality about them. You may even look for a woman who reminds you of your mother. Your ideal woman is the Madonna. Androgenous, athletic or model-thin women don't appeal to you in the least; you much prefer big-breasted fertility goddess-types. Nor are you interested in feminists or women who are individualistic, independent or career-oriented. You're looking for an old-fashioned homebody who adores children, loves to cook and will devote herself totally to you and the family.

Venus in Leo

Highly creative, it is very important to you to express yourself in some artistic manner. You love beauty in all its myriad forms and want to make your own, special contribution to the world of art. Painters James McNeil Whistler and Peter Paul Rubens, film makers Stanley Kubrick and Vittorio de Sica, and composer Claude Debussy are a few examples of Venus in Leo.

You have a strong sense of drama and your creations often are vibrant, bold and ornate as well as imaginative. Certainly there is nothing timid or subtle about the way you express yourself, and your art may even be somewhat garish and gaudy. For instance, P. T. Barnum, whose art form was the circus, had his Venus in Leo.

Venus also is associated with physical beauty and adornment, so this placement could signify an interest in fashion design, hair styling, modeling or fashion photography. For example, the birth charts of clothing designers Yves St. Laurent, Pierre Cardin and Coco Chanel all feature Venus in Leo. Whatever form your creative expression takes, you want recognition for it. You have no intention of being a "starving artist" living in obscurity. You are proud of your talent and believe that fame and fortune are your just due, and you want your name to be known and respected.

Love is also extremely important to you. In fact, you can even elevate love to an art form. Love may be an artistic stimulant for you; perhaps you compose love songs or write beautiful sonnets to your lover or paint his/her portrait.

You love being in love, being the center of your lover's attention, being involved in the dramatic spectacle of romance. An incurable romantic, you might shower your partner with gifts, songs, flowers and attention (and expect the same sort of demonstrations of devotion in return). Ardent and passionate in affairs of the heart, you throw yourself into your romances with such enthusiasm and fanfare that at times you seem to be playing a part in an opera (or soap opera). If the truth be known, Romeo is one of your favorite literary characters and the image of the "Latin lover" appeals to you. For all your theatrics, however, your affection is real and you are capable of deep devotion and loyalty in relationships. You want a stable, committed and loving partnership, complete with children and a beautiful home that is your castle. And no matter how long you and your partner are together, the romance never goes out of your relationship.

Women with this planetary position see themselves as heroines in gothic romance novels. You want to be courted in high style, to be adored and pampered and treated like a queen by your lovers. Flattery will get your partner everywhere with you, and you need to be told you are beautiful at least a dozen times a day. Terribly vain, you spend plenty of time and money on your appearance and ask your mirror on a regular basis "who's the fairest in the land?" You enjoy wearing the latest (and showiest) clothes, jewelry, hairstyles and see no reason for keeping a low profile. You love to see heads turn when you make your entrance, and whether or not you are a great beauty, you have a sense of style and grandeur that sets you apart from "ordinary mortals." Actress Lauren Bacall is a good example of Venus in Leo. You're nobody's docile pet or slave, however. Strong-willed and individualistic, you are usually the dominant partner in any relationship.

Men with Venus in Leo are most attracted to women who are glamorous, exceptionally beautiful, even a bit gaudy. Your ideal woman is the movie star, the Las Vegas showgirl, the California golden girl. Looks count for everything, and you want a lover who's a perfect 10. Who cares if she can't spell her own name? You want to show her off as a gorgeous accessory, the way you would a new sports car or a custom-made suit. Though you may not end up with this sort of woman as your life partner, you never stop looking and dreaming.

Venus in Virgo

This is not an especially creative placement for Venus—you are too cautious and self-critical, afraid to try new things and insecure about your abilities. If you can't be Rembrandt, why bother? However, if other factors in your chart give you artistic talent, your artwork will be masterful in its precision, neatness and detail. Patient and meticulous, you are capable of doing intricate, painstaking work and might express yourself well in such areas as engraving, drafting, needlepoint, quilting, woodcarving or jewelry making.

Since function is as important to you as form, you might choose to create practical, useful objects, or those which have substance and an earthy, tactile quality to them. For example, architect and furniture designer Le Corbusier and sculptors Alexander Calder and Henry Moore had Venus in Virgo. So did Henry Ford, whose art form was the automobile. And chef Julia Child, known for her culinary artistry, also has Venus in Virgo.

In relationships, too, you are cautious and practical. Not given to storybook romances, you are more interested in relationships that function efficiently and orderly on a day-to-day basis. A solid, down-to-earth partnership that provides both parties with their basic needs and makes life easier for everyone would appeal to you more than a whirlwind love affair.

Although your ideal lover may not be a knight on a white charger or a fairy princess, you can be quite picky about your partners. You have a very exacting set of specifications which candidates must meet if they want you to consider them. You might not expect your lover to be a great beauty, but if s/he isn't squeaky clean, punctual and hard-working you'll quickly scratch him/her off your dance card. You're also concerned with etiquette and want your partner to have impeccable manners. The birth chart of etiquette expert Emily Post, for example, features Venus in Virgo. Once in a relationship, you have a tendency to find fault with your partner and to complain long and loud about all those annoying little habits you just can't stand. You expect your partner to be perfect and have trouble accepting a few human failings.

You want desperately to feel needed by your partner, and work hard to make yourself indispensable in his/her life. Perhaps your paycheck is absolutely essential to your partner's survival. Or, you may stoically take care of all the details of running the home—cooking, cleaning, childcare, etc.—so efficiently that life would be impossible without you. You show your affection by doing practical things for your loved ones—making sure they have clean clothes and nutritious meals, for instance—rather than showering them with words of endearment or lavish gifts.

Women with this Venus placement in their birth charts pride themselves on being neat, well-organized, efficient and dependable. Being able to take care of the many details of life makes you feel good about yourself as a woman. You probably try to be "superwoman," however, working a full-time job outside the home, then assuming complete responsibility for the house and kids, too. This is partly because you don't know how to say no, and partly because you aren't satisfied with the way others do things.

To you, cleanliness is a sign of femininity, and you wouldn't be caught dead wearing dirty jeans or a paint-splattered sweatshirt. Nor would you feel comfortable in flashy or overtly sexy clothing that might draw attention to you. You prefer to fade into the background and usually dress in modest, conservative, neatly pressed outfits.

Men with Venus in Virgo are most attracted to women who are unassuming, unpretentious, even a little shy. Neatness is more important to you than beauty in a partner, and you're turned off instantly by unkempt hair and dirty fingernails. Your ideal partner is conscientious, dependable, intelligent, modest and practical. She can tune her own car, comprehend income tax forms, make cakes from scratch and keep the household running on budget. She's always there when you need her, but doesn't demand a lot of praise for what she does and never tries to upstage you.

Venus in Libra

You enjoy art and beauty in all their myriad forms, and want to fill your life with lovely things. Creative and sensitive to color, harmony and balance, you probably have artistic ability. Artists Pablo Picasso and Robert Indiana, writers T. S. Eliot, Albert Camus and D. H. Lawrence (whose novels are about love and relationships) are some examples of Venus in Libra. Whether or not you are an artist yourself, you have an innate sense of aesthetics and are able to appreciate fine art, music, theatre, literature, etc., and might be a collector or patron of the arts.

Relationships of all kinds are central in your life. Friendly, gracious and good-natured, you have many friends and acquaintances and love to socialize. Your manners are impeccable and you are known for your diplomacy and tact. Able to get along with just about anyone, you are the perfect guest at social gatherings, the ideal co-worker and a good friend to all.

You don't like being alone and function best—personally and professionally—in partnerships. It is especially important to you to be involved in a love relationship at all times. For you, love makes the world go 'round and you aren't complete without a lover. However, you don't usually pursue a prospective partner actively; your way is to make yourself attractive, then sit back and wait for him/her to come to you. Your idea of love is moonlit nights, soft music, wine and roses, where everyone lives happily ever after. There's nothing sordid or tempestuous in your romantic fantasies.

Because love is vital to your happiness, you tend to place more emphasis on the relationship and your partner than on yourself. You are always ready to compromise to maintain the partnership, and to put your loved one's wellbeing in front of your own. Perhaps you don't even know what you really want, since your happiness is dependent upon your partner's; if s/he is satisfied you are, too. You eagerly adopt your lover's interests, friends, beliefs, lifestyle, etc., and can be something of a chameleon.

You want everything about your relationships to be nice all the time, and can't stand arguments or anger. The consummate peacemaker, your motto might be "don't make waves." Thus, you rarely speak your mind or stand up for yourself in a relationship for fear of causing friction or opposition. You'd rather go along to get along. Once involved in a relationship, you are faithful and loyal to your partner. Even if you aren't satisfied in the partnership you are loathe to end it because you can't stand to make a scene or have anyone mad at you. You'd rather slip out the back door when your mate isn't looking or write a "Dear John" letter than confront the situation openly.

Women with this planetary position are extremely feminine in a conventional sense. Actress Grace Kelly, for example, had her Venus in Libra. You enjoy wearing beautiful clothing, cosmetics, perfume, jewelry, and your appearance is very important to you. You devote much time and energy to making yourself look your best and tend to be terribly vain. You might place so much importance on your looks that you fail to develop other qualities, and are more devastated than other women when old age takes away your trump card. You also pride yourself on your pleasant disposition and refinement. Easily offended by coarseness, you equate femininity with grace, good manners and physical beauty. You can't bear to get your hands dirty, dislike sports of all kinds (unless your Sun is in Sagittarius) and wouldn't be caught dead without your mascara.

Men with Venus in Libra are attracted to traditionally beautiful women. Your female ideal is the "perfect lady," delicate, sweet-tempered, refined, intelligent, with looks like Catherine Deneuve's. She never changes diapers, pumps her own gasoline, perspires or swears. You are turned off by strong-minded, independent women or those who are highly competitive—in business or private life. You are looking for a woman who will complement you, not one who is fully-formed in herself.

Venus in Scorpio

Superficial beauty and art that is purely decorative have little appeal for you. Instead you are fascinated by what goes on at the deepest levels, behind the scenes so to speak, and regardless of the form your creativity takes it will deal with hidden motivations, the dark side of human nature or the mysteries of the Universe. Mystery writer Agatha Christie, science fiction writer H. G. Wells and film maker Martin Scorcese are examples of Venus in Scorpio. Your art may border on the macabre or be disturbing in some way. Certainly it is anything but pretty. Often your subject matter is death and transformation. You pursue your muse with passion and intensity, and can become obsessed with your art to the exclusion of all else. However, your perseverance and focus allow you to develop your talent to a high level.

Or, you might express yourself through one of the metaphysical arts. The birth charts of telekenic Uri Geller and psychic Jeanne Dixon, for example, feature Venus in Scorpio.

No one takes love and relationships more seriously than you do. You are seeking nothing less than complete merger with a partner—body, mind and spirit. You aren't frivolous with your affection and open your heart to few. Extremely emotional, you realize how strong your feelings are and how deeply you can be hurt if a love affair doesn't work out, therefore, you are skeptical and cautious about getting involved. Once you commit yourself in love, however, you do so totally and permanently. You take the vow "till death do us part" seriously, and are a devoted, romantic and passionate lover.

You invest so much of yourself in your mate and become so emotionally entwined that you have trouble separating your feelings from his/hers. It is as though you are Siamese twins joined at the heart. Therefore, if you lose your lover or if s/he betrays you, you feel like you have lost part of yourself. This is the reason for your infamous jealousy and possessiveness. If a lover rejects you or breaks off the relationship—particularly if the cause is another wo/man—you are likely to seek revenge. For you, a broken heart can be fatal.

Your relationships are intense, punctuated by emotional upheavals. Either you and your lover are in the throes of romantic ecstasy or clawing at each other's throats. You thrive on emotional excitement and excess, and would be bored in a partnership that functioned smoothly most of the time. If things become too calm and predictable, you might provoke your partner into a dramatic scene just to get your emotional adrenalin flowing. You are the type who believes that love is never so good as after a heated fight.

Power is usually a factor in your relationships, and it can be a heady aphrodisiac. You enjoy seeing the power you have over your lover, and may use it in manipulative ways. You want to be in control of the partnership and power struggles between you and your mate may be the source of many of your arguments.

Often you seem to fall in love with someone who isn't right for you, or with someone you can't have for one reason or another. There can be a degree of self-frustration and destructiveness in the way you approach love relationships, for one of Scorpio's roles is to demolish the ego. Regardless of how unsuitable or unattainable your love object is, however, you refuse to give up and may become obsessive in your pursuit of him/her.

You may find that you are changed by your relationships, in subtle or profound ways, and that every love affair has a deep, transformative effect on you.

Women with Venus in Scorpio project a powerful sensuality and magnetism that can be both enticing and intimidating. There is something mysterious about you that makes you irresistible to many men, even if you are not especially pretty. To you, part of being feminine is expressing your sexuality. You enjoy being seductive, and seeing the effect you have on men reinforces your sense of yourself as a woman. Perhaps you dress in a way that is overtly provocative. Or, you might like to wear clothing that either makes you look tough, such as black leather, or exotic outfits and bizarre combinations that attract attention.

Men with this planetary position are most interested in women who are dark, intense, mysterious and obviously sexual, the kind you wouldn't think of taking home to meet your mother. No cheerleader types or Miss Americas for you—your ideal woman is the femme fatale or the porno queen. For example, *Hustler* magazine publisher Larry Flynt has his Venus in Scorpio. You're also looking for a partner who is strong and not easily dominated by you, someone who will make you struggle to win her love. To you, nothing of value comes easily.

Venus in Sagittarius

If you have artistic ability you probably express it in a way that shows your sense of fantasy and humor. Though you may be as serious as anyone about your art and self-expression, you seem to have more fun with it. Whether you're writing an adventure story or designing a skyscraper, you don't hesitate to depart a bit from stark reality, to exaggerate and include a touch of whimsicality. You have a vivid imagination and a special talent for keeping your audience entertained. Authors Jonathan Swift, Robert Louis Stevenson, Louis Carroll and Mark Twain, and film maker Frederico Fellini are some good examples of Venus in Sagittarius. You enjoy art that is bigger than life and not so harsh; in your opinion, art should take us beyond the mundane and broaden our perspective by introducing us to all sorts of possibilities. The birth charts of impressionists Georges Seurat and Claude Monet, and abstract painter Jackson Pollock, for example, feature Venus in Sagittarius.

In relationships, you are equally expansive and curious. Friendly, out-going, adventurous and optimistic, you love to socialize and often are the life of the party. Your list of friends, acquaintances and lovers is extensive and includes people of all kinds. You see no reason to limit yourself to only one partner and miss out on other possibilities. Your motto might be "you only go around once," so why not try everything you can while you've got the chance. Consequently, you'll have problems if your lover isn't as free and easy as you are and insists on fidelity or permanence. You mean well and don't want to hurt anyone's feelings, so you tend to promise what you can't deliver. If you get caught in an awkward amorous situation, your first line of defense is to lie with a smile. You can be terribly fickle, flirtatious, superficial and self-indulgent in matters of love. To you, it's all good fun. If your Sun is in Capricorn or Scorpio, you'll tend to be more serious and willing to make commitments, though you might subscribe to the old double standard: it's okay for you to run around but your partner better not try it.

You tend to idealize the concept of love, so much so that it is impossible for you to find a flesh-and-blood mate to fulfill your romantic fantasies. You are looking for a fairy princess or knight in shining armor, and may prefer chasing your dream to settling into a real-life, day-to-day partnership.

Generous with your time and money, you enjoy showering your friends and lovers with gifts. You like to go out on the town with your partner and do things in grand style. Cuddling up with your lover in front of the fireplace isn't exactly your idea of a good time; you'd rather play a few games of tennis, have a sumptuous dinner, go to the theatre, then dance the rest of the night away. Anyone who's involved with you had better have plenty of energy.

You want your partners to expand your horizons, to expose you to new ideas and experiences. Perhaps you choose lovers who will play the role of teacher for you, or you might enjoy teaching them what you know. Another possibility is that you could be attracted to people from other countries or cultures. For you, relationships are growth-producing opportunities and you learn something from everyone you meet.

Women with Venus in Sagittarius pride themselves on their sense of humor, gregariousness and cheerful dispositions. It is important to you to be well-liked and to have lots of friends and admirers. The more popular you are, the better you feel about yourself as a woman. Quantity is more important than quality. You also may enjoy sports and are especially concerned with looking physically fit. A dedicated follower of fashion and fads, you are always eager to try the latest trend. Actress and fitness enthusiast Jane Fonda, for example, has her Venus in Sagittarius.

Men with this planetary position are most attracted to active, vivacious, friendly and fun-loving women. No intense, possessive or highly emotional types need apply. You want a partner who's more of a buddy than a lover, someone with whom you can do things and share ideas and experiences. You admire knowledge and worldliness, and are fascinated by women who have done things and know things you don't. Tall, slim, athletic women with long legs probably appeal to you most.

Venus in Capricorn

Although this sign position doesn't in itself signify artistic talent, if other factors in your chart denote creative ability you probably will express it in a traditional, conservative or practical manner. Your tastes are conventional and reserved, and you look to the past for inspiration, using forms and techniques that are "tried and true." Perhaps you will not discover or express your artistic interests until later in life, and you may have to overcome blocks of some kind that stand in the way of your creativity—family responsibilities, financial concerns, lack of education or fear of failure.

It is important for you to create something material and tangible, that is useful and will endure for generations to come. Thus, your preferred art form could be architecture. Or, you might be a collector of art, an investor in antiques and/or "old masters" (rather than someone who takes a chance on unknown artists). Another possibility is that you would make a business of art.

In relationships, you are cautious, practical and traditional. You seek stability and permanence in both romantic and business partnerships. Not one to take relationships lightly, if you make a commitment to another person you stick by it faithfully. One-night stands and brief affairs don't interest you much. You like constancy, predictability and the security that comes from an established partnership with clearly defined parameters and patterns. Therefore, your relationships have a better chance than most of enduring. Actor Paul Newman, for example, has his Venus in Capricorn and his marriage to Joanne Woodward is one of Hollywood's few long-term partnerships. However, your desire for stability and permanence can cause you to stay in a relationship that is no longer satisfying, or one that has ceased to grow and develop. People with this planetary placement can let themselves and their relationships get "in a rut," and become more of a habit than a joy.

When it comes to matters of the heart, you are a realist, a pragmatist. You aren't the type to fall head-over-heels in love with someone, and usually want to know your lover for a long time before making a commitment. You may even view love relationships as a business arrangement, and are more likely to marry for money, status, security or convenience than out of passion. Therefore, others might consider you cold-blooded or mercenary. Eva Braun, mistress to Adolf Hitler for fifteen years, is an example of Venus in Capricorn. You aren't very romantic or affectionate, and tend to be reserved and constrained when it comes to expressing your feelings for your partner. What you lack in romance, however, you make up for in loyalty. Duty-conscious and reliable, you won't shirk your responsibilities to your loved ones or dump your partner of many years for a younger, prettier face.

Though you appear to be aloof, unfeeling or superior in love matters, in truth you are terribly shy and sensitive. You often hesitate to make a move for fear of being rejected. Perhaps there is some obstacle—physical, emotional, financial or otherwise—that keeps you from involving yourself in love relationships. For example, French painter Henri Toulouse-Lautrec, whose abnormally short stature interfered with his love life, had Venus in Capricorn. You undervalue your attractiveness and are afraid that others don't like you. Because love to you is serious business, you usually won't take a chance if you aren't certain of the outcome beforehand. Thus, you may miss out on many romantic opportunities or wait until rather late in life to form a love relationship.

Women with Venus in Capricorn view maturity and wisdom as desirable qualities in a woman and, therefore, are less likely than others to dread growing older. You also tend to be career-oriented, and might place work ahead of marriage and children. Being successful professionally makes you feel good about yourself as a woman, and you certainly don't believe businesswomen are less feminine than homemakers. Entrepreneurs Elizabeth Arden and Helena Rubinstein are two good examples of Venus in Capricorn. However, your attitudes toward love and relationships are traditional and somewhat old-fashioned, so you may have difficulty reconciling your professional ambitions with your conservative views about male-female partnerships.

Men with this planetary position are most interested in women who are mature, refined, no-nonsense types. Your ideal woman looks like she just stepped out of *Town and Country* magazine. Her public image is proper and dignified, but in private she's sensual and passionate. Classic beauties with old-fashioned values and blue-chip stocks are the stuff of which your romantic fantasies are made. You also might be attracted to women who are older than you.

Venus in Aquarius

The Renaissance may have been the pinnacle of artistic achievement, but as far as you're concerned only the most modern and innovative art forms are worth considering. You might be interested in computer graphics, neon sculpture, holographs, electronic music or experimental theatre. Or, you could choose to express your creativity and inventiveness through aerospace or automotive design. Anything new, different, untried or unorthodox appeals to you. Your willingness to go where others haven't and your lack of concern for what the critics think enable you to break new ground. German architect Ludwig Mies van der Rohe, who was known for designing sleek contemporary buildings and furniture, is a good example of Venus in Aquarius.

In relationships, you have little regard for what society, your family or peers think. Your partner's religion, race, age, background or status isn't important to you. In fact, you enjoy pairing up with someone who is totally unlike yourself. "Vive la difference" might be your motto. You are eager to experience people and things that are new and unusual. But you also get much satisfaction from shocking more traditional people with your unorthodox behavior, and actually thrive on negative feedback. You want to do whatever "isn't done."

You insist on having lots of space and independence in your relationships, and can't bear possessiveness or jealousy. An open-ended arrangement that allows you to experiment freely would be more satisfactory than a conventional, monogamous partnership. French writer Simone de Beauvoir is a good example of Venus in Aquarius. She maintained a lifelong relationship with Jean Paul Sartre but never married him, retaining her right to see other men when she pleased. You are easily bored and need plenty of excitement, stimulation and change in your love life.

Fairness and equality are most important in your relationships. Both partners must have equal say and contribute fairly to the partnership. You won't last long in a love affair with someone who is either too domineering or too submissive.

You're looking for a lover who is also a friend, someone with whom you can share ideas and experiences. Not especially romantic or affectionate, you can seem detached, unloving and overly cerebral. Often you'd rather debate an intellectual concept than make love. You enjoy a good argument with your partner from time to time—for you, conflict adds spice to the relationship and you grow bored if things between you are peaceful for long.

Women with Venus in Aquarius value their individuality highly and have no intentions of letting a man tell them what to do. You consider yourself everyone's equal and are probably a supporter of women's rights. Feminists/writers Gertrude Stein, Gloria Steinem, Erica Jong and Amy Lowell are a few good examples of Venus in Aquarius. As far as you're concerned, a woman's place is anywhere but in the home. You want to be respected for your intelligence, and use your mind rather than your looks to attract others. Being independent, outspoken and avant garde, even a little outlandish at times, reinforces your sense of yourself as a woman. For example, legendary rock singer Janis Joplin had her Venus in Aquarius. You "march to a different drummer" and love to provoke traditionalists with your progressive ideas, behavior, dress, lifestyle.

Men with this planetary placement find intelligent, free-spirited, unorthodox women most attractive. You are looking for someone who is different, unpredictable, eccentric, who stands out in a crowd. No cookie-cutter beauty queens for you—your feminine ideal is definitely one-of-a-kind, and not necessarily good-looking in the usual sense. You also like women who stand up for themselves, speak their minds and refuse to let you overpower them. In short, you enjoy a bit of a challenge and a strong partner you can consider your equal.

Venus in Pisces

You have a wonderful imagination and a keen sensitivity to color, tone and rhythm, and might possess great artistic ability. You hear the music of the spheres and your inner world is full of visions of exquisite beauty or horror. Painter Vincent van Gogh, composers Johann Sebastian Bach and Felix Mendelsohn, singers Billie Holiday, Marvin Gaye, Barbra Streisand and Ella Fitzgerald, writers Elizabeth B. Browning, Jules Verne and Edgar Allen Poe, and film maker Francis Ford Coppola are some good examples of Venus in Pisces. This position can be indicative of the creative genius or the madman. Your imagination sometimes overwhelms you and your hypersensitivity can make it difficult for you to deal with the harsh and ugly side of life.

Though you might have plenty of talent, you tend to be lazy about developing it. Being an artist requires discipline and effort, but you'd rather dream about your creations than work to bring them to fruition. You could benefit from the influence of a strong, pragmatic manager or partner, someone who will push you to do your best.

In relationships you are inclined to be overly idealistic. You are looking for the perfect lover and nothing less than Apollo or Aphrodite will do. As a result, you usually end up disappointed by mere mortals. You might reject all possible lovers because none meets your unrealistic standards. Or, you may deny your partner's flaws and see him/her in the light of your romantic fantasies, just as Don Quixote imagined the prostitute Aldonza Lorenzo was the virtuous lady Dulcinea. Your capacity to delude yourself is infinite and your unwillingness to look at your partner's true character can cause you to get involved with people who aren't right for you or who take advantage of you. Even if you end up in a relationship that is happy and enduring, you probably have a good many false illusions about your lover and the partnership in general.

Extremely emotional and romantic, you want to be able to share your deep, intense feelings with your lover and to relate to him/her on an intuitive level. So sensitive and attuned are you to your partner that you seem to be linked psychically. Ideally, you'd like to erase the physical boundaries between you and become totally enmeshed in each other. What you are looking for—a soulmate, a spiritual union—is hard to find on the Earth plane.

A sucker for a hard-luck story, you have a soft, forgiving and gullible heart. You want to help those who are less fortunate than yourself and thus may fall for someone who seems to need you, someone you can "save." For instance, a person who has a substance abuse problem or some other emotional or physical disability awakens your compassionate feelings and your desire to be needed. You often mistake pity for love. In relationships, you tend to see yourself as the savior/martyr, sacrificing your own best interests for your partner, and doing so makes you feel virtuous. However, this is a subtle form of manipulation, for in reality you are attempting to make over your lover, and you might be surprised to find that s/he resents you for it. You appear to be meek and passive in the relationship, but you actually have a great deal of hidden power.

Women with this planetary position can seem almost ethereal. Your idea of femininity is being gentle, delicate, graceful and helpful. It may be hard for you to assert yourself because, to you, it's "unladylike" to go after what you want or to stand up for yourself. You may even feel that you don't deserve to get what you want, that it's better to give than to receive. Therefore, you might let yourself be pushed around by your partners (unless your Sun is in Aries or Aquarius). Because you don't have a very clear image of who you are and tend to undervalue yourself, you are easily influenced by others and try to become what you believe others want you to be.

Your love of beauty, color, texture, etc., might inspire an interest in fashion. Even as an adult, you enjoy playing dress-up, creating different illusions with costumes and makeup, and you may be quite photogenic.

Men with Venus in Pisces are attracted to women who are passive, fragile, sensitive and pretty in a delicate, china-doll way. You tend to put women on a pedestal and are looking for a fairy princess rather than a human being. Your ideal woman is Cinderella. Strong-willed, outspoken or independent women don't interest you much. Nor do you find earthy or sensual women very appealing. Both types are too threatening. You want someone who needs you, is completely devoted to you, who professes her undying love in poetry and song—but you almost prefer to worship her from afar because touching her would destroy the fantasy.

Chapter Seven

Mars

Mars orbits the Sun in 687 days, however, it usually takes about two years to complete its passage through all twelve zodiacal signs due to periods of retrogradation.

Mars is one of the planetary embodiments of the masculine force and its glyph is used widely as a symbol for man.

Martian energy is assertive, projective, active, separating; its function is to differentiate the individual from the collective. How you project yourself outwardly, aggressively into the world and the way you go after what you want will be shown by the placement of Mars in your birth chart.

Along with the Sun, Mars is connected with your sense of self, identity, independence, individuality and self-sufficiency. Its position suggests areas where you are inclined to be self-centered, willful and unable to see another's point of view.

Confidence and courage also are associated with Mars. A well-placed Mars indicates a strong belief in yourself which allows you to face danger undaunted. However, Mars' position also shows the areas where you can be impulsive and impatient, where you will leap without looking.

Your energy level and vitality are affected by Mars' position in your chart. A strongly-placed Mars gives an abundance of natural vitality, stamina, recuperative ability and physical strength.

Along with the Sun and Jupiter, Mars is a source of enthusiasm and youthful optimism. A cosmic internal combustion engine, Mars generates the impetus for facing challenges and bouncing back from defeats. It shows how you confront opponents, whether you respond with "fight or flight" tendencies, and how you handle conflict in your life. Mars is competitive and combative, and many athletes, entrepreneurs, career soldiers and adventurers have it prominently placed in their charts.

Mars is the planet of desire. Its sign describes the "color" of your desires as well as the *modus operandi* you use to pursue them. What you desire—fame, love, money, freedom—also will be indicated by Mars' sign, house position and aspects.

The desire for sexual expression is associated with Mars. How and where you use your sexual energy, your attitudes toward sex, and what you find stimulating are indicated by Mars in your birth chart. Whether your libido is strong or weak, free-flowing or obstructed, will be shown by Mars' sign and aspects.

Mars is usually more accessible to men than to women. Men generally identify with Mars; women sometimes project it onto the men in their lives. In a man's chart, Mars suggests what strokes his "male ego" and how he would like others to see him, as well as what characteristics he respects in other men. In a woman's chart, Mars can represent her ideal man and it shows what masculine qualities she is likely to find attractive.

In order to get a complete picture of how this energy will express itself in your life, it is important also to examine Mars' house position and aspects to other planets in your chart.

Mars in Aries

You are energetic, aggressive and highly competitive, a combination that strongly suggests athletic potential. Football great Joe Namath and basketball stars Kareem Abdul-Jabbar and Larry Bird are good examples of Mars in Aries.

However, you also have a "short fuse" and may tend to let your temper get in your way, as is the case with baseball team manager Billy Martin, whose Mars is in Aries. You also might have difficulty disciplining yourself and focusing your abundant energy and desire unless you also have some stabilizing factors (such as a prominent Saturn) in your chart.

Impulsive and overly confident, you usually leap before you look. Action is your middle name, and you rarely think about the consequences of your actions before you do something. You never let an obstacle stand in your way. You charge ahead, undaunted by risks; in fact, the more dangerous a venture is, the more eagerly you tackle it—whether you're speculating in the stock market or sailing single-handed across the Atlantic. Sometimes you accomplish tremendous feats of daring and courage, other times you are simply reckless and foolhardy. You love challenges, even conflict, and want to keep things stirred up; peace and harmony bore you. For instance, some sources place Mars in Aries in the birth charts of both Iraq and Lebanon.

You have a strong sense of self, but little understanding of others. Assertive to the point of being pushy, you don't know how to go easy or be patient. Your impetuousness can cause you to be accident prone. At times, you seem rather like an exuberant, roughneck kid, unaware of your own strength or your affect on others. Subtlety and tact are unknown to you. Blustering and blunt, you have a way of saying the wrong thing at the wrong time and can offend others with your coarseness or brute force.

The ultimate individualist, you can't bear to have anyone else tell you what to do or how to do it. The word compromise isn't in your vocabulary and since you rarely value others' opinions you are likely to have trouble in situations that require teamwork. If you can't do it on your own you are at a loss. Fortunately, you have the drive and vitality to accomplish more than a dozen people and usually function best when you can do everything yourself. Once you get going, it's hard to keep up with you, but your attention span is short and you tend to run out of steam and interest rather quickly. Better at starting things than completing them, your life may be littered with half-finished projects.

Your sex drive is strong, but you lack true sensuality. Sex, to you, is a contest and a form of physical release—sort of an intimate boxing match—and your romantic quotient is zero. You also tend to be a bit rough, pushy and concerned only with your own satisfaction. Unless Libra or Taurus is prominent in your chart, you are probably more interested in adding notches to your bedpost than with having a meaningful relationship.

Men with this position can be the ultimate "macho men." A "man's man," you love hanging around the gym with the other guys, hunting and going out drinking with your buddies. Writer Norman Mailer and actor Clint Eastwood are two good examples of Mars in Aries. You'll stand up to anyone about anything, and never walk away from a fight. In fact, you often are the instigator. You particularly enjoy provoking authorities, and there is a rebellious, individualistic spirit in you that won't bend to the powers that be. American patriot Nathan Hale and Latin American revolutionary Che Guevarra are two such examples of Mars in Aries. The feistiness and violence inherent in this planetary position can indicate lack of feeling and compassion, and you can be cruel at times. Some extreme examples of Mars in Aries are the Marquis de Sade, murderer Richard Speck, and Army Lieutenant William Calley who was convicted of the 1967 My Lai massacre.

Some women with this position are just as assertive and competitive as their male counterparts; others project this part of themselves onto the men in their lives. You may be attracted mostly to strong, aggressive men, athletes, "muscle boys" or "macho men."

Mars in Taurus

Rather than chasing madly after your goals, you pursue them with dogged determination. You may take longer than some to achieve your desires, and you might not do it with so much flair and daring, but your accomplishments are more enduring. Once you decide you want something, you are not easily discouraged and you often succeed because of your persistence and single-mindedness.

One thing you are likely to pursue is wealth, and you'll invest all of your energy to this end. Material possessions and creature comforts are important to you and you'll do whatever you have to so you can have them in abundance.

Another area in which you might choose to focus your energy is the arts. Taurus stabilizes Martian energy, giving you the patience and perseverance to spend years developing and perfecting your talent. Artists Edgar Degas, Paul Klee,

Salvador Dali, James McNeil Whistler and M. C. Escher are some examples of Mars in Taurus. Architecture and interior or furniture design in particular might interest you. You appreciate beautiful things and even if you don't have much talent, you probably enjoy art and might collect it.

This Mars placement indicates great sensuality and sexuality, and satisfying your physical desires is probably first on your list of priorities. No one understands the pleasures of the flesh like you do. Sex is never far from your thoughts and you have a tendency to be led around by your libido. You invest so much time and energy into fulfilling your body's appetites that you might overlook other areas of life. Your approach to sex is straightforward and uncomplicated, devoid of fantasies or fetishes. Your only sexual problems might be insatiability and lack of discrimination. For example, Catherine the Great of Russia, who was known for having many lovers, had her Mars in Taurus.

You don't radiate with energy the way people who have Mars in fire signs do, and unless you have several planets in Aries or Sagittarius, you probably aren't very athletic. However, you have tremendous endurance and muscle strength and are capable of doing more physical work than almost anyone. Even if you appear rather lethargic and overweight you are remarkably powerful, and beating you in a fight is much more difficult than it looks. You're a lover, not a fighter, though, and it takes a lot to make you mad. You also have great resistance to illness and stress.

Though you can be stubborn, you are generally easy-going and cooperative and are able to set your ego aside when teamwork or compromise is needed.

Men with this position pride themselves on their sexual prowess. Your measure of a man is how many times he can make love in a night. Earning lots of money and owning expensive and showy things also makes you feel good about yourself as a man.

Women with this planetary placement might be attracted to teddy bear-like men who are both strong and gentle. You want someone who is affectionate, sensual, good-natured and down-to-earth. No James Dean types for you. Your masculine ideal is dependable, stable and a good provider, someone who'll praise your cooking and keep you warm at night. A man who enjoys doing the cooking himself is even better.

Mars in Gemini

Much of your energy goes into mental activity and you are passionate about ideas. Your mind is never still, always racing from one thought to another. You are interested in almost everything, but rarely focus on any subject for long—there is always something else more fascinating just around the corner and you don't want to miss anything. Because you try to cover so much intellectual territory, you only manage to skim the surface quickly, rarely taking the time to examine any area in detail. Your mental breadth is greater than its depth. Always hungry for information, you are a voracious reader and lifelong student. You love gathering data and are a human library of disassociated facts, figures and trivia, however, your tendency to look at the pieces rather than the whole can cause you to miss the bigger picture.

Sharing what you know with others is as important to you as knowing it in the first place, and you love talking with other intellectually-oriented people. You express your ideas loudly and forcefully, and at times can be quite argumentative. And since you rarely censor your speech, saying whatever comes into your mind without considering the effect your words might have, you often "put your foot in your mouth" or hurt others' feelings inadvertently.

Your desire to communicate your thoughts to others may inspire you to become a writer. For example, the birth charts of writers Saul Bellow, Joseph Heller, Herman Melville, Flannery O'Connor, Sir Arthur Conan Doyle, Virginia Woolf, F. Scott Fitzgerald and James Joyce all feature Mars in Gemini. You have the energy and drive to create volumes of text, however, you'll probably need a good editor to pare down your excess verbiage.

So much of your energy is channeled into mental and verbal activity that you almost never stop talking. Teaching, lecturing or public speaking are other ways in which you might express yourself. You probably have a strong voice and can put a great deal of fire into what you say. Civil rights leader and powerful orator Martin Luther King, Jr., for example, had his Mars in Gemini.

Highly sociable, you enjoy meeting new people and see every interaction as a potential learning experience. This is especially true when it comes to sexual relationships. You eagerly pursue new experiences and partners, and find it difficult if not impossible to remain faithful to one person for long—you might miss out on someone more interesting. For you, sex is a game, not something to be taken too seriously, and you love to flirt. You'd almost rather talk about it than do it, however, and rarely keep bedroom secrets to yourself. Your mind is definitely your most active erogenous zone, and unless Scorpio or Taurus is prominent in your chart, you may be good at preliminaries but probably lack real passion, feeling or stamina.

You are high-strung and have lots of nervous energy, but may lack physical vitality or endurance. You have a tendency to burn yourself out through stress and mental strain, and might need to force yourself to get more exercise as a way of balancing the physical with the mental.

Men with this planetary placement pride themselves on their intelligence and verbal dexterity. To you, intellectual fortitude is the measure of a man and you want badly to be respected as a formidable thinker. French philosopher René Descartes, who stated "I think, therefore I am," had his Mars in Gemini. You collect vocabulary words the way athletes collect trophies and the only muscles you care about building up are your mental ones. Versatile and adaptable, you know something about almost everything and are probably a "jack of all trades, master of none."

Women with Mars in Gemini are attracted to men who are intelligent and well-spoken. Jacqueline Kennedy Onassis, for example, has her Mars in Gemini and John F. Kennedy (whose Sun was in Gemini) fit her masculine ideal. You're not interested in the strong, silent types—you want a man you can talk to, who can be your friend, and share ideas and experiences with you. Tall, slender, agile men might appeal to you most.

Mars in Cancer

Mars has a difficult time expressing itself through this sign, for the two energies are radically different. Mars is active, assertive and individualistic; Cancer is passive, introverted and desirous of union with significant others. The physical vitality as well as the courage and confidence inherent in Mars are diminished when the planet is placed in Cancer. You might find it hard to assert yourself or to go after what you really want in an aggressive, decisive way. Instead, you tend to pursue your desires in a round-about or stop-start manner, changing your course of action from day to day.

One thing you will strive to achieve is security, and you may invest a great deal of energy to this end. You might seek security in material wealth and work hard to acquire as many financial assets as possible. Or, you could find security in your family and put lots of your energy and enthusiasm into your family life. Perhaps much of the activity in your life is centered around your home and/or family.

Though you are not naturally a fighter, you are like a mother bear when it comes to protecting your home and children and would defend them to the death if need be. This fierce protectiveness extends to all members of your family and your expanded family—co-workers, neighbors, fellow citizens—and you might be known for your vociferous patriotism and loyalty.

You are strongly sexual and sensual, but are really only fulfilled within the structure of a committed, stable relationship. Sex without emotion seems meaningless and empty. You are happiest when you can share your powerful feelings with a partner to whom you are devoted and with whom you are comfortable and secure. Once involved in an intimate relationship, you aren't likely to be unfaithful and couldn't bear disloyalty from your lover. Infidelity threatens the sense of security you find within the relationship.

Highly emotional, you can be rather "touchy," easily upset and volatile. Most likely, you are very susceptible to emotional stress and tension, and your feelings are quickly engaged. Thus, your emotional responses—particularly anger—sometimes seem disproportionate to the situation. Sensitive to what you envision as attacks on you personally, you tend to over-react with defensiveness when you believe you are being challenged in some way. You might feel vulnerable or weak, and try to compensate by attacking first or hardest.

Men with Mars in Cancer may have a particularly difficult time accepting and dealing with the great sensitivity and emotion they experience. Perhaps you choose to channel this sensitivity into an artistic field. Since Cancer is the sign of children, nurturing and the creative process, you might put your energy into birthing "children of the mind." Writers Honoré de Balzac, Alexander Pushkin, James Fenimore Cooper and Lord Byron, painters Pablo Picasso and Marc Chagall, and musician/composer Johannes Brahams are a few good examples of men who applied Mars in Cancer in creative ways. However, it is also possible that you may feel weak or unmasculine and over-compensate with excessively "macho" behavior or attempt to appear manly through use of violence, as was the case with Chicago crime boss Al Capone, whose Mars was in Cancer. Perhaps you harbor much anger toward women—especially if Mars is stressfully-aspected by Uranus or Pluto—and either denigrate them or try to assuage your feelings of inadequacy through sexual "conquests." For example, German philosopher and misogynist Arthur Schopenhauer had his Mars in Cancer.

Women with this planetary placement are most attracted to men who are warm, affectionate, romantic, nurturing and sensitive. You find it rather endearing to see a man cry and are put off by "tough guys" who hide their emotions. A devoted family man, who loves children and takes care of his mother, touches your heart. You also want someone who is a good provider, who can give you a nice home and financial security. Slightly plump homebodies who enjoy cooking and like nothing better than to cuddle up with you in front of the fire appeal to you most.

Mars in Leo

You project an image of confidence, self-sufficiency and vitality that makes people notice you immediately. Charismatic and gregarious, you see yourself as a natural leader and because you believe so strongly in your own importance and ability, others are inspired to follow you. American guru Baba Ram Dass, for example, has his Mars in Leo. Ambitious and egotistic, you are likely to channel your abundant energy into becoming "somebody." You want to be recognized and admired by all. However, you can be arrogant and vain, forgetting that a king depends on his subjects as much as they depend on him. In your self-centeredness, you often fail to realize the needs of others and thus turn off those whose adoration and respect you so desperately desire.

You love being "center stage" and excel when called on to perform for an audience. For example, baseball star Reggie Jackson played his best in Championship and World Series games when millions are watching; his Mars is in Leo. You possess an innate sense of the dramatic and are completely unselfconscious, therefore, you might choose to channel your energies into acting. Actresses Goldie Hawn, Cher and Sophia Loren, actors James Dean, Gary Cooper and Jackie Gleason, rock musicians Bruce Springsteen, Paul McCartney and Ringo Starr, comedienne Bette Midler, and playwright Neil Simon are a few good examples of Mars in Leo.

Your drive to express yourself might also find an outlet in one of the other art forms. The birth charts of artists Joseph Turner, Aubrey Beardsley and Paul Gauguin, architect/designer Le Corbusier, and writers Vladimir Nabokov, William Blake and Ezra Pound all feature Mars in Leo. Not only are you highly creative, you also have plenty of energy, determination and the self-esteem to keep believing in yourself regardless of what the critics say. Though you might be stung initially by criticism, you never admit defeat and bounce back from disappointments easily. However, you may lack discrimination and, if your talent is second-rate you probably won't realize or admit it. Although you can apply much vigor and stamina toward achieving your objectives, you really don't want to have to work your way up the ladder, and may be lazy and impatient about "paying your dues" before reaping the glory. You expect overnight success and instant fame.

Excessive pride is one of your most likely pitfalls. You are always ready to accept praise for your accomplishments, but rarely take the blame for any failures. It is almost impossible for you to concede to a fault or mistake, or to accept advice from someone else. Since you won't acknowledge your errors you can't learn from them, and consequently are destined to repeat them.

You take great pride in your skills as a lover, and may be quite boastful about your sexual prowess. Affectionate and physically demonstrative, you enjoy the drama and excitement of a passionate affair. Though it bolsters your ego to have many sexual partners, you aren't as fickle as someone with Mars in Sagittarius or Gemini, and can be content in a monogamous relationship so long as your lover pays plenty of attention to you. You expect total devotion from your mate and would see infidelity as an insult to you personally. But because you believe your partner already has the best there is, you'd probably be the last to know if s/he had other interests.

Men with Mars in Leo usually have a high opinion of themselves and their masculinity, but still desire constant flattery and ego-reinforcement from friends and lovers. You don't feel you have to do much of anything to earn the appreciation of others—your companionship should be enough. Good-natured and optimistic, your positive attitude and childlike enthusiasm endear you to many. You enjoy being magnanimous with people you like and can be generous with your time, money and talents. Since you don't feel threatened by others, you willingly use whatever influence or power you have to help them achieve recognition, and enjoy playing the role of mentor or patron. Should one of your protégés "make it," however, s/he better dedicate the best-selling novel to you or give his/her first-born son your name.

Women with this planetary placement are most attracted to dynamic, charismatic, larger-than-life men. Status is important to you in a mate, and you want someone who is well-known, respected and admired by all. The more important his is, the better. You are seeking vicarious fame and want to bask in his reflected glory. Big, blond, "Greek gods," beach boys and movie/rock star types appeal to you most.

Mars in Virgo

You are hard-working and conscientious, focusing much of your energy into your job. When something needs to be done you are the one who does it, and you manage to accomplish more than most people through efficient, practical organization of time and resources. This is the position of the office manager, production supervisor or shift foreman, the dynamo behind the scenes who actually runs the show and without whom the operation couldn't function. You tend to be a perfectionist and have little patience with yourself or others when they make mistakes. However, your ambitions are modest and you have no desire for fame, fortune and power (unless Leo is prominent in your chart). Because your ego is smaller than most and you don't stand up for yourself, you may not receive the credit you deserve.

In fact, you are fearful of having to assert yourself and may "choke" in situations that require aggression. Perhaps you feel weak or vulnerable, unable to protect yourself physically. Rather than moving outwardly with force and vigor, you often hold your energy in check, which results in a build-up of tension. The way you are most likely to release this pent-up aggression is through complaining, irritability and nervous habits. Stress and unexpressed anger also can cause you to have problems with your stomach or digestive system. Not only are you more susceptible to stress than most people, you don't possess a great deal of natural vitality, therefore you need to take good care of your health through proper diet, rest and exercise. Yoga, in particular, might appeal to you since you probably don't have much interest in competitive sports.

Although you may not be willing to fight for yourself, you often stand up for the rights and well-being of others, particularly those who are less fortunate than yourself. For example, former U. S. President Lyndon Johnson, who was a champion of the common people, had his Mars in Virgo. You are especially concerned with helping the sick and handicapped, and might choose to focus your energy into medical work. When it comes to nursing the ailing, you can be tireless in your efforts. You need to feel needed. Clara Barton, founder of the American Red Cross, is a good example of Mars in Virgo. So are renowned scientist Linus Pauling, missionary Albert Schweitzer, Nobel Peace Prize winner Mother Teresa and Dr. Benjamin Spock.

Though your sex drive is strong you might not feel comfortable about expressing it and tend to be a bit puritanical. You could even be somewhat fearful of letting your passion loose, of giving in to such overpowering sensations. It's hard for you just to relax and enjoy yourself, without worrying or judging. Therefore, you may repress much of your desire and be critical of people who are more sexually open or indulgent. At the same time, though, you envy them. Your perfectionism also might cause you to suffer from performance anxiety.

Men with Mars in Virgo often pride themselves on their efficiency, organization skills and dependability. You can be a workaholic and expect everyone else to devote as much energy and effort as you do to the job. Working makes you feel good about yourself and your ego is gratified if you believe you are indispensible. Though you aren't looking for lots of prestige and money for your contributions, you'll become cranky, complaining and negative if others don't recognize and appreciate how much you do. You want to serve in some way and might be happier in a support or service position than one that is highly visible.

Unless fire signs are prominent in your chart, you may be somewhat insecure about your masculinity and might feel you are a bit of a "wimp." You fear you won't be able to assert yourself when necessary. Perhaps you have more brains than brawn and lack athletic ability. However, you may attempt to overcompensate for your timidity with excessive bravado, as did writer Ernest Hemingway, whose Mars was in Virgo.

Women with Mars in Virgo are attracted to modest, unassuming, shy men. No Rambo types for you. You are looking for someone you can depend on, who is gentle, considerate, hard-working and practical. Cleanliness is high on your list of priorities, too, and it is much more important to you that your partner be neat than good-looking.

Mars in Libra

Your passions never rule your thinking and you rarely act in haste or anger. Concerned with justice and fairness, you don't let your ego get in the way of your decisions and actions. Your objective, unemotional approach could enable you to be a good judge, manager, general or diplomat. Former heads of state Abraham Lincoln, John Adams, Winston Churchill, Jawaharlal Nehru and Nazi General Erwin Rommel all had Mars in Libra.

However, you often have difficulty asserting yourself and going after what you want in a direct, decisive manner. Instead your tendency is to think too much before you act and, because you usually can see value in both sides of every issue, you vacillate or change your course of action several times before reaching your goal. Or, you may defer to others and let them decide for you.

Aggression in any form seems threatening to you, and you don't deal well with confrontations, arguments, forcefulness or physical combativeness. When faced with challenges, you may experience anxiety rather than positive stimulation. If possible, you'd like your environment and relationships to be balanced, harmonious and congenial at all times. Your desire is to unite with others rather than oppose them, and you'll always seek a way to work with others instead of against them if possible. You want to make friends, not adversaries.

Consequently, you might not enjoy sports (unless fire signs predominate in your chart). There's too much antagonism and competitiveness involved—and too much chance of getting injured, or at least dirty! Since you don't possess a lot of natural vitality either, you may not like to exert yourself physically. Unless other factors in your chart provide energy and stamina, you probably need to get more rest and take better care of yourself than most people.

One area in which you are likely to be assertive is relationships. You invest much of your energy into pursuing and maintaining relationships of all kinds, but especially romantic ones. Although you are never pushy or forceful, once you decide you want someone you'll exert gentle and continuous effort toward establishing a partnership with him/her. You might even make love your life's work.

For you, sex is always best within the context of a loving and stable relationship, and you find casual affairs unfulfilling. Instead of being excited by the novelty of a new sexual encounter, you usually feel anxious, apprehensive or insecure. For you to enjoy sex you also must be getting along well with your lover; a disagreement before bed will turn you off completely. Though you are very affectionate and romantic, your sex drive is rather low. You tend to overly idealize sex, expecting emotional as well as physical satisfaction. When it comes to lovemaking, you are conservative and cautious, reluctant to try anything new or different. You want everything about the experience to be nice, neat and predictable. No spontaneous, impassioned encounters in parked cars or elevators for you, and clean sheets, soft music and candlelight are more powerful aphrodisiacs than triple-X movies or exotic underwear.

Art is another area into which you might channel much of your energy and effort. Impressionist painter Georges Seurat and composer/musician Felix Mendelssohn are examples of Mars in Libra. You can be passionate about art and aesthetics, and might even feel invigorated by the act of creating something of beauty.

Men with this Mars placement pride themselves on their refinement and good taste. However, you can be terribly vain about your looks and the image you present. You enjoy dressing fashionably and like to impress people with your knowledge of music, art, fine wines, etc., and would rather discuss the classics than football. You know the best restaurants and tailor in town, and are more likely to have an art dealer than a stock broker or bookie. To you, fastidiousness and the ability to get along with everyone are virtues in a man. Tactful, sociable and well-mannered, you are the perfect dinner guest, a pleasant and amiable friend and every mother's ideal son-in-law.

Women with Mars in Libra are attracted to men who are intelligent, sociable, impeccably dressed, squeaky-clean, with perfect manners and good taste—old-fashioned "gentlemen." You are intimidated by forceful, passionate men and prefer a partner who is more restrained. "Jocks" and cowboy-types are too coarse for you; you want someone who is totally civilized and as far removed from the physical world as possible.

Mars in Scorpio

You have tremendous will power and drive, and are able to focus all your energy on your objective. Once you make up your mind to do something you either achieve it or die trying. You can be ruthless in the pursuit of your goals, and to those who try to stand in your way you show no mercy. No adversary is too formidable—even governments or religious institutions. You are an extremist, however, and can become obsessive in your quests, losing sight of reason or practicality and refusing to compromise or change once you've set your course of action. Your all-or-nothing attitude can cause you to triumph or lose spectacularly.

You may have the ability to transform others or situations in some way. Sometimes you accomplish this by manipulating their unconscious desires, sometimes you inspire the masses with your fearlessness and passion. For example, Mohandas Gandhi, Martin Luther, George Washington and Mao Tse Tung all had Mars in Scorpio. However, the transformations you affect need not take the form of confrontation with the powers that be. Jonas Salk, for instance, transformed medicine, Orville Wright changed transportation for all time, and Jimi Hendrix left the music world irrevocably altered; all three had Mars in Scorpio. You might influence others to kick drugs, change careers or take up occult studies, and thus transform their lives and outlooks in some important way. Or, you may develop your potential for psychic healing and use this power to benefit humanity.

Intensely passionate and sensual, you are likely to put a great deal of your energy into sex. You exude an almost animal magnetism that makes you extremely attractive to the opposite sex, regardless of how good-looking you are. You have an active and powerful libido, and are fascinated with sexuality in all its expressions. Novelist Henry Miller, *Cosmopolitan* magazine publisher Helen Gurly Brown and *Hustler* magazine publisher Larry Flynt are three examples of Mars in Scorpio; sex is an important factor in the work of all three. For you, the sex act is a way to merge with your partner, emotionally as well as physically. You may be a consummate lover with an uncanny understanding of your own and your partner's deepest desires. Or, you might be afraid of the strength of your own passion and attempt to repress it, lest it take control of you. Power struggles and issues of domination could play a part in your sexual expression, and you might use your sexuality to manipulate others. You are jealous and possessive of your sexual partners and, if betrayed, are likely to become vengeful, perhaps even violent. In the extreme, you might be cruel or perverse, obsessed with the dark side of sexuality.

Men with Mars in Scorpio like to think of themselves as being "forces to reckon with." Though you might not be the type to start fights in bars, you are like a poisonous snake coiled and ready to strike and can be ominous if provoked. You certainly won't run away from a confrontation and seem to be fearless in the face of danger. Power is important to you, but you probably prefer to wield it from behind the scenes, and you want to be in control of everyone and everything in your environment. As a result, you tend to be domineering, unwilling to trust others or delegate authority to them. Proud of your prowess, you might emphasize your sexuality or use it to get what you want.

Women with Mars in Scorpio are often attracted to men who project an image of power. This could mean take-control types, authority figures or those who are in important business/government positions. Or, you might be fascinated by men who attempt to appear tough or mean, such as "biker" types or petty criminals and thugs. You like your men to be overtly sexual, but you're looking for someone who is strongly emotional and passionate as well. Dark, smoldering, intense men of few words probably interest you most. Because this planetary combination sometimes signifies sexual frustration, you might find yourself continually involved with men who aren't good for you or who don't give you what you want. In the extreme, you could be attracted to men who are cruel or abusive toward you. And, because Scorpio is the sign of transformation, it's quite likely that you will be transformed in some way by the men in your life.

Mars in Sagittarius

Restless and energetic, you need lots of physical activity and have trouble sitting still for long. You want to be on the move as much as possible. Your boundless curiosity and adventurousness may inspire you to explore distant realms, and you enjoy nothing better than traveling. Writer Jack Kerouac, best known for his novel *On the Road,* and Captain John Smith, one of the first Europeans to journey to the "new world," are good examples of Mars in Sagittarius.

You probably enjoy sports and have natural athletic ability as well as energy, speed and enthusiasm. Tennis champion Jimmy Connors, for example, has his

Mars in Sagittarius. Since Sagittarius is associated with the legs, you might excel at skiing, running, soccer, basketball or bicycling. Or, your love of speed and gambling could make you an auto- or horse-racing enthusiast. Unless you have some stabilizing factors in your birth chart, though, you may not have the discipline and determination to develop your talent fully; you want to have a good time and once it becomes work you lose interest.

You have a tendency to scatter your energy, to try to do too many things at the same time and spread yourself too thin. Because your attention span is short and your interests many, you often start things but fail to finish them, and are inclined to promise more than you can deliver. It seems that you are always late and rushing madly from place to place, like the rabbit in *Alice in Wonderland.*

Friendly, witty and good-natured, you have many associates, people with whom you like to do things and have fun. You love to talk, but prefer to keep the subjects light and humorous, and often entertain friends with jokes and amusing stories. Comedian George Burns, for example, has his Mars in Sagittarius. You have a vivid imagination and might channel your energy and enthusiasm into creating a colorful fantasy world as did authors Lewis Carroll and Mark Twain, both of whom had Mars in Sagittarius. Too often, however, you prefer the fantasy land you've imagined to the responsibilities of the material world.

You believe that you are invincible, and your irrepressible confidence and optimism usually get you through the tough times, so that it seems as though you were born under a lucky star. Often you succeed because you never stop to think about failing. Racketeer "Lucky" Luciano, for example, had his Mars in Sagittarius. You are the quintessential salesperson or con artist, and sometimes even manage to convince yourself that your snake oil really works. Even if one of your fanciful schemes doesn't pan out, however, you bounce back from defeats with hope in your heart and a smile on your face, and it's hard to stay mad at you for long. To you, it's all a game and the playing is what counts.

You approach sex as if it, too, were a game to be enjoyed, but not taken too seriously. It's difficult for you to commit to one person, partly because you don't want to limit your opportunities and partly because you are afraid of serious involvements. You are terrified of being "trapped" in a relationship. In this area as in so many others, you are better at starting things than finishing them.

Men with this planetary combination are proud of their sense of humor, positive attitude, athletic ability and playfulness, and see wit and optimism as desirable qualities in a man. You enjoy nothing more than watching a ball game or going out drinking with the boys. But when things get too serious you become uncomfortable and you fill your life with activity to avoid dealing with important issues. Free and easy with your money and time, you like to impress others with your generosity. Responsibility, however, isn't your strong suit and things like mortgage payments and business meetings tend to slip your mind.

Women with Mars in Sagittarius find humorous, upbeat, fun-loving men most appealing. You want a partner with whom you can go places and do things, not someone who will sit quietly with you in front of the fireplace. In particular, you might be attracted to athletes and/or tall, active, robust men who make you laugh.

Mars in Capricorn

Ambitious, hard-working and determined, you channel much of your energy into your career and have a tendency to become a workaholic. You believe in making it on your own, through your own efforts. Able to focus and direct your energies productively, you don't waste effort, and therefore accomplish more than most people. You pursue your desires with cautious, steady, well-planned steps and won't attempt something unless it seems to be a sure thing. No flash-in-the-pan schemes for you. Patient and persevering, you are willing to wait for what you want. Not only do you want your achievements to last, you have a strong sense of responsibility and commitment to your company and/or community and aren't likely to bail out if the going gets tough.

Quite likely, you have managerial ability and are good at organizing others and delegating responsibility. Your common sense and practicality could be advantageously applied in almost any area of business. However, your tendency to be overly cautious and skeptical can cause you to miss out on opportunities at times, and your fear of the unknown might lead you to look to the past for answers. Former U. S. President Ronald Reagan, who has his Mars in Capricorn, is a good example of this. Taking risks is difficult for you and you have trouble breaking out of old habit patterns and traditions in order to try new ideas.

Somewhat pessimistic, you are inclined to look for trouble, often expecting the worst. Perhaps you lack self-confidence because you are all too aware of your limitations. Other people may see you as somber, withdrawn, rigid. Certainly you take your responsibilities seriously and are anything but frivolous, however, you may need to "lighten up" a bit.

Although your natural vitality is not great, you have tremendous endurance and strength of will that enable you to overcome illnesses. As a child, you might have been rather sickly or limited in some way, but your energy and health usually improve as you mature. Your self-reliance, stubbornness and tendency to dig in your heels in the face of adversity could result in a long, independent life.

Your sex drive is strong and you have a hearty appreciation of all physical and sensual pleasures. However, you probably conceal your desires behind a carefully controlled and dignified exterior. In public you appear cool, refined, even uptight, but in private you are not shy about expressing your lustfulness. Perhaps you might attempt to repress your powerful sexuality since it is important to you to always be in control of yourself, and you wouldn't want your libido to get out of hand. You might even be a bit insecure about your sexual ability, and men in particular may suffer from performance anxiety or fear they are not desirable. Actor/director Woody Allen, who often depicts this type of character in his movies, has his Mars in Capricorn. However, you are likely to retain your sexual appetite until late in life and amaze younger partners with your vitality.

Men with Mars in Capricorn might have had difficulty being children. You couldn't wait to grow up and always seemed more mature and serious than other boys. Not until you were nearly forty did you start to become comfortable with yourself. You pride yourself on your common sense, practicality and stability and look askance at men who behave like overgrown adolescents or shirk their responsibilities. To you, a "real man" is one who heads a prosperous company and is a respected member of his community.

Women with this planetary combination often seek a substitute father in their partners. You want a man who is the strong, silent type, who takes charge of problems and manages them efficiently. Serious, mature, dependable and dignified men appeal to you most and you are put off by boisterous, childish or carefree types who show no signs of achieving material success. Your ideal man is tall, dark and handsome, a protector and provider on whom you can lean and who will always take care of you.

Mars in Aquarius

You are concerned with the world of ideas, particularly those of an unconventional or progressive nature, and you invest much energy in mental pursuits. Always eager to learn new things, you want to be challenged intellectually.

It is important for you to be able to think and speak freely. Often you find yourself at odds with accepted "truths." You enjoy being thought of as "different," a unique individual. As a result, you may become involved in unpopular political causes, avant garde art movements, or be on the cutting edge of scientific or technological advances. Astronomer Nicolas Copernicus and artist/inventor/scientist Leonardo da Vinci are two good examples of Mars in Aquarius.

Because Aquarius is a fixed sign, you can hold rather stubbornly to your opinions. When you believe in something, you believe passionately and express your ideas with evangelistic zeal. Though you consider yourself open-minded, you really regard your way of thinking as the only "right" way. You love discussing ideas and your "discussions" frequently escalate to heated debates. You enjoy nothing better than a good intellectual argument with a worthy opponent. Others may find you extremely opinionated, but you see no virtue in being wishy-washy.

You are always ready to stand up or fight for what you believe in. The birth charts of U. S. political leaders Edward Kennedy and Adlai Stevenson, for example, feature Mars in Aquarius. You have the energy and enthusiasm to stir others to action and could be effective as a labor organizer, politician, team captain, project head or leader of a group dedicated to social change. However, you lack diplomacy and can alienate people with your abrasive and self-righteous approach. From time to time, you might find yourself in trouble with authority figures: parents, teachers, employers, even the law.

One of your purposes in life is to break down old structures and change outworn traditions so that new ones can take their place. In the extreme, however, this expression might take the form of terrorism, for Aquarius is also the sign of revolution and violent upheavals. Rash and explosive, Mars in Aquarius can indicate the "rebel without a cause" who rails against any authority or established order and wants change for the sake of change alone.

Easily bored, you require a high level of excitement and stimulation. Sexually, you are intrigued by anything new or unconventional. You consider yourself open-minded about sexual issues and may want to experiment with all sorts of sexual behaviors and partners. For you, variety certainly is the spice of life. Actress Mae West, who had Mars in Aquarius, was known for her unabashed sexual remarks. She once commented that when it came to choosing between two evils she'd always pick the one she hadn't tried yet.

Men with this planetary position usually pride themselves on their intelligence and uniqueness. You want to be seen by others as open-minded, unconventional, independent, a free-thinker, and you admire these characteristics in other men. Stereotypical male roles don't interest you and you don't need to appear "macho" to feel masculine. Nor are you threatened by strong, independent women and probably you are more egalitarian than most men.

Women with Mars in Aquarius are attracted to men who are intelligent, forthright, progressive, independent, egalitarian and/or unusual in some way. Actress Joanne Woodward, for example, has Mars in Aquarius and both she and her husband Paul Newman (whose Sun is in Aquarius) are involved in numerous progressive political activities. All sorts of men from all age groups, races and backgrounds interest you—the differences keep things from getting dull. Most importantly, your partner(s) must be your friend(s). You want a companion with whom you can share ideas, and you probably have many platonic male friends, too.

Mars in Pisces

You have a great deal of trouble asserting yourself and tend to be rather shy, withdrawn, even timid. Passive and peace-loving, you have no desire to behave aggressively or engage in any sort of contest or combat with others. You believe in "turning the other cheek" and are more likely to respond to an assault with forgiveness or retreat than with violence.

This attitude stems from your keen sensitivity to the feelings of others—not only humans, but animals and plants as well. You can almost feel another's pain yourself, and thus cannot bear to inflict injury on anyone or thing. Instead you are likely to strive to improve the lot of all defenseless or underprivileged creatures, and the only fight you might engage in willingly is the fight to end cruelty and tyranny in the world. Crusader and political activist Ralph Nader, botanist George Washington Carver and abolitionist John Brown are some good examples of Mars in Pisces.

You are private and inclined to withdraw from outer-world activity, unless you have a number of other planets in sociable signs. What activities you do engage in are probably of a personal, inner-directed nature. For artists and persons involved in spiritual pursuits, such isolation and introspection is essential. Highly imaginative, you probably channel much of your energy and enthusiasm into some sort of artistic endeavor. Your sensitivity to color, tone and rhythm might incline you to painting, photography, dance, music or poetry in particular. For example, the birth charts of musicians Miles Davis, Bob Dylan and Herbie Mann, poet John Milton, and artists Vincent van Gogh and Michelangelo all feature Mars in Pisces.

Unless fire signs are prominent elsewhere in your birth chart, this placement of Mars signifies a lack of natural vitality, energy and resistance to illness. You probably need plenty of sleep and are more susceptible to contagious diseases than most people. Allergies, too, might trouble you because you are so hypersensitive to everything in your environment. Although you may not enjoy athletics or any sort of physical activity, you could increase your stamina and vigor through regular exercise.

Because Pisces is more concerned with cosmic realms than with the physical world, you might not have much interest in sex. In order for you to be satisfied physically you need to be emotionally involved, too. You are extremely idealistic and romantic about sexual matters and your expectations might be of a fantasy, storybook sort that are impossible to achieve in real life. In extreme cases, this placement could indicate celibacy for religious reasons or self-denial so that all your energy can be used for your art.

Men with Mars in Pisces often feel somewhat insecure about their masculinity. Perhaps you have trouble accepting your sensitivity and emotionalism, believing that such things are signs of weakness. You might fear that you could not defend yourself against an attack or take care of yourself in difficult circumstances, and these fears make you feel inadequate. You are proud of your artistic/musical ability, however, and want to be respected for this talent. You also admire creativity in other men. If you are involved in religious/spiritual pursuits, you find strength in your beliefs and practices, and want to be recognized for your spirituality. Men who are able to accept their sensitivity, vulnerability and strong emotions as positive qualities see these as desirable characteristics in a man.

Women with this planetary combination are attracted to men who are gentle, peace-loving, romantic and emotional. Blustering, rough or "macho" types don't interest you in the least. You find the sensitive artist or selfless, saintly humanitarian much more appealing.

Your heart is touched by someone who appears helpless and needy, and consequently, you have a tendency to fall for men who have problems, such as substance abusers, or those who are physically or emotionally ill. As a result, you might find yourself continually getting involved with dependent partners who are not capable of taking care of themselves, and end up sacrificing yourself for them.

Overly idealistic, you may be disappointed frequently by the men in your life because you refuse to see them as they really are, viewing them instead through the mist of your illusions. Actresses Elizabeth Taylor and Marilyn Monroe, for whom maintaining a satisfying relationship proved difficult, are two good examples of Mars in Pisces. You are seeking the perfect lover, a soulmate, but what you are looking for cannot be found on the Earth plane.

Chapter Eight

Jupiter

Jupiter takes about twelve years to travel through all twelve signs of the zodiac and it remains in each sign for approximately one year. In Roman mythology, Jupiter was king of the gods, the equivalent of the Greek's Zeus.

The largest planet in our solar system, Jupiter aptly represents the principle of expansion. It is linked with all things that encourage you to expand your horizons, that broaden your understanding of the Universe and your place in it. Therefore, such things as higher education, the publishing industry and journalism, long distance travel, philosophy, psychology, religion and mythology are all part of Jupiter's domain. In the birth chart, Jupiter's sign, house position and aspects indicate where you are likely to be expansive, and how you grow in knowledge and experience through or as a result of the society in which you live.

Traditionally, Jupiter has been considered the "greater benefic," the planet of good luck, a sort of cosmic rabbit's foot. Its placement suggests areas in which you are inclined to be lucky or to benefit through fortunate associations. The growth it brings comes easily, without requiring much effort from you. However, too much of a good thing—too much growth and expansion—is not always desirable, and Jupiter also indicates where you tend to be excessive and indulgent. For instance, Jupiter in the first house could expand the physical body;

in this position the planet might enhance vitality but at the same time increase your weight and make obesity a problem. And, because you don't have to work for Jupiter's "gifts," you don't always appreciate them, so the planet also reveals the areas in which you are likely to rest on your laurels and be lazy.

The experiences you have in connection with Jupiter are generally pleasurable, even if the end results are not. For example, the person who has Jupiter in the first house and gains too much weight probably enjoys the experience of eating and drinking excessively, even though s/he may not like being fat. Therefore, Jupiter's position in the birth chart shows what you enjoy in life, what gives you pleasure and how you have fun.

Finally, Jupiter is an indicator of your worldview, your philosophy of life, your "religion" in a broad sense, and your ideals. Its sign and house placement tell much about the gods/goddesses you worship and respect, while aspects to it show how comfortable you are with your own personal Divinity and how easily you express your *weltanschauung.*

Jupiter in Aries

You expand your understanding of yourself and the world around you by taking chances. Always "pushing the outside of the envelope," you like to test your own limits, often pitting yourself against extreme odds and risking life and limb in the process. Auto-racing champion Mario Andretti, for example, has his Jupiter in Aries. The more dangerous or difficult the challenge, the more you long to accomplish it. You want to go where no one has been before, to do what they say can't be done. You truly believe that you never know what you can do until you try.

The thrill you get from attempting some feat of daring makes it all worthwhile. You love to feel the adrenalin rushing through your veins, and are at your best in life-or-death situations that require instantaneous action. Whether your arena is Wall Street, the tennis court or the battlefield, you are known for your courage, energy and desire to win. Taking risks gives you a pleasurable sensation akin to sexual excitation and you experience such a "high" that you barely feel pain or fear. Your exaggerated need for adventure, however, can lead you to take foolish chances or to endanger others.

You resent having to play by the rules and have little respect for tradition. Always seeking new ways to do things, you are a pioneer, a renegade. Mary Baker Eddy, who founded the Christian Science Church, avant garde artist Salvador Dali, Cuban leader Fidel Castro and oil tycoon John Paul Getty are good examples of Jupiter in Aries. You can be abrasive, callous and excessively antagonistic in your attempts to break with old conventions and consequently make more enemies than friends. However, you don't care much whether others like or approve of you; you idealize independence and individuality and are not interested in being accepted by any group. Your "god" is the individual, and in your opinion society will destroy the individual if given the chance.

In the extreme, (especially if Jupiter is stressfully aspected by Mars, Uranus or Pluto) you might totally disregard others and lack feeling to such an extent that you become cruel or bloodthirsty. Kevin Bianci, known as "the Hillside Strangler," is one such example of Jupiter in Aries. You glorify aggression and violence and tend to see the use of force as the only way to settle disagreements.

Success and/or recognition usually come as a result of your adventurousness, aggression, daring or competitive spirit. Your natural vitality, enthusiasm and, perhaps, athletic ability also might bring you good fortune.

Jupiter in Taurus

You use your sensory awareness to expand your understanding of the world and your place in it. Through touching, seeing, smelling, hearing and tasting what life has to offer you grow and enlarge your knowledge and experience. A true hedonist, you derive great enjoyment from all physical pleasures and have a tendency to over-indulge in food, drink, sex, drugs, etc. When it comes to sensual gratification you have trouble setting limits for yourself—you simply want to experience everything.

Your innate understanding of the material realm may enable you to make money easily. In financial areas, you seem to have the Midas touch. Billionaires Aristotle Onassis and Howard Hughes are two good examples of Jupiter in Taurus. You also love all beautiful things and covet material possessions, therefore your desire to own as much as possible contributes to your money-making ability. The "god" you worship is money. Expanding your physical resources is so important to you that you invest a great deal of effort into acquiring wealth and building up your holdings. However, your excessive appetite for material things can cause you to spend more than you make and you might find yourself frequently in debt because of your extravagance.

Perhaps you express your love of beauty through art, and you probably have some natural talent and aesthetic appreciation. Because you want to be productive and to transfer your interests into physical form you might not be satisfied with just admiring the creations of others—you want to create something of lasting, physical beauty yourself. Thus, you may achieve recognition or benefit financially from your artwork. For example, the birth charts of painters Henri Matisse, Pablo Picasso and Joan Miró, sculptor Helen Frankenthaler, architect Frank Lloyd Wright and film maker Stanley Kubrick all feature Jupiter in Taurus. Music, too, could bring you fame, fortune, or at least enjoyment, and since Taurus is associated with the throat you might have natural singing ability. Songwriter Cole Porter and singers Dean Martin and David Byrne are good examples of Jupiter in Taurus.

In its most fundamental expression, this planetary position could signify exceptional physical gifts. You might have been blessed with more than average strength, robustness or beauty, or you may benefit in some way from your physical characteristics. Body builder Charles Atlas and entertainer Raquel Welch are two good examples of Jupiter in Taurus.

Jupiter in Gemini

You believe you can learn just about anything by reading a good book on the subject. Your understanding of life, the world around you and your place in it comes from reading everything you can get your hands on: the classics, religious texts, newspapers and magazines, *National Geographic,* popular novels and how-to guides. Through reading, you become aware of things you would never be able to experience directly. But although you may have plenty of "book learning" your "real life" understanding might be rather limited.

You also learn and grow by exchanging ideas with others: talking, writing letters, attending classes and lectures, and through all other forms of communication. Because you also want to share what you know with other people, you may become a writer, teacher or lecturer so that you can help them to expand their knowledge, too. A lifelong student, you are always studying something new; as a result, you probably know a little bit about almost everything. However, because you are interested in so many areas and lack focus and mental discipline, you tend to be a dabbler, never acquiring more than a superficial understanding of anything.

You derive great pleasure from learning and may have been the only kid in your class who didn't mind going to school. Learning comes easily to you, and you are especially adept at communication. Perhaps you can speak several foreign languages or have a gift for oratory. For example, Rev. Jesse Jackson, who is a powerful and charismatic speaker, has his Jupiter in Gemini. However, you can be verbose. Or, you might possess special writing talent. Success and recognition could come to you as a result of your writing and/or speaking skills. The birth charts of many notable authors feature Jupiter in Gemini, among them Honoré de Balzac, Alexander Pushkin, Sir Arthur Conan Doyle, Charles Dickens and Dashiell Hammett. Songwriters/composers Paul Simon, Carole King and Nicholas Rimsky-Korsakov are also good examples of Jupiter in Gemini.

Because Gemini is associated with the hands, your manual skills might be exceptional. Perhaps you are talented at such things as handcrafts, drawing, carpentry, typing or handball. For example, fighter Mohammed Ali has his Jupiter in Gemini.

Your pleasures in life are usually of an intellectual sort. Reading is particularly enjoyable to you and you prefer curling up with a good book to going out on the town. You're not a misanthrope, however—far from it. Talking with friends—in person or on the telephone—is one of your favorite pastimes. Once you get going, it's hard to shut you up. You also love to play games that exercise your mind or add to your storehouse of information: card games, crossword puzzles, chess, *Trivial Pursuit*, etc. Though you might not be very active physically, your mind is never idle.

You glorify intelligence and the "god" you worship is the mind. First on your list of important people are those who possess exceptional mental ability or writing talent, and you'd like to be respected for these things yourself. For example, publisher Joseph Pulitzer, who established the Pulitzer Prize to acknowledge and encourage literary ability, had his Jupiter in Gemini.

Jupiter in Cancer

Your family is likely to contribute to your expansion and growth in a way that you find positive, easy or enjoyable. Perhaps family ties open doors for you professionally. Or, your family's money might enable you to study at the best schools, travel widely and meet influential people. The home in which you were raised was probably a supportive and nurturing environment, and your mother (or nurturing parent) in particular, encouraged you to "reach for the stars." Because of your family and the environment in which you grew up, your personal and/or professional growth has been easier.

This supportive environment might include your town or even your country, and you may feel that your home and/or homeland have benefitted you significantly. As a result, you are likely to be quite patriotic, a champion of your community and nation. The "god" you worship might be your country. You admire and uphold traditional, family-oriented values and glorify the image of home, motherhood, family and country. Evangelist Billy Graham and actor John Wayne are two good examples of Jupiter in Cancer. However, it is here that you also tend to be excessive, even sanctimonious and pejorative.

Perhaps you achieve success or recognition by appealing to these sentiments in others, or through creating an idealized image of "home" with which others can identify. For example, artist Winslow Homer, whose paintings often depict pleasant, everyday country scenes, had his Jupiter in Cancer. So did conductor Arthur Fiedler (whose Fourth of July performance with the Boston Pops orchestra became a tradition) and lyricist Oscar Hammerstein.

Some of your greatest pleasures in life might be associated with your home and family. You love holidays and want to gather your loved ones around you in your own home (or the ancestral one) to celebrate the traditions you hold dear. Your children are a source of joy, and through them you are given an opportunity to grow in a positive way and to expand your understanding of yourself and the world around you.

Jupiter in Leo

Your growth and expansion are linked to your self-expression. Quite likely, you possess an abundance of creativity and it seems that the more you use it, the more creative you become. For example, the birth charts of artists Amedeo Mondigliani and Aubrey Beardsley, writers Victor Hugo, Isak Dinesen, F. Scott Fitzgerald and Simone de Beauvoir, and opera composer Richard Wagner all feature Jupiter in Leo. You find it easy to express yourself artfully and the experience is pleasurable and invigorating for you. Unlike some people, you rarely find yourself without inspiration or suffering from writer's block—the creative juices just keep on flowing in you. Art and creativity might be the "god" you worship. However, because self-expression comes easily to you, you may lack the diligence and discipline to develop your talent fully.

You possess a strong sense of the dramatic and can be quite flamboyant in the way you go about expressing yourself. For example, film makers Federico Fellini and George Lucas have Jupiter in Leo. So did painter/film maker Andy Warhol. Art forms that allow you to exaggerate and be theatrical, such as acting and performing musically, might appeal to you most. Not at all shy or self-conscious, you love being center stage, and seem to blossom with attention and adoration. Singers Mick Jagger, Diana Ross and Cab Calloway are good examples of Jupiter in Leo. So are actresses Bette Davis and Joan Crawford, actors Robert De Niro and Yul Brenner, and comedians Chevy Chase, Groucho Marx and George Burns. Tremendously self-confident, you are certain that you will accomplish whatever you try and your optimism contributes to your success.

A born leader, you radiate enthusiasm and assurance and inspire others to follow you. You believe your rightful place is at the top, and may rise easily to a position of power and/or glory.

Jupiter in Leo, however, can indicate an inflated ego and excessive pride. You could become so wrapped up in yourself and your art that you ignore the rest of life. And, you might think so highly of yourself and your creations that you can't accept criticism or admit to mistakes. You may be so self-satisfied and puffed up with your own importance that you barely notice others, except as an audience for your performance. French King Louis XVI is a good example of the arrogance of Jupiter in Leo.

Jupiter in Virgo

Through helping others, you expand your knowledge and awareness of yourself and the world in which you live. You achieve personal growth by providing others with some sort of service, and you might excel in fields such as medicine, nutrition, animal welfare or through assisting the underprivileged or the handicapped. Menial work that others may find unpleasant offers you a sense of satisfaction, and you enjoy knowing that what you do benefits humanity. Perhaps you will even achieve recognition for your efforts, even though fame and fortune are not what you seek.

When exaggerated, however, your concern for the health and well-being of all turns into excessive worrying, even paranoia. You spend a great deal of time and energy fretting over your diet and trying to defend yourself against germs. Perhaps you are a fanatic about cleanliness, immunization or health foods, and the "god" you worship might be medicine.

You have a penchant for detail, and are extremely orderly and precise in all you do. Engraver Albrecht Dürer, for example, had his Jupiter in Virgo. However, you sometimes carry your meticulousness to extremes, over-refining or overworking everything and wasting time and energy on insignificant details.

You enjoy facts, figures and organizing information, and could use your analytical abilities to great advantage in fields like accounting, statistics, medical research or computer programming. For example, economic analyst John Kenneth Galbraith has his Jupiter in Virgo. Be careful not to over-analyze situations or focus so intently on specifics that you miss the big picture.

Virgo is associated with work. You probably derive much satisfaction from working—you need to be busy constantly and would not be content living a life of leisure. However, you are inclined to overdo it in this area and become a workaholic, unable to relax and enjoy other things in life.

This is one of the most modest and unassuming positions for Jupiter. You aren't looking for glory or prestige (unless Leo is prominent in your chart) and are content to work efficiently behind the scenes. Rather than bringing you public acclaim and notoriety, Jupiter may give you good fortune in a more personal and private way.

Jupiter in Libra

You are likely to experience some sort of growth and expansion as a result of your relationships. Perhaps a fortunate marriage or business partnership enables you to achieve greater success or recognition than you would have on your own. Or, because of your relationships you might expand your horizons through travel, higher education, philosophy or religion. Your partners in love and/or business open doors for you—professionally, personally, intellectually or spiritually—and you come to understand yourself and your place in the Universe better through them.

You seem to be lucky in love and never lack admirers. Love is certainly your game, and you not only play it well you enjoy it immensely. Your relationships make you feel good about yourself and you are never happier than when you are in love. Because you are so fond of companionship, however, you may get involved with someone just so you won't be alone. You are sometimes indiscriminate in your choice of partners and might be more concerned with quantity than quality.

Friendly, good-natured and diplomatic, you are popular with both sexes and your social calendar is always full. It is quite likely that your social contacts will benefit you in some way, and you might have connections in high places that prove advantageous to you. In your professional life, you would probably be more successful and content working with other people—in a partnership or group—than by yourself.

Libra is the sign of the arts, therefore, you might find opportunities for personal growth in some artistic field. Perhaps you will even become recognized and respected for your talent. Composers/musicians Johann Sebastian Bach, Wolfgang Amadeus Mozart, George Gershwin and John Mayall, painters Paul Cézanne and Marc Chagall, and sculptors Henry Moore and Alexander Calder are some examples of Jupiter in Libra. Unlike some artists who agonize over their work, you enjoy what you do and being creative comes easily for you. However, you might take your ability for granted and be lazy about developing it fully.

You also like being in the company of artistic people. Even if you don't have talent yourself, you are able to recognize it in others. You might become a collector or patron of the arts, and thus help gifted artists grow and expand themselves. For example, John D. Rockefeller, who was a great supporter of the arts, had his Jupiter in Libra.

Jupiter in Scorpio

By exploring the hidden realms, you broaden your understanding of the Universe and your place in it. You want to find out what goes on beneath the surface, what the core truths are, and may study metaphysics to increase your knowledge. Superficial explanations aren't enough for you—you want to comprehend life's great mysteries: birth, death, regeneration. You also want to experience the other worlds that exist beyond the apparent one and discover the forces that operate there. Quite likely you possess psychic ability of some kind; certainly, understanding metaphysical concepts comes easily for you. Occultist Aleister Crowley, astrologer Llewellyn George, psychic Uri Geller and hypnotist Franz Mesmer are some good examples of Jupiter in Scorpio.

Your fascination with the great unknown might lead you to teach or write about mysterious realms or occurrences, thus expanding others' awareness, too. Perhaps you will even become successful or well-known for this. For example, the birth charts of writers Stephen King and Jules Verne, and director Alfred Hitchcock all feature Jupiter in Scorpio.

Another possibility is that you could benefit in some way through clandestine activity, or by working behind the scenes. Joseph Kennedy and Al Capone, who amassed fortunes in bootlegging during Prohibition, are two such examples of Jupiter in Scorpio. Or, you might become known for exposing hidden activities, as is the case with "60 Minutes" host Harry Reasoner, whose Jupiter is in Scorpio.

Issues of power and control are likely to play a part in your life. You assume authority easily and are comfortable in positions of power, even those which give you the power of life and death over multitudes of people. For instance, the birth charts of former U. S. President Ronald Reagan, former Secretary of State Henry Kissinger, former Presidents Radhakrishnan of India and Chiang Kai-shek of Nationalist China, and former French Emperor Napoleon all show Jupiter in Scorpio. Wielding power not only comes naturally to you, you enjoy it immensely. Power might be the "god" you worship. Your tendency is toward excess in this area, however, and you must be careful not to become abusive, manipulative, dictatorial or cruel.

Sex, too, is associated with Scorpio. Referred to by Shakespeare as "the little death," sex still is surrounded by fear and mystery, and often is used as an instrument of power and control. With Jupiter in Scorpio, you may possess a strong sexual appetite or exude a powerful sensuality that large numbers of people respond to. Perhaps you will benefit in some way from your sexuality. Singers Elvis Presley and Madonna, and actor Humphrey Bogart, all of whom became stars at least partly because of their sex appeal, are examples of Jupiter in Scorpio. Since the expansiveness of Jupiter often encourages excess, you may be inclined to be sexually indulgent and promiscuous, or to use sex to manipulate or dominate others.

Jupiter in Sagittarius

You believe you are here to learn and experience everything life has to offer, and your motto might be "the sky's the limit." Restless and curious, you want to see the world, and nothing makes you happier than being on the road, meeting new people and exploring new territories. For example, Admiral Richard Byrd, the first person to journey to the North Pole, and American pioneer Daniel Boone both had Jupiter in Sagittarius. You expand your understanding of the Universe and your place in it through traveling; for you, traveling is not just a form of entertainment, it is a quest for truth and wisdom. Not only do you benefit personally through your travels, you might also open up new worlds for others and thus expand their knowledge as well. Astronomer Nicolas Copernicus, who determined that the planets revolve around the Sun, is a good example of Jupiter in Sagittarius.

Your thirst for knowledge makes you a lifelong student. You love learning new things and if you aren't enrolled in a formal study program, you probably are an avid reader, watch educational television programs, listen to radio talk shows, or take correspondence courses. You also enjoy sharing what you know with others and might excel as a teacher, writer, publisher or lecturer. The birth charts of writers Hermann Hesse, William Blake, Truman Capote, astrologer/writer Marc Edmund Jones, and film maker/writer Woody Allen, for example, feature Jupiter in Sagittarius. Being a foreign correspondent might be your ideal profession, allowing you to travel widely and write about your adventures. Newsman Chet Huntley is another good example of Jupiter in Sagittarius. Although you are interested in practically everything, you often lack the focus and perseverance to finish what you start. Thus, you probably know a little bit about many things and have a broad overview, but aren't proficient in any one area.

Your desire to understand the Universe and your place in it could inspire an interest in philosophy and/or religion. Protestant reformer John Calvin, Pope John Paul I and Rosicrucian Max Heindel are a few examples of Jupiter in Sagittarius. The modern state of Israel, which was established for religious purposes, has its Jupiter in Sagittarius. Once you believe you've found the truth, you long to spread the word to one and all and have a tendency toward proselytizing. Quite likely, you are an eloquent and inspirational—though somewhat verbose—public speaker. Though your intent may be to educate and enlighten, in your zeal you can be self-righteous and intolerant of others' freedom to believe as they choose. Iranian religious leader Ayatolla Khomeini, for example, has Jupiter in Sagittarius.

This placement of Jupiter also can signify natural athletic ability. You have an abundance of energy, speed and agility, and since Sagittarius is associated with the legs you might excel at sports such as running, bicycling, soccer, basketball or ice skating. For example, basketball great Wilt Chamberlaine, skating champion Peggy Fleming and ballet dancer Mikhail Barishnikov have Jupiter in Sagittarius. Perhaps even more important, though, are the optimism, self-confidence and fun-loving enthusiasm you bring to the sports arena; you never lose your childlike love of the game and your belief that you can win, regardless of the odds. However, you may lack discipline and determination, unless this is provided by other factors in your chart, such as a prominent Saturn or Pluto.

In its own sign, Jupiter's tendency toward exaggeration and excess is even more in evidence. In the extreme, your gregariousness and "good time" attitude can lead to laziness, over-indulgence in food, drink, drugs and socializing, escapism to avoid work or responsibilities, and possibly compulsive gambling. Unchecked, your restlessness and fun-loving spirit might make you a rolling stone, unable to keep a steady job, hold on to a dime or commit to a relationship.

Jupiter in Capricorn

Through work, you expand your understanding of yourself and your place in the world, and some of your most important learning experiences are likely to come to you through your career. Actually, you enjoy working and derive much pleasure from seeing a job well done. However, you might become a workaholic since so much of your self-esteem and your satisfactions in life are connected to your job.

You possess natural managerial ability, have a good head for business and are known for your shrewdness, common sense, reliability and diligence. Willy Brandt, former Chancellor of West Germany, and British Prime Minister Margaret Thatcher are good examples of Jupiter in Capricorn. Supervising and organizing operations gives you a sense of satisfaction and you like being in a position of responsibility. You assume authority easily and are comfortable in a decision-making role, believing that no one is quite as capable as you.

Status is important to you and you want to have the respect of your peers, your community and society in general. Though you are ambitious, you do not desire glory or riches as much as honor and authority. For instance, you would prefer being president of a college to being a movie star. Success, however, is likely to come to you slowly, little by little and as a result of your own efforts, rather than being dropped in your lap by Lady Luck.

In the extreme, your ambition might cause you to do just about anything to achieve your goals and you may believe that "the ends justify the means." For example, the birth charts of Nazi leader Aldolf Hitler, former U. S. President Richard Nixon and his Attorney General John Mitchell feature Jupiter in Capricorn. Above all, you are a pragmatist and you do what you believe must be done without letting your emotions or ideologies get in the way. Thus, others often see you as cold and calculating.

You respect traditions, and unless something has stood the test of time, you don't place much value on it. Consequently, you tend to stick with what you know rather than taking chances on new ideas, techniques or practices, and you can be extremely rigid and old-fashioned. The "god" you worship might be tradition. Upholding the status quo benefits you, and through becoming part of the establishment you are likely to increase your wealth, status and/or sense of security. Therefore, you see no reason to make changes or "rock the boat." You might even become well-known as a result of your conservative views, as is true of writer and political talk show host William F. Buckley, Jr., whose Jupiter is in Capricorn.

You also seek security, stability and a predictable, well-defined, orderly life. Thus, you might go to the "right" schools, work hard, plan carefully, hold on to your resources, invest in blue chip stocks, support the established order and associate with people who can benefit you so as to provide the best possible future for yourself and your descendants.

Jupiter in Aquarius

You seek knowledge and understanding in many different and often unusual ways, and your search for truth is unbounded. Unlimited by conventions and accepted belief systems, you eagerly explore new ideas, and might be on the cutting edge of science, technology or "new age" thought. Because you look at things in a different light, you may make important discoveries that others miss, and your insights could help expand humankind's understanding of the Universe and our place in it. French scientist Marie Curie, who isolated radium, Jonas Salk, who developed a vaccine for polio, Gus Grissom, who was one of the first astronauts, and Albert Einstein, who developed the theory of relativity, are some good examples of Jupiter in Aquarius.

Intellectually-oriented, you enjoy learning, respect knowledge, and are especially interested in abstract or modern fields such as computers, science, aviation, alchemy, astrology and electronics. The "god" you worship might be science or metaphysics. Your personal growth and learning are likely to take place outside the ordinary channels, however. Perhaps you are self-taught, or your education has been erratic or atypical in some way.

You see yourself as a member of the world community and are interested in improving the lot of humankind. Your interest in universal brother/sisterhood, equality and human rights could lead you to become involved in causes that address these issues, and working for social change makes you feel good about yourself. In fact, you may never be happier than when you are protesting injustices.

Often your ideas conflict sharply with conventional ones, and you enjoy being seen as a renegade. You gravitate toward avant garde or progressive views, especially in politics and religion, and could benefit through organizing or working with an ideologically-based group. For example, Russian occultist Madame Helena Blavatsky, founder of Theosophy, had Jupiter in Aquarius. However, you tend to be overly idealistic and impractical, and many of your utopian ideas simply won't work in the real world. Strongly opinionated, you rarely hold your tongue and are sometimes quite tactless and antagonistic when it comes to expressing your beliefs. You also can be self-righteous and evangelical, intolerant of people who are more conservative.

Through being "different," trying new things, and breaking the rules, you develop a broader understanding of yourself and the world in which you live. One of your functions is to expand the awareness of others, too, and enable them to go beyond the boundaries of accepted thought, behavior and experience. You have the ability to help people see things in a new light, to make them think about things, and to open their eyes to alternative possibilities. You may even achieve success or recognition for your unusual ideas and/or lifestyle. French painter Edouard Manet, considered by many to have been the first "modern artist," had his Jupiter in Aquarius. So did dancer Isadora Duncan, who was seen as a radical and bohemian in both her dancing and her personal life. Both of these individuals broke with tradition and caused others to view art in a new way—and outraged conservatives in the process.

In your desire to be unique, however, you may go overboard and adopt odd or iconoclastic attitudes and/or behaviors just for the sake of being different. You love playing the eccentric and have fun shocking those who are more traditional.

Jupiter in Pisces

You probably possess much artistic talent, and expressing it—through painting, music, photography, dance or poetry—comes easily and naturally for you. Musicians Franz Schubert, Felix Mendelssohn, Rimsky-Korsakov, Stan Getz, Stevie Wonder and Ella Fitzgerald, painters Rembrandt, Paul Klee, JeanBatisse Camille Corot, universal genius Leonardo da Vinci, writers Johann von Goethe, George Orwell, Edna St. Vincent Millay and J.R.R. Tolkien, and actor/film maker Orson Welles are some of the many famous artists with this Jupiter position in their charts. Through the use of your imagination, intuition and creativity you grow and expand your awareness of the Universe and your place in it. You derive great satisfaction and an exhilarating feeling of well-being and self-confidence from your art. Perhaps you will even achieve recognition for your creativity and might get a "lucky break" that results in your success.

However, unless your chart contains other factors that provide some discipline and perseverance, you might spend more time dreaming about the symphonies you'll write or the paintings you'll paint than actually doing it. On its own, this combination indicates laziness and lack of focus. You want things to come easily and may give up too quickly, rather than working diligently toward a goal. You also are a perfectionist, and if you can't be the best at something you won't even try.

Your wonderful imagination enables you to see and hear things others don't—a valuable gift when used artistically. However, you have a tendency to let your imagination run away with you sometimes, and you could experience hallucinations, paranoia, or simply have trouble separating fact from fantasy. At times, your dream world and fantasy life might be more real to you than the physical realm.

For you, the unmapped territory of the subconscious holds great fascination, possibly because the boundary between your own conscious and subconscious is not so distinct as it is in most people. You also may realize that this is the source of your creativity. Quite likely, you have an interest in psychic development and/or psychology and see them as ways to get in touch with the inner realm. For example, psychiatrist Sigmund Freud had his Jupiter in Pisces. So did writer Edgar Allen Poe, whose psychological thrillers revealed his understanding of what goes on in the depths of the human mind. You want to expand your horizons to encompass all worlds of existence—inner and outer—and all levels of experience.

Your sensitivity to realms outside the physical may result in strong spiritual beliefs. Regardless of what religion you embrace, your faith is an important part of your life and brings you joy and comfort. Perhaps you will even devote your life to your religion, as a monk/nun, spiritual teacher or leader. In the extreme, you might become so fervent in your beliefs that you are self-righteous and intolerant of others'. Or, you might escape into your spiritual life as a way of avoiding the difficulties of the "real world."

Your desire to escape the harsh realities of earthly life could cause you to turn to alcohol and/or drugs, or to withdraw into yourself to avoid facing your problems and responsibilities. With Jupiter in Pisces, your ideal is not to be found in this world and your hope is that you'll find it in another, more perfect one.

Chapter Nine

Saturn

It takes Saturn about twenty-nine years to complete its passage through the twelve zodiacal signs, and the planet remains in each sign for approximately two and one-half years.

Through the ages, Saturn has been much maligned and traditional astrologers have called this planet the "greater malefic," the grim reaper and Satan. It is linked with the Devil card in Tarot, and has been connected with all sorts of evils, including chronic diseases, losses, frustration, loneliness, hardship, poverty, old age, even death. Just about every unpleasantness in life has been blamed on Saturn at one time or another.

But Saturn is hardly an ill wind that blows no one any good. Like all the planets, Saturn performs a necessary role and represents an essential principle: contraction and limitation. Jupiter, discussed in the last chapter, represents the principle of expansion. These two work together to maintain balance, for too much expansion leads to excess and waste, while too much contraction results in rigidity and stagnation.

Saturn's sign and house position and its aspects to other planets in the birth chart show areas where you are likely to feel restricted or deficient in some way. As a result, this planet often reveals what you consider inadequate, stunted and/or problematic in yourself. Often you feel sensitive and vulnerable about these areas of "weakness" and someone can "push your buttons" by triggering your Saturn. Because you usually feel inferior about areas in your chart that are influenced by Saturn, you may work hard to improve upon them. As a result, these parts of your character over time might actually become your strengths because you have put so much effort into developing them—though it is doubtful that you will ever view them as such.

Saturn is linked with work and sometimes is thought of as the astrological taskmaster. Its placement in your chart shows what you will have to work for in life and what things don't come easily to you. However, you probably appreciate Saturn-related gains more than Jupiter-related ones because you had to overcome obstacles to earn them. Saturn signifies slow, incremental growth, cautious, steady movement toward a goal, tenacity and practicality.

Tests and trials are also are associated with Saturn, and the areas in which you are likely to be tested are revealed by Saturn's position in your chart. Every seven years or so, when transiting Saturn makes a stressful aspect to your natal Saturn, you are given a sort of cosmic exam to determine how successfully you are managing the areas in your life that are related to your natal Saturn placement.

"Lord of Karma" is another of Saturn's monikers. Astrologers frequently connect this planet with the past—either the past events of this lifetime, or, if you believe in reincarnation, issues you've carried over from previous incarnations as well. Though this may sound rather ominous, karma only has a negative connotation because most of us don't like the idea of getting exactly what we deserve. Although we'd rather Saturn had a little pity, this planet's job is to show us where we are deficient and force us to correct the deficiency. Saturn doesn't create problems, it merely illuminates them. The more you resist making the necessary changes, however, the more pain Saturn must inflict, since frequently it seems we won't correct something until life becomes so painful that we have no other choice. It is often through suffering, though, that we learn and grow; in the words of Rudolf Steiner, "Wisdom is crystallized pain." Thus, Saturn also is the planet of wisdom and the insight that comes with age.

In her book, *Saturn: A New Look at an Old Devil*, Liz Greene makes an insightful analogy between Saturn and the Beast, from the story "Beauty and the Beast."[1] The Beast is the dark face of the handsome prince, and until you make friends with the Beast inside, your prince won't come.

Saturn in Aries

You probably have trouble asserting yourself and going after what you want in an aggressive manner. At times, it might seem as though some internal or external obstacle blocks you every time you try to push forward. This does not mean necessarily that you are timid or weak, but rather that you are reluctant to behave forcefully and don't like confrontation. However, you may feel that you are unable to stand up for yourself or to compete, and might experience anxiety whenever you have to be aggressive.

Your anger is kept carefully in check and you rarely let your temper get the better of you. Usually, you seem cool and in control, able to act rationally and with moderation even in the heat of the moment. Therefore, you could be good at such things as leading troops in battle, managing an athletic team or directing new business ventures. For example, U. S. Generals George Washington and Douglas MacArthur had Saturn in Aries. Perhaps one of your tests in life is to learn to be a leader in times of stress.

Cautious and pragmatic, you carefully plan your actions and aren't likely to do anything impulsively. In most situations you play it safe and hesitate to take chances. You are inclined to overestimate the dangers involved and the strength of your adversaries. As a result, you sometimes miss out on opportunities because you are afraid to risk much and because you do not act quickly or decisively enough.

Men especially might see this as a weakness and overcompensate for their lack of daring by engaging in dangerous activities so that no one can say they lack courage or are unmanly. Another possibility is that you might test yourself and put your life on the line in an attempt to confront and overcome your trepidation. For example, daredevil Evel Knievel and race car driver Mario Andretti have Saturn in Aries. One of your tests in this lifetime might be learning to take calculated risks and face challenges in practical ways that will produce tangible results, instead of engaging in foolish acts of bravado or rashness for no good reason.

Unless Mars is strong in your chart or you have several planets in fire signs, this Saturn placement can indicate lack of vitality, strength and enthusiasm. You aren't very playful and sports probably don't appeal to you much. However, you have determination and can focus your energy and discipline yourself so that, if you do have athletic ability, you could be quite successful. Runner Herb Elliot, who first broke the four-minute mile, is a good example of Saturn in Aries. Perhaps his test was to break through old limits (Saturn) and introduce new possibilities (Aries) into his sport.

Saturn in Taurus

Your tests in life are likely to revolve around issues of material possessions and physical resources. How you acquire and use your resources will be important, and you may learn many significant—though perhaps difficult—lessons in this area.

Probably you will have to work for whatever you get, rather than being born to wealth or winning a fortune in the lottery. If money does come to you as a result of something other than your own efforts, it may turn out to be a burden in some way, so that you don't really enjoy your wealth. Perhaps your freedoms are limited by material responsibilities and you feel trapped by your possessions. Or, you might find that your financial position isolates you from other people.

At some time in your life you probably experienced poverty, and as a result, you might live in fear of being needy again. If you were born into a poor family, you may feel you are inferior to those who have more money than you do. You might connect personal worth with material worth and be very sensitive and defensive about what you see as a deficiency in yourself. Therefore, as an adult, you might try to build the self-respect you so desire by accumulating wealth. You also may value others in direct relationship to their portfolios.

Money and possessions give you a sense of security that goes beyond the ability to provide for yourself and your family, and even if you have more money than you could ever spend, you never seem to get enough. You may be avaricious and greedy, stubbornly holding on to your possessions as if your life depended on them—for to you, at some deep inner level, it does. However, if you compromise your principles to obtain wealth or profit through the misfortune of others you might end up losing everything. Or, you could discover that your gains were not worth what you sacrificed for them. Thus, the test of Saturn in this life might be what are you willing to do for money? Your attachment to your possessions, too, may be tested and, if you don't come to realize this easily, you could be forced painfully to face up to the fact that security does not come from material things.

Your body, too, is one of your physical resources and how you treat it and use it will be significant in this lifetime. For example, entertainer Raquel Welch, who has Saturn in Taurus, has used her great physical beauty to earn a fortune. Singer Barbra Steisand, who also has Saturn in Taurus, is another good example of someone who has benefitted financially from developing and utilizing her physical resource—her voice. If you neglect or abuse your body, or use your sexuality to control or manipulate others, however, you are likely to suffer for it, for Saturn always insists that you assume responsibility for your actions.

Saturn in Gemini

In some way, you are likely to experience difficulties in the area of communication. Perhaps your early education was restricted or inadequate, interfered with by poverty, childhood illness, poor schools, family troubles, etc. Or, maybe a learning disability, speech defect or other problem caused you to get a slow start and you had to work hard to catch up later. You might have had to teach yourself everything you know, mostly through trial and error.

As a result, you feel inferior in terms of your intellect, education or communication skills, and you probably are quite sensitive about this. Because you believed you were deficient in these areas, you may have put forth Herculean effort to improve yourself, so that now you are more than adequate. However, it is also possible that early impediments to your intellectual and verbal development caused you to fear and dislike learning, so that as an adult you still find yourself mentally blocked. This does not mean that you are stupid or unable to learn, but rather that your negative attitude toward education and your fear of being inferior could be standing in your way.

Speaking before groups might be especially hard for you, and your writing style may be stilted and self-conscious. Your test in this life, however, could be to learn to use your intellect and/or communication skills effectively. This might even mean that you work to improve communication systems, perhaps through delivering mail, editing manuscripts or repairing telephones, office machines or computers. If you neglect your mental development or misuse you powers of communication, however, you will have to pay the price. For example, Colonel Oliver North, who abused his position as a spokesperson for the U. S. to negotiate illegal weapons deals, has his Saturn in Gemini.

Your mind works in a logical, orderly fashion, and you are good at planning, organizing, analyzing, researching and retaining information. Quite likely, your powers of concentration and your memory are also good. A practical thinker, you want to be able to apply what you know so that it produces tangible results. You have common sense, a head for business, and the ability to focus intently on facts, figures, technical data. Whether writing or speaking, you get to the point and don't waste words, and you rarely speak unless you have something to say.

Because Gemini is associated with your immediate environment and travel near your home, you might experience frequent delays, frustrations and difficulties driving or taking public transportation in and around your community. Neighbors and/or siblings, too, could present problems for you and you may find it hard to communicate with them. Finally, Gemini's connection with the hands could indicate restrictions or tests related to your hands and, perhaps, a need to develop manual dexterity. Fighter Joe Louis, who had Saturn in Gemini, is a good example of someone who worked hard and steadily to develop his manual skills.

Saturn in Cancer

Many of your tests in life involve your family and home. Although your family also may provide you with a sense of structure and permanence, you might be burdened or limited in some way by family responsibilities or be called on to make personal sacrifices for your family. Perhaps you will have to work hard to support your family. Or, family ties and obligations could make it necessary for you to remain in your hometown and pass up opportunities elsewhere. Family expectations might force you into a role that is not of your own choosing, such as running a family business or upholding your family's societal position. Queen Elizabeth I of England and former U. S. President John F. Kennedy, for example, had Saturn in Cancer. Your sense of duty toward your family is strong, and though you probably feel some resentment about the hardships you've had to endure because of them, you are not likely to run out on them.

Though you feel an inextricable bond with them, there is a lack of closeness and warmth between you and your family members, almost as though some unseen obstacle blocks the emotional connection you desire. Perhaps you feel your parents didn't love you; perhaps work demands, death, illness or divorce caused you to be separated from them. For example, actress Candice Bergen, who always felt her father was more devoted to his famous puppet Charlie McCarthy than to her, has Saturn in Cancer. Whatever the reason for the absence of positive interaction between you and your parents, the deficiency causes you a great deal of pain and you are quite sensitive about the deprivation you experienced. You might try to deny it to yourself, or overcompensate by attempting to create the family you never had.

Your mother (or nurturing parent) in particular might have been a stern disciplinarian who limited your fun and freedom as a child, controlled your self-expression or burdened you with responsibilities at an early age. Even in adulthood, you probably feel restrained by her and your relationship with her might be problematic. Singer Liza Minelli, who had a difficult relationship with her mother Judy Garland, is a good example of Saturn in Cancer.

Although you may be critical of your family, you are also a staunch defender of family members and won't allow anyone else to speak badly about them. Perhaps you view yourself as the guardian of your family honor and traditions.

Toward your own children, you are strict, rigid and rather aloof. Though you may love them very much, it is difficult for you to demonstrate it openly. You worry about them—often to excess—and tend to be overly protective of them, restricting them in much the same way as your parents restricted you. In reality, your protectiveness toward your children stems from your own fear of losing them. Another possibility is that you may have wanted children but never had them. Your test in life may be to learn to express your feelings toward your family members, and to become less dependent and attached to them.

Your physical home could represent security and stability for you, and you might be strongly attached to it. Even if it makes many demands on you, in terms of hefty mortgage payments or constant repairs, your home creates a bond between you and your family and/or community. You may feel an obligation to provide a home for your family, or to keep up the old homestead.

Since Saturn is associated with work, another possibility is that you might work in an area that is related to the home, family and/or children—real estate, architecture, pediatrics—and through your efforts, learn important life lessons.

Saturn in Leo

Although you want to be creative and may even have artistic ability, you probably have trouble expressing your talent. In some way, you seem to be blocked. Perhaps demands from family and/or work take up so much of your time that you have no energy left for creative pursuits. Possibly you were criticized by your parents, or were discouraged from pursuing an artistic career because it wasn't practical. Or, you may never have had a chance to develop your talent, so that now it lies unformed within you like a diamond in the rough. You might even have a physical limitation that makes it hard for you to do what you want to do. For example, the great German musician and composer Ludwig von Beethoven, who had Saturn in Leo, was deaf.

You probably feel inadequate in this area and see only your shortcomings. Self-expression is important to you and because you feel deficient in this area, you tend to be quite sensitive and defensive about your creative ventures. You might be reluctant to let anyone else see your drawings or poems and you don't take criticism well. Quite likely, your extreme seriousness and your unreasonably high expectations of yourself make you so tense and judgmental that you block the flow of your creative juices. In short, you are standing in your own way.

Because Saturn is the planet of work and pragmatism, you might put your creativity to work in some "safe," practical area such as carpentry, drafting, editing or repairing musical instruments. If you do devote yourself to your art, you may never make any money at it, or you might not be recognized during your own lifetime. For example, French impressionist painter Georges Seurat, who had Saturn in Leo, sold very little of his work while he was alive. Regardless of the route you take, success probably won't come easily for you and you will have to work hard for whatever recognition you get. Perhaps your test in this life is to learn to apply yourself diligently to your creative pursuits without expecting easy rewards and overnight fame.

Because the sign Leo is connected with self-confidence, ego, optimism and courage, you also might experience tests involving your self-esteem. Perhaps you have suffered setbacks or criticisms that caused you to lose confidence in yourself. You might discover that your low opinion of yourself or your timidity are inhibiting your creativity, and you may have to work on improving your self-image and confidence before you can become a good artist. In order to make it in the art world, you need a healthy ego and a strong enough belief in yourself that you don't care what the critics say.

Children, too, are an expression of your creativity. Therefore, you might experience tests, difficulties and responsibilities raising your children that will teach you important life lessons. Maybe you feel your children restrict you or are a burden in terms of time, energy and money. The responsibilities of raising children might be more than you are comfortable with, however, you are very conscious of your duty and try hard to do what you feel is best for them. Or, perhaps you always wanted children, but never had them.

How you develop and use your creativity will be important in this lifetime, and though you probably will experience problems related to your self-expression, your greatest growth can come from this, too.

Saturn in Virgo

You are likely to experience difficulties in connection with work and service to others, but it is here, too, that you will learn your most important life lessons. Your tests in life may be related to your attitudes about providing service to others, what and who you serve, and how you treat those who serve you. Perhaps it will be necessary for you to learn humility, or to work to improve conditions for those who are less fortunate than you are by helping them to help themselves. In serving others you may be required to make some sort of personal sacrifice, as is true of Rose Kennedy who sacrificed her sons to her country; her Saturn is in Virgo. You might have to give up opportunities for wealth, status and power, or be obliged to work hard and perform unglamorous tasks thanklessly. However, great personal growth can result from your modesty and compassion.

The workplace itself might be a testing ground for you, and you may have to work long and hard without much help from others. Whatever you accomplish will be through your own efforts, rather than because you know the right people or got a lucky break. Neatness and organization are extremely important to you; the expression "a place for everything and everything in its place" certainly applies to you. At your best, you make things run smoothly by taking care of all the details; at worst, you can become so rigidly attached to order and routines that the ritual means more than the result. Conscientious, hard-working and perfection oriented, you are willing to work at low-paying, low prestige jobs so long as you feel what you are doing is worthwhile. However, you often have trouble standing up for yourself at work and might sell yourself short, allowing employers or more ambitious people to take advantage of you. Unless other factors in your birth chart offset this inclination, you may lack ambition and assertiveness, and prefer to stay in the background assisting others and letting them take the credit.

Highly critical of yourself, you might lack a sense of self-worth and probably undervalue your abilities. You feel inadequate and are afraid of being incompetent at your job, therefore, you can be rather sensitive and defensive about work-related issues. You believe you must be perfect, and your perfectionism can result in ulcers, digestive problems, skin irritations and other stress-related illnesses.

One of the tests associated with this Saturn placement is understanding the connection between mind and body—how each affects the other—and learning to integrate their functions. You probably have an interest in nutrition, medicine and other issues that involve health. You might even work in one of the health-related fields. In this way, you can combine your concern for people in need, your desire to serve in some practical way, and your fascination with the body and how it functions. Surgeon William Mayo, one of the founders of the Mayo Clinic, is a good example of Saturn in Virgo. Whether or not you pursue healing professionally, you probably are fond of "doctoring" yourself and your family members. You might be an avid vitamin and/or pill popper, a fussy eater or constant dieter, and perhaps are a bit neurotic about germs.

Your overly-critical nature can cause you to focus more on what's wrong than what's right. For example, French writer Victor Hugo, whose novel *Les Miserables* centers on misfortune and suffering, had his Saturn in Virgo. You are inclined toward negativity, irritability and excessive complaining, and one of your tests in life might be to learn to see things in perspective, be less pessimistic, and "lighten up."

Saturn in Libra

Partnerships of all kinds may prove troublesome for you, and in your relationships with other people you probably will experience your share of disappointments, frustrations and delays. Through relationships, however, you are likely to learn your most significant life lessons and grow in many ways. If you believe in karma, this position of Saturn could signify "fated" associations and karmic lessons to be learned through your relationships.

Perhaps you will be denied a meaningful relationship, at least until you are mature enough to balance your needs and desires with another person's. Indeed, one of your tests in life might be finding this delicate balance and learning to compromise without sacrificing yourself. Although relationships are very important to you, it may seem as though you are unlucky in love. External or internal obstacles—cultural, ethnic or religious barriers, age differences, poverty, work or family obligations— might stand in the way of your happiness. Your relationships could develop very slowly, or you might have to wait a long time for a lover to become available. Physical problems, such as illness, handicaps or ugliness, could make it hard for you to attract partners. French artist Henri Toulouse-Lautrec, who was shunned by women because of his short stature, is a good example of Saturn in Libra.

You may feel you are unlovable, and your inferiority complex could repel prospective partners. Or, you might be so desperate for love that you cling to any likely candidate, and thus drive him/her away with your expectations. Because you believe you are inadequate and undesirable, you tend to be quite defensive and sensitive about love and relationships. Afraid of being rejected, you might shut yourself off from other people and refuse to get involved because you don't want to be hurt. You are cautious and conservative in love, and your cold, aloof, disinterested demeanor can cause potential partners to give up on you and go looking for someone more accessible. For example, French painter Edgar Degas, who had Saturn in Libra, cut himself off from friends and lived as a near recluse.

The sign Libra also is connected with art, and both Degas and Toulouse-Lautrec turned their emotional energy to creating great works of art. Saturn in Libra can suggest a need to channel love and attention into artistic pursuits, therefore, you might be blocked from relationships with other people so that your time and energy can be devoted to another cause. Perhaps your tests and growth experiences will come through the arts.

Your relationships may be a burden to you in some way. Some sort of sacrifice could be necessary, and your partner or the relationship itself might make great demands on you. For example, the Duke of Windsor, formerly King Edward

VIII of Great Britain, had to give up his throne as a result of his marriage; he had Saturn in Libra. Perhaps your independence will be limited by your partnership, or the relationship might require you to shoulder heavy responsibilities.

This is a good placement for business partnerships, however, since Saturn is associated with work and Libra with all types of committed partnerships. Perhaps you and your mate share career goals and work together effectively in business. Work might be an important and solidifying part of your love relationships, or you might meet romantic partners through your job.

Once you establish a relationship, it is likely to endure. You are not frivolous with your affection and tend to be a traditionalist, preferring marriage to less structured, casual love affairs. A devoted and dependable partner, you take your commitment and the relationship very seriously and won't give up when the going gets tough. You are willing to work hard to make a partnership a strong and lasting one, and though they may not be easy, your relationships ultimately can be very successful.

Saturn in Scorpio

You are intent upon understanding the forces that operate behind the scenes. Perhaps you are interested in the inner workings of Earth and the Universe. For example, Russian writer Immanuel Velikovsky, who theorized about major transformations on Earth and in the cosmos, had Saturn in Scorpio; so did chemist and physicist Marie Curie, who discovered the secrets of radioactive materials. Your search might lead you to explore the depths of the human psyche, or to probe the hidden activities of businesses, organizations or governments to find out what goes on inside, as did former FBI director J. Edgar Hoover, whose Saturn was in Scorpio. Surface appearances mean little to you; you are searching for deeper meanings and core truths. One of your life lessons might be how you use this knowledge.

Knowledge is power, and power—over yourself, other people, your environment—is what you are really seeking. You may fear that you have little control over your own life and this sense of helplessness might lead you to attempt to dominate people and situations. For example, former Chinese leader Mao Tse Tung, who rigidly controlled the people and politics of The People's Republic of China, had Saturn in Scorpio. So does British Prime Minister Margaret Thatcher. How you exercise your power, whether you use it to limit and manipulate others or to help them, probably will be a significant issue for you in this life. You may have opportunities to do great good or great harm, and the choice you make could be one of your "tests."

One of the secrets you might try to unmask is death. Death and life afterwards—the ultimate transformation—fascinate you. You may even believe that through understanding death you will have more control over it, or at least your response to it. For example, Elisabeth Kübler-Ross, who researches and writes about death and dying, has her Saturn in Scorpio. So did writer Truman Capote, whose best-selling book *In Cold Blood* was about murder. All forms of destruction and rebirth are of interest to you, and you might even work in such areas as renovating buildings, reconstructive surgery, cancer research or weaponry.

Sex, another of life's great mysteries, is probably an important issue for you. Hugh Hefner of *Playboy* is a good example of Saturn in Scorpio. However, you might find sex frightening or frustrating; your inclination is to tense up and try to control the experience, yet in order to enjoy sex you must relax and give in to your body's sensations. Perhaps you are quite sensitive about your sexuality and feel somewhat inadequate or undesirable. In the extreme, you might deny yourself sexual satisfaction; or, you could attempt to control or dominate your partners because the power sex has over you is threatening.

At your core lurk intense and turbulent emotions, but you may try to block them from your consciousness, afraid of being overwhelmed if you open up your "Pandora's box." If you refuse to make friends with your Minotaur, however, you might project your fears into the outer world and believe that people are "out to get your" or that you can't trust anyone. At times, you have a dark view of life and expect the worst to happen. Painter Vincent van Gogh, whose fears caused him to commit suicide, had his Saturn in Scorpio.

Maybe you have experienced a traumatic loss of some kind that transformed your life. In fact, your life sometimes seems to be a series of difficult ups and downs, and you long for stability and permanence. As a result, you might attempt to create security in your life by holding on too tightly to everything and everyone—partners, your job, money or property—that you believe might provide some structure for you. Any "loss," even changes, can seem almost life-threatening to you, and you run a risk of becoming rigid, stubborn and miserly, afraid even to give up things that are no longer useful to you. Consequently, you might inhibit your own growth and creativity because you can't just relax and let things take their course. You need to learn to let go and not fear change, to let the old die so the new can be born. Most of all, you need to develop trust—in yourself and the powers that be.

Saturn in Sagittarius

Knowledge is very important to you, but you may have been denied the education and opportunities for growth that you desire. Consequently, you might feel that you are not as well-educated, widely-traveled or wise as you would like to be, and are defensive and sensitive about what you see as an inadequacy in yourself. Perhaps you will work hard to educate yourself and attempt to overcome the limitations placed on you. This planetary position suggests an education in the "school of hard knocks," and your knowledge is likely to be gained through personal experience rather than books.

Your tests in life are likely to be connected with your religious or philosophical views, and you may be faced with difficult decisions and learning experiences in this area. Indian leader Mahatma Gandhi, civil rights leader Rev. Martin Luther King, Jr., and clergyman Norman Vincent Peale are some examples of Saturn in Sagittarius. Your beliefs are important to you and they provide you with a sense of structure and order in life. As a result, you might hold on tightly to traditions and dogma, and see any opposition to your beliefs as threatening to your personal stability. Conservative in your views, you resist change and can be rather narrow-minded and severe at times. By refusing to entertain new ideas, however, you limit your understanding of the world and your place in it, therefore, one of your tests could be to broaden your philosophical horizons and break away from rigid, authoritarian dictates that are inhibiting your growth.

Another possibility is that you have become disillusioned with orthodox views and have rejected all religious and philosophical beliefs as impractical, useless or unfounded. This planetary position can be indicative of someone who has trouble accepting anything on faith. You might need to prove something to yourself before you can believe it. For example, French statistician Michel Gauquelin, who has Saturn in Sagittarius, had to "prove" astrology through statistical research before he could accept its validity. However, your skepticism may cut you off from intuitive knowledge and insights that cannot be quantified according to physical laws. Perhaps you need to learn to trust your intuition and to develop a worldview that is based on your own experience, rather than relying on some "authority" to tell you what to believe.

Sagittarius is an idealistic sign, but with Saturn positioned here you may have suffered painful disappointments that caused you to exchange your youthful optimism for pessimism. You have the ability to bring your dreams to fruition, however, and to build castles here on Earth rather than in the sky. One of your life lessons might be learning to combine your idealism with common sense and hard work, so that your dreams can be manifested in the physical world.

Saturn in Capricorn

Ambitious, pragmatic and hard-working, you invest much of yourself in your career and your greatest tests in life are likely to involve some aspect of your work. You have plenty of common sense and when it comes to managing resources, organizing or planning, no one does it better. Known for your diligence and dependability, you readily assume responsibility and usually do more than your share. You can have trouble delegating authority, however, and usually believe that if you want it done right you have to do it yourself. Therefore, you probably have lessons to learn about trusting others. How you use your authority also could be important in this lifetime.

Despite your obvious capabilities, however, professional success may not come easily or quickly for you, and you will have to work for whatever you get. You probably will have to climb the corporate ladder in slow, determined steps. As you pursue your goals, you might experience many frustrations, obstacles, delays or setbacks that will test your perseverance. Perhaps success will be denied you until rather late in life, or at least until you have gained the maturity to handle it, and what you are willing to do to get to the top could be significant.

Your work is very important to you and you feel most comfortable in the business world. Structured, impersonal, unemotional environments suit you best, and unless Cancer is prominent in your chart, you may feel more "at home" in your office than your home. People with this planetary position can become workaholics who don't allow themselves time to get to know their families—or themselves. One of the lessons you might need to learn is to balance work with play, professional life with personal.

You aren't looking for fame, however, and prefer to remain in the background, controlling things from behind the scenes. In fact, you may be rather self-conscious and shy, and don't like drawing attention to yourself. Although you desire prestige and status and want to be respected for your competence, you have little interest in publicity or glory (unless Leo is prominent in your chart).

Cautious and conservative, you are inclined to stick with tried-and-true methods and shy away from anything new or different. Fear of failure is a powerful motivating factor in your life. You rarely take chances, find change threatening and are the last to update your techniques, products, behavior or ideas. An arch traditionalist, you can become rigid, dogmatic and stubbornly mired in the past. For example, conservative U. S. Senator Strom Thurmond has his Saturn in Capricorn. Your excessive prudence could be limiting your potential, however, and you might be forced to give up your old habits and securities—perhaps by circumstances that seem to be outside yourself—in order to grow. Or, you may find yourself hindered by entrenched powers, traditions or bureaucracies and have to break away from the established order before you can achieve your goals. For example, Soviet leader Mikhail Gorbachev, who desires social and economic reforms but is limited by restrictive, established political forces, has his Saturn in Capricorn.

Because you respect the past, you may be interested in history, geology, archeology or anthropology. Anthropologist Margaret Mead, and Charles Richter, who developed the Richter scale, are good examples of Saturn in Capricorn. You want to be able to explain, order and quantify your life and everything in it, and before you can make sense of something you must make it tangible. Through studying the past you are able to understand the present better and your place in the natural order of things.

Your public image and your position in your community are of great concern to you. Sensitive about what others think of you, you support the status quo, play by the rules and do what you think is expected of you. Emily Post, arbiter of etiquette, had her Saturn in Capricorn. Keenly aware of your duty and your role as a member of society, you tend to put society's needs ahead of the individual's and would sacrifice personal freedoms to maintain stability in the society. But you must learn to find security within yourself, instead of looking for it in the outer world, for if you allow others to define right and wrong for you, you relinquish your right to be a self-determining individual.

Saturn in Aquarius

This is a difficult combination, since Saturn's function is to limit and solidify while Aquarius' is to break up. Saturn represents the past, Aquarius the future. Consequently, if you have this planetary placement in your birth chart, you might feel torn between the two extremes. For instance, Salvador Dali, who is known for his avant garde art and his unconventional behavior, was also a supporter of fascism; he has Saturn in Aquarius. At best, you are the practical idealist who finds ways to incorporate both energies and make tomorrow's dreams a reality today. Perhaps you work in a scientific or technological field and are able to bring new ideas down to Earth so they can benefit humankind. However, your inventions and discoveries and how they are used could be an important test in this lifetime, and you must bear the responsibility for your creations. Robert Oppenheimer, father of the bomb, is a good example of Saturn in Aquarius.

Your concern for humanity could lead you to work for the betterment of people everywhere. Perhaps you are striving to help others achieve their independence or to eliminate social barriers and restrictions that limit and burden people. Missionary and humanitarian Albert Schweitzer, for example, had Saturn in Aquarius.

Quite likely, you are fascinated with the future, but your vision of it is rather bleak. Aquarius is the sign of freedom and individuality, and Saturn is the planet of authoritarianism and restriction. Therefore, you probably believe that in the future your independence will be limited in some way and your individuality will be hampered by the authorities. Writers George Orwell and Ayn Rand, whose birth charts feature Saturn in Aquarius, expressed this view in their books *1984* and *Atlas Shrugged.*

One of the things you fear most is loss of liberty and you may be particularly sensitive and defensive about your rights. Perhaps you interpret any rule or regulation as an attempt to limit your freedom, and you might over-react and rebel against even reasonable laws and responsibilities. The opposite response is also possible. You may have great difficulty handling independence and try to clamp down on yourself and everyone else. The responsibility of making your own choices and expressing your individuality frightens you, and you look to "authorities" to tell you how to live your life. You are afraid of change and intolerant of anyone who is "different," and feel you must cling to the status quo or everything will dissolve into chaos. For example, fundamentalist preacher Jerry Falwell has his Saturn in Aquarius. Your fear, however, is the result of your own rigidity and your reluctance to let go and allow even small changes into your life. Whichever way you respond to this energy, one of your life lessons is learning to balance liberty and responsibility, change and stability, new and old.

Whether or not you want to, it may be necessary for you to break with the past in order to express your own uniqueness. You might even appear to be something of a revolutionary, and could encounter hostile resistance from traditionalists. England's King Henry VIII, who broke away from the Church of Rome so he could divorce his first wife and marry Anne Boleyn, is a good example of Saturn in Aquarius. So is Swiss psychiatrist Carl Jung, whose interests in the occult ran counter to the prevailing attitudes of the psychological community. Your decision to break away from the old ways may cause you much pain and difficulty, but it is necessary if you are to grow.

Saturn in Pisces

You are extraordinarily sensitive—to people, your environment, the psychic realms—but your sensitivity may frighten you and make you feel vulnerable or defenseless. At times, you can be a bit paranoid and depressive, and have a tendency to look on the dark side. Perhaps you believe others are out to get you and that you are helpless; or, you might focus on life's evils and think that the world is an awful place. Thin-skinned and easily hurt, you fear that nothing you do will make things better, so you simply give up without trying. Too often, you play the role of the victim or martyr, and unless you have fire signs prominent in your chart or a strongly-placed Sun and/or Jupiter, you can become stuck in a morbid and self-destructive rut. One of your life lessons could be how you use your sensitivity.

A more constructive way would be to channel your sensitivity into artistic, spiritual or psychic work. You have the ability to tap into energies of which other people aren't aware, and could bring those energies down to Earth and use them to benefit humanity. American psychic and healer Edgar Cayce, for example, had Saturn in Pisces. So did French painter Paul Gauguin, film maker John Huston and occultist Francis Israel Regardie. This planetary placement can give you the grounding and focus to utilize your heightened awareness in some practical manner.

Your spiritual beliefs might be very important to you; perhaps your religion is the cornerstone of your life and provides you with a sense of security and structure. Conservative and traditional in your beliefs, you are inclined to follow one of the more orthodox and established faiths. Or, you could go to the opposite extreme and reject religion altogether because it isn't practical and can't be proved. For example, the birth charts of Karl Marx, founder of socialism, and French existentialist writer Jean-Paul Sartre both feature Saturn in Pisces.

Perhaps you never had an opportunity to develop your artistic or musical talent fully. Or, you might have been discouraged or kept from expressing it, maybe by parents who believed that being an artist wasn't a practical or suitable occupation. Thus, you may feel you are inadequate in this area and can be quite sensitive to criticism. Most likely, you are a perfectionist and overly critical of yourself; therefore, if your efforts fall short, you quickly give up in discouragement. You need to use the perseverance of Saturn and work diligently to develop your skills. Another possibility is that you are afraid of getting in touch with your subconscious self—the source of your creativity—and as a result, you block the flow of artistic energy and inspiration. Your test in this life might be finding ways to open up the channel between your conscious and subconscious.

Your sensitivity enables you to feel a kinship with all living things, and because of your keen awareness of other realms and dimensions you understand your connection to everything else in the Universe. You can't bear to see any creature suffer and might work in some way to alleviate pain in the world. Marine biologist and writer Rachel Carson is a good example of Saturn in Pisces. Perhaps you embrace one of the nature religions, or are involved in efforts to save our planet from pollution and bring peace to the world. With this placement in your chart, you have the ability to combine compassion with pragmatism and find workable ways to manifest the Divine on Earth.

Notes

1. Liz Greene, *Saturn: A New Look at an Old Devil* (New York: Samuel Weiser, Inc., 1976), p. 9.

Chapter Ten

Uranus

The first of the "outer" or transpersonal planets, Uranus takes about eighty-four years to complete its trip through the zodiac and remains in each sign for approximately seven years. Therefore, people who are born within a few years of each other will have the same sign placement of Uranus in their birth charts. The result is a "mini-generation" of individuals who have a common Uranus denominator, and who thus vibrate to a unique tone that sets them apart from all other groups. You share certain attitudes, emotions, behaviors and responses with everyone else in your Uranus-group.

Uranus is the planet of change, but it also is associated with freedom, individuality, equality, humanitarianism, anarchy, chaos, revolution, sudden upheavals, the unexpected, instantaneous insights, unconventional attitudes and behavior, modern ideas and technology, and anything that is new, different or unusual. Around the time Uranus was discovered (1781) there were all sorts of significant changes going on in the world. Some of these, such as the French and American Revolutions, involved the Uranian issues of freedom, self-determination and revolution. Some involved sudden advances in technology and thought, such as the harnessing of electricity and the advancement of the concept of democracy. It was also a time of outrageous behavior and styles, especially among the upper classes, and of heightened awareness and expression in art, music and literature. Whether these were the result of Uranus' discovery or a synchronistic condition, is a matter of opinion.

The influence of the outer planets tends to be more social than personal, and the effects associated with their sign positions are expressed and felt more in the outer world than on an internal, individual level. This is not to say that you don't experience the energy of Uranus in your own life—for certainly you do—but rather that your response to this energy is to try to manifest it on a larger scale, in ways that affect your society or the world community. You respond to the vibration of the outer planets as part of a group whose members all share a common bond and are working toward the same purpose, (though you may not be conscious of this). The outer planets link us to others of our own kind and make us aware that we are part of something larger than ourselves, integrally connected to the rest of humanity.

Because Uranus is the planet of change, the sign in which it is placed shows the things you and your Uranus-group, consciously or unconsciously, will attempt to change. And because it is the planet of independence and individuality, the changes you seek and affect usually provide more freedom, greater opportunity for unique expression, and equality in the areas related to the sign in which Uranus is positioned. Tension, antagonism and destabilization often result as you and members of your group break away from established traditions. The house in which Uranus is placed and the aspects it makes to other planets in your chart are also important in its interpretation.

Uranus in Aries

Uranus was in Aries this century from April through October 1927, again from January 1928 until May 1934, and from October 1934 through March 1935. Aries is the sign of individuality and the self as separate from society; therefore, those of you who have Uranus in this sign in your birth charts will experience and be involved with changes that affect the individual's role in society. Aries also is associated with war, the military, and all forms of conflict and competition, including sports, so your Uranus-group might be responsible for bringing about changes in these areas, too.

Much of the world was in turmoil during Uranus' most recent trip through Aries. The United States and Europe were in the midst of economic chaos. In China, the warlords who had held control since the end of the Empire were overthrown and the country was embroiled in civil war. Militaristic regimes were increasing their power in Germany, Italy and Japan. Japan and China were at war, and conflicts and unrest that would lead to World War II were building around the globe.

Those of you who were born during this explosive time are yourselves explosive, assertive, impulsive, antagonistic, reckless, outspoken, even violent. You also are daring, courageous and adventurous, and eager to confront challenges and danger—on the battlefield, the sports arena or in the boardroom. Not easily intimidated, you have the single-mindedness and strength of character to go after what you want aggressively, no matter what the odds against you are, and may see yourself as a modern-day David fighting Goliath. This is the stuff of which heros and heroines are made. Civil rights leader Martin Luther King, Jr., is a good example of Uranus in Aries. So is legendary marshall Wyatt Earp, who pitted himself against the outlaws of the American wild west. However, this fearlessness, aggressiveness and love of adventure can lead some Uranus-in-Aries people to endanger others or even to engage in lives of crime, as was the case with the notorious outlaw Jesse James.

Issues of individual rights and expression versus society's rules and conventions often arise for people with this Uranus placement, as was true of the individuals mentioned above. Those of you with Uranus in Aries insist on complete freedom to do as you please, and see the individual as being more important than society. Perhaps you believe society interferes too much with personal freedoms, and you might embrace a civil libertarian viewpoint or work to do away with government regulations and restrictions. Soviet leader Mikhail Gorbachev, who is attempting to loosen some of the U. S. S. R.'s confining policies and attitudes, is a good example of Uranus in Aries. In the pursuit of your own desires, however, you can be reckless and irresponsible, and sometimes show total disregard for others.

During the mid-nineteenth century, when Uranus also was in Aries, many of the great industrialists, interested only in their own purposes, exhibited a lack of concern for the health and safety of their workers as well as for the environment. This same "rugged individualism" and willingness to push ahead without considering the consequences, however, was what made the Industrial Revolution possible in the United States and Europe. Uranus in Aries signifies the self-made men and women whose pioneering spirit, energy, independence and vision result in major breakthroughs in science, technology and industry. American inventors Thomas Edison and Alexander Graham Bell are two good examples of Uranus in Aries.

Those of you born while Uranus was in Aries this century have been responsible for the development of computers, aerospace technology, sophisticated military hardware, medical techniques and equipment, and many other scientific advances. You are interested in discovering new things and new ways to accomplish your aims, and are inventive and original in your thinking and methodology.

Uranus in Taurus

Uranus was in Taurus during this century from June through September 1934, then again from April 1935 until May 1942. Taurus is associated with material and earthly resources of all kinds—money, movable property, physical stamina and sexual energy—therefore, these are the areas in which your "mini-generation" will experience and affect changes.

Those of you with Uranus in this sign were born during a time of unparalleled economic turmoil and sudden, dramatic ups and downs that wreaked havoc with people's sense of security and stability. In the United States, millions first saw the Depression wipe out their savings and jobs almost overnight—and often their self-worth as well—then found themselves catapulted into a war that profoundly altered the country's economic and strategic position in the world. Germany first experienced rampant inflation and economic chaos, then the infamous reign of Adolf Hitler (whose Sun, interestingly, was in Taurus). Europe was ravished by a war that not only destroyed the lives of millions, but also overturned powerful monarchies and reorganized entire nations. Communist and socialist ideologies, which espoused a more equitable distribution of wealth and power, were popular in many parts of the world, and new socially conscious economic programs, such as the American Social Security system were established.

The people born into this period of economic crisis and upheaval encapsulate the essence of the time. To some extent your own financial situation and your attitudes toward money, material stability and values, continue to be influenced by the unrest that was your birthright. In addition, your sense of self-worth and your need for stability are affected by Uranus' placement in Taurus. Author Barbara Raskin describes the unique insecurities of people born during this turbulent time in her book *Hot Flashes.*

Perhaps your personal earnings—and your attitudes toward money—have fluctuated greatly over the years. American political activists Jerry Rubin and Rennie Davis are interesting examples of Uranus in Taurus. In the sixties they decried capitalism, then a decade later reversed their position and joined the economic establishment. Even if your own finances are stable, you might fear sudden loss and stockpile material wealth in an attempt to provide yourself with a sense of security. Or, you may believe in freeing up the world's resources and dispersing them more evenly among all people. Another possibility is that members of your Uranus-group might strive to change financial policies and institutes and make them more open and fair.

Sex also is associated with Taurus. One of the people who was responsible for bringing sex out of hiding and opening up discussion about sexual problems and taboos was Sigmund Freud, who was born during the last passage of Uranus through Taurus. As this century's Uranus-in-Taurus people reached adulthood, the birth control pill became available and some countries began instituting family planning programs. Yours was the first mini-generation to enjoy the sexual freedom that accompanied new methods of contraception and new attitudes toward sex and reproduction.

Uranus in Gemini

Uranus was in Gemini during this century in August and September 1941, and again from May 1942 through early June 1949. Those of you born with this Uranus placement have experienced and been responsible for changes in the education system, changes that resulted in more openness, individuality and equality. Most of you with this planetary placement attended public school systems that were authoritarian, unimaginative and stultifying. In an attempt to change this limited system, many of you chose to pursue careers in education and were responsible for breaking away from the traditional methods of teaching. Open classrooms, alternative study programs, greater freedom of expression and more emphasis on students' rights were initiated by members of your Uranus-group. Those of you who went to school in the southern United States were the first to experience the integration of the public schools, a change designed to create more equitable educational opportunities for all children.

Gemini also is the sign of communication, and the most notable and significant changes affected by your "mini-generation" are in this area. Those of you with Uranus in Gemini have been responsible for revolutionary, technological advances in the way we communicate. Although earlier generations may have designed the first computers, it was your Uranus-group who improved and expanded the technology and made it available to a broad audience. Under the leadership of people with Uranus-in-Gemini, all sorts of sophisticated electronics and telecommunications systems that not long ago would have seemed like science fiction have proliferated and become part of our daily lives. As a result of your inventiveness, worldwide communication has been opened up, accelerated and made easier than most people would have dreamed possible.

As children, you were the first group to grow up with television—another major breakthrough in communication. Suddenly the world was opened up and laid bare for all to see. With the invention of the television, the way people received information changed radically, and that information could be conveyed instantaneously from any spot on the globe—even from outer space. Those of you with Uranus in Gemini saw the world from a different perspective than earlier generations did.

Another "first" for your Uranus-group was the development of electronic music as a form of communication. Rock-and-roll, and its many variations, burst on the scene with your mini-generation and many of the bards of this new musical language had/have Uranus in Gemini. Paul McCartney, Jimi Hendrix, Mick Jagger, Janis Joplin and Eric Clapton are only a few who found rock music an exciting new vehicle for communicating their ideas and emotions. Along with this new music came revolutionary changes in musical equipment. In a few short years, an entirely new industry blossomed. The invention of stereo systems and other technology related to the electronic music field irrevocably altered the way people listened to and produced music.

Uranus in Cancer

Uranus was in Cancer this century from September to November 1948, again between June 1949 and August 1955, and from February until June 1956. Those of you born during this period are responsible for making changes in the family structure, and these changes have provided greater freedom, openness and equality in this area.

Many of you in this "mini-generation" were raised in families with a rigid and unquestioned hierarchy. Father was the breadwinner and head of the household, mother was the nurturer, and the children (usually three or more) were the possessions of their parents. It seemed to you that there was very little diversity or flexibility in this well-established order—especially if you were white and middle-class. Nor was there much in the way of equality in the family unit: Father, as wage-earner, had decision-making power, mother was expected to acquiesce to him, and the children had virtually no say over their lives.

You found this condition limiting, even stifling, and questioned its validity. Out of curiosity as much as rebellion, you began experimenting with all sorts of "alternative" lifestyles, breaking through the walls of tradition and shocking the more conservative older generations with your ideas and behavior. England's Princess Diana is a good example of a Uranus-in-Cancer person rebelling against the restrictions of a rigidly-defined family order.

As your Uranus-group became a significant force in society, you destroyed the old patterns and attitudes about what constituted a "family" and replaced the traditional model with a variety of options that had been inconceivable before: single parents, blended families, homosexual couples, unmarried men and women living together openly, interracial marriages, househusbands, career mothers, and many others.

Most notable among the changes you affected was creating new and broader roles for women. Though this revolution was begun by members of earlier Uranus-groups, the Uranus-in-Cancer people were the first to live these changes on a wide scale and to be comfortable with these new concepts. Along with the changes in women's roles came greater equity in the family structure, for as women became wage-earners their independence grew—and so did their power. No longer totally dependent on men to support them, the Uranus-in-Cancer women have demanded more egalitarian relationships.

Children of Uranus-in-Cancer people are seen as unique individuals with rights and options, too, rather than simply being the property of their parents. Italian educator Maria Montessori, who encouraged children to develop their abilities through freedom of movement and expression, had her Uranus in Cancer. You and your Uranus-group tend to be more open with your children and less authoritarian, and you allow your children greater autonomy, freedom and choices. You are more likely to consult your children before making decisions that will affect their lives and give them a voice in the daily operation of the family, rather than leaving all power in the hands of Father.

However, you may be a bit lax when it comes to discipline, and probably expect your children to be more independent than they are capable of being. Perhaps you feel confined by the demands and restrictions of parenthood, and refuse to sacrifice your individual goals and desires for the benefit of your children. Or, you might decide not to have children at all because you feel they would tie you down. Women in this Uranus-group spend more time apart from their children—working or pursuing other activities—than their mothers did, so that the children must become self-sufficient and self-determining at an earlier age.

People with Uranus in Cancer are more likely than previous generations to break away from the lifestyles, ideas and expectations of their own parents. You pursue the career directions, friendships and behaviors that please you, rather than succumbing to parental pressures to "follow in their footsteps" or to fulfill their dreams. Thus your relationship with your parents might be somewhat tense, or you may distance yourself from your parents and other family members. Instead of viewing blood relatives as your family, you could feel a greater kinship with your friends and relate to them as your "family."

Uranus in Leo

Uranus was in Leo during this century between August 1955 and January 1956, from June 1956 through October 1961, and from January until August 1962. Leo is associated with self-expression in all its forms: artistic creativity, the entertainment industry, childbearing, romance and egotism. Those of you who have this Uranus position in your birth charts will experience and be responsible for making changes that provide greater freedom, individuality and openness in these areas.

Uranus' entrance into Leo signaled an end to the U. S. government's "black listing" of artists and entertainers for their political ideologies. Those of you who have this Uranus placement in your birth charts encapsulate the energy of this time and you insist upon creative freedom and the right to express yourselves without censorship. You believe that restrictions of any kind interfere with the creative process and you want to be able to do and say what you please, to try new things and to be uninhibited by social conventions or government regulations.

Sometimes you go to extremes to assert your individuality; you enjoy being outrageous and provocative in expressing yourself and like to project the image of the eccentric free spirit. Dancer Isadora Duncan, known for her renegade style on and off stage, is a good example of Uranus in Leo. So are rock singers Michael Jackson and Madonna, and tennis star John McEnroe. You also can be extremely willful, egotistical, selfish and stubborn in your beliefs and behavior. At the very least, you are outspoken and/or unconventional in your creative expression, as were American writer Gertrude Stein, British artist Aubrey Beardsley, German author Thomas Mann, French composer Maurice Ravel and American magician Harry Houdini, all of whom had this Uranus placement in their birth charts. You reject traditions and your creations often display boldness, self-assurance, ingenuity and originality.

Uranus' most recent passage through Leo also heralded major changes in the entertainment industry, particularly in the music field. The first rock 'n' roll stars began performing during this period and electronic music was born. Members of your "mini-generation" have been involved in the development of rock music, electronic equipment and audio technology, music videos, and a multi-billion-dollar industry that did not exist before you were born. You also are among the first to use computer graphics technology in artistic ways.

Leo also is connected with romantic love—the self-centered, idyllic, fun-filled early stages of romance, not the committed, day-to-day, "in sickness and in health" love of long-term partnerships. The Uranus-in-Leo group came of age in a time of relatively unrestricted romantic and sexual expression, after the legalization of abortion and before the discovery of AIDS, and therefore, you were more free to experiment with all sorts of romantic relationships than earlier generations had been. "Love" became more casual, easy and open than at any other time.

You seek excitement, change, new experiences and independence in love affairs and find the responsibilities and limitations of deeper attachments less attractive. The attitudes of your "mini-generation" toward love, romance and sex are less inhibited and more egalitarian than those of other Uranus-groups. You may be more willing to experiment with unconventional or alternative relationships and are less pejorative about other people's love lives and sexual expression.

Uranus in Virgo

Uranus was in Virgo during this century from November 1961 to January 1962, then again from August 1962 through September 1968, and briefly in May and June of 1969. Virgo is the sign of work, service and physical health, therefore, those of you who were born with this Uranus position in your birth charts will experience and be involved in changes in these areas.

Uranus' trip through Virgo prompted large-scale concern for the needy peoples of the world. In the United States, government programs like the Peace Corps and VISTA were established to help the poor at home and abroad learn to help themselves, and young people from the wealthy and middle classes chose to work in these programs. Others pursued teaching careers, especially in "special education" areas designed to help children with mental or physical handicaps, as a way of serving their fellow humans. Social consciousness was at an all-time high during this period; helping others and doing socially useful work was considered more important by many people than wealth, fame or prestige.

Those of you who have Uranus positioned in Virgo might be responsible for stirring up public awareness about social and economic inequities in the world. You want to find ways to assist those who are less fortunate than yourselves to become self-supporting and independent, and may work to bring this about. Former U. S. President Franklin D. Roosevelt, who had Uranus in Virgo, created government programs during the Great Depression to provide work for those who needed it.

Physical health also is associated with Virgo, and as Uranus moved through Virgo it aroused public interest in health issues. Concerns about environmental pollution and adulterated food, and how these affect health were brought to the fore during this period. As a result, natural foods, vegetarianism, vitamin supplements and alternative health care options proliferated, and millions of people changed their diets because of increased awareness about health. Public outcries against environmental contamination brought about the establishment of the Environmental Protection Agency in 1970. Uranus-in-Virgo health-consciousness also produced changes in work-related health, and led to the formation of the Occupational Safety and Health Administration (OSHA) in the United States in 1970. Uranus' passage through this sign triggered Virgoan concern for the health and well-being of all life forms, and during this transit the Endangered Species Acts was created to protect animals, birds and marine life.

Those of you who have Uranus in Virgo in your birth charts are interested in health issues, and your Uranus-group might be responsible for establishing national medical insurance and progressive public health care programs. Or, you could be involved in improving the design and use of health-related products and/or therapies. Perhaps you are a proponent of alternative health care and unconventional medical practices, and might help bring new techniques, practices or ideas into public awareness. You may consider traditional medicine and the medical establishment too restrictive, conservative, authoritarian and inhuman, and may strive to instigate changes in the health care industry that provide more openness and rights for patients. Because of your interest in the connection between mind and body you might find ways to use "mind over matter" to treat illnesses, or discover cures for diseases that are related to attitude and lifestyle.

Uranus in Libra

Uranus was in Libra this century from October 1968 until November 1974, and from April until September 1975. Libra is the sign of partnerships—in love and business—and of art, women, peace, and legal matters. Therefore, these are the areas in which people with this planetary placement will experience changes that produce greater freedom, equality and openness.

During the time that Uranus was in Libra, relationships and attitudes about love, marriage, sex and commitment were shaken to their very foundations. This was the era of "free love" and the "sexual revolution," and the men and women who became adults during this period had decidedly different ideas about relationships than previous generations. Couples began living together and raising families without getting married; homosexuality became more open. Extended families, interracial relationships, group living situations, casual sex, "wife-swapping" and other relationship alternatives proliferated.

The Women's Movement of the early seventies irrevocably altered women's perception of themselves and their place in the world. Suddenly, women began to think of themselves as equal partners and demanded more balance, fairness, individuality and rights in their relationships. Many women rebelled against the traditional concept of the "woman's place," and rather than accepting without question the role of housewife and mother they opted for careers in the business world. Some decided to postpone marriage and children until they had established themselves professionally, others wanted to be career women and mothers both, still others chose to stay single or childless. Uranus in Libra inspired women to claim greater independence for themselves and make new choices in their love relationships.

The legalization of abortion in the U. S. in 1973 was, perhaps, the most significant liberating factor for American women in this century—and it occurred while Uranus was in Libra. Without the burden of unwanted pregnancy, women were free to make their own decisions in life.

The destabilization and turbulence that are Uranus' trademark focused on relationships during the planet's passage through Libra. Divorce rates soared and new laws were enacted to make divorce faster and easier. People entered into partnerships without making lifetime commitments and left when things got tough. However, as divorce became common, it also lost its stigma, and people who had stayed together unhappily for years finally were able to break free and begin new lives.

Children who were born during this time often experienced a home life and parental relationships that were altogether different than those of earlier generations. The home in which the child was raised was probably less structured than those of previous generations. Perhaps there was more equality between mother and father. Both parents may have worked outside the home, so the child developed autonomy at a young age. All sorts of unconventional living arrangements could have been part of the Uranus-in-Libra child's upbringing. Perhaps the parents were separated or divorced, so that the child experienced some sort of upset or destabilization in the home.

Everyone is the encapsulation of the time in which he or she was born, and those of you born with Uranus in Libra are more likely than other Uranus-groups to be concerned with equitable, open or avant garde relationships that allow for independence and individuality within them. Probably you will always insist on a great deal of freedom, change and excitement in your relationships, and it could be difficult for you to settle down with one person for long. You might change partners frequently, or maintain relationships with more than one person at a time. For example, Joseph Smith, who founded the Mormon religion in New York state in 1830, and is reputed to have had fifty wives, had Uranus in Libra.

Perhaps you will be responsible for creating legislation that provides true equality for women. Or, you simply may live your beliefs and, as your "mini-generation" gains influence in the world, your independent lifestyle and attitudes toward relationships will create greater openness for all.

Libra is also the sign of peace and harmony, but with Uranus positioned here, you may not experience much tranquility. Instead, you might have to deal with frequent upsets, turmoil or chaotic situations. Perhaps you find peace and quiet dull and prefer to have excitement and change in your life. For example, the Viet Nam War was raging during Uranus' passage through Libra, and interestingly, Ho Chi Minh, president of North Viet Nam, had Uranus in Libra in his birth chart. So did Adolf Hitler. Both saw their countries torn apart by war while they were in power.

Uranus in Scorpio

During this century, Uranus was in Scorpio from December 1974 through April 1975, then again from September 1975 until November 1981. Scorpio is associated with all things that are hidden—occult knowledge, unseen worlds, the unconscious, secret activities and organizations, hidden resources, sexuality—therefore, these are the areas that your Uranus-group will change in order to provide more openness and freedom.

During the years when Uranus was in Scorpio, more and more people underwent some form of therapy to open up the hidden recesses of their psyches. New types of therapy were developed and psychoanalysis lost its stigma. Many individuals also began delving into occult fields and the ancient mysteries, and publications that revealed long-secret knowledge proliferated. Those of you who have this planetary placement in your charts might be interested in probing these hidden realms, as was true of astrologer Dane Rudhyar, who was born during the last passage of Uranus through Scorpio.

Space exploration during this period exposed new information about the mysterious worlds beyond our own planet. Your Uranus-group could be responsible for even greater discoveries in our Universe, or for inventing the technology that will allow us to travel through space in the future. For example, scientist Immanuel Velikovsky, whose views about events in our solar system were years ahead of their time, and astronomer Nicolas Copernicus, who invented the telescope, both had Uranus in Scorpio.

Uranus in Scorpio also brought the secret activities of the government and powerful organizations out into the open. In the United States, the most notable of these exposures was Watergate, which changed the public's attitude toward government behavior and policies and brought about a new desire for openness in politics. The CIA's role in the destabilization of other countries also began coming to light, as did some of the hidden horrors of the Viet Nam War and its effects on the veterans who fought there. Those of you with Uranus in Scorpio might be involved in uncovering the surreptitious operations of big business, multinational banks, government or other powerful institutions and in forcing them to be more equitable and truthful. For example, former Chief Justice Earl Warren, who presided over the investigation of John F. Kennedy's assassination, had Uranus in Scorpio.

Hidden behavior and taboo subjects, particularly sex, also are in Scorpio's domain, and during the most recent passage of Uranus through this sign sex became more open and free than ever before. Frank depictions of sexual activity became popular in movies, and sex was an open topic for television, advertising, and books like *The Joy of Sex*. This new attitude of sexual freedom brought about a more relaxed approach to sexual activity. Greater numbers of people were engaging in casual sexual encounters and experimenting with unconventional sexual practices. Homosexuality came out of the closet and gay rights movements gained momentum.

Those of you with Uranus in Scorpio are probably quite open-minded about sex, and your Uranus-group might be responsible for initiating new attitudes toward sexual liberation and openness. Controversial psychiatrist and scientist Wilhelm Reich, whose work, theories and politics centered on issues of sexual freedom, had Uranus in Scorpio. You also might enjoy experimenting with a variety of sexual practices and partners, and are uninhibited in your sexual behavior (unless other factors in your chart suggest otherwise). Infamous Italian lover Casanova is a good example of Uranus in Scorpio.

Uranus in Sagittarius

Uranus was in Sagittarius when this century began and remained there until December 1904. In November 1981, Uranus again entered this sign, where it will be through November 1988 (except for a period between February and May of 1988 when it moves briefly into Capricorn). Sagittarius is associated with expanding horizons; anything that helps us grow or increases our understanding of ourselves and the world in which we live is related to this sign. Higher education, religion, philosophy and long distance travel all help broaden our knowledge, therefore, those of you who were born with Uranus in Sagittarius will experience and bring about changes in these areas.

Around the turn of the century, when Uranus was last in Sagittarius, unconventional religions whose belief systems diverged from the prevailing Judeo-Christian attitudes of the Western world, became popular and many people explored mysticism, ancient religions and secret spiritual societies. During Uranus' most recent passage through Sagittarius, huge numbers of people once again are rejecting orthodox religions and turning to other beliefs systems—Eastern philosophies, astrology, witchcraft, Native American teachings, ancient religions—and literature that reveals formerly hidden knowledge is now widely available.

Those of you who have Uranus in Sagittarius in your birth charts might be interested in unconventional religions or have spiritual beliefs that are avant garde or radically different from those of the general public. Occultist Manly P. Hall, for example, had this planetary placement in his chart. So did Martin Luther, who broke away from the Catholic Church and formed his own religious movement.

Uranus in Sagittarius also signifies major changes and breakthroughs in travel. In 1903, for example, when Uranus was last in this sign, the Wright brothers made their famous flight at Kitty Hawk and introduced the world to air travel. The automobile had its real beginning at this time, too, with the founding of the Ford Motor Company in 1903. During the more recent Uranus-in-Sagittarius period, the Voyager space probe journeyed to the outer planets for the first time, increasing our understanding of the solar system. Those of you who have this planetary placement in your charts may be interested in or responsible for new developments in the travel field. Aviation pioneer Charles Lindbergh, for example, had Uranus in Sagittarius. Perhaps the first people to journey to other planets will be members of this Uranus-group.

This planetary position also is responsible for changes in education. When Uranus was last in Sagittarius the progressive education movement in the United States, influenced by the philosophies of Rousseau, Froebel and others, introduced industrial, social and agricultural subjects into the school curriculum. Changes in the education system during the most recent transit of Uranus through Sagittarius include a marked increase in the number of students attending private primary and secondary schools rather than public institutions, and enormous increases in the price of higher education. Computers, both as a field of study and a tool to aid study, have revolutionized educational programs at all levels. Sagittarius is associated with religion, and while Uranus has been in this sign, church-operated schools in the United States have proliferated. The debate over the church's role in public education has intensified, and attention has been focused on issues such as the teaching of evolution, school prayer and censorship of textbooks.

Those of you who have Uranus in Sagittarius in your birth charts are interested in and might be involved with creating, developing or promoting new methods and fields of study. Perhaps you feel there is a need for greater freedom and individuality in education, and will work to bring this about. Or, having been born during a time when quality education seems to be beyond the reach of all but the wealthy, you may attempt to make learning more accessible to all who want it. You could rebel against the influence of religion in the schools or go to the opposite extreme and strive to strengthen the connection between church and state in terms of the public education system. Whatever path you take, you are sure to be involved in changes that affect what and how we learn.

Uranus in Capricorn

In this century, Uranus was in Capricorn from December 1904 through January 1912, and from September to November 1912. In February 1988, Uranus once again entered this sign, where it will remain until January 1996.

Capricorn is the sign of structures, traditions, big business, the established order, patriarchal authority, the physical world and its boundaries, and responsibilities, controls and limitations. These things, therefore, are what your "mini-generation" will be involved with changing, in order to bring about more openness and equality. During Uranus' last passage through Capricorn, for example, Albert Einstein introduced his theory of relativity (in 1905), which changed our concept of matter and the structure of the Universe. Another person who was instrumental in altering our understanding of the Universe was astronomer/astrologer Johannes Kepler; he had Uranus in Capricorn in his birth chart.

Your Uranus-group probably will be concerned with the influence big business has on the democratic system, and could witness or be involved with breaking up its control over individual lives and world freedom. The practices and policies of large, multinational corporations will come under attack during this period, and the public may insist that banks and other powerful institutions disclose their activities. This could be a chaotic time, as monetary systems and the institutions that control the world's financial structures are upset. The stock market crash of 1987 and the corresponding fluctuations in world currencies could be a precursor to the upcoming changes Uranus is sure to bring. Interestingly, former U. S. President Ronald Reagan, whose economic policies have been responsible to some extent for this confusion and destabilization, has his Uranus in Capricorn.

In the coming years, we might see a loosening of the rigid structure of the status quo so that it becomes easier for more people—especially women and minorities—to obtain a "piece of the pie." Conflicts between the "haves" and the "have nots" are likely, and countries where the disparity between rich and poor is great could experience the most severe disturbances. The struggle now raging in South Africa is a good example. There may even be revolutions or attempts to overthrow the ruling authorities in some parts of the world, or at least movements to revise the established order. Whether the changes are accomplished easily or through violence and turmoil depends on how willing those in authority are to relinquish some of their control. As those of you who were born with Uranus in Capricorn reach adulthood and gain power, you might bring about greater equality and openness, in both business and politics.

During the last passage of Uranus through Capricorn there were wars and disputes throughout Europe, Russia, Turkey and Japan, and the conflicts that eventually escalated into World War I began boiling. These wars not only toppled old ruling powers, but also resulted in the realignment of national borders.

Capricorn also is the sign of traditions and conservative beliefs, and as Uranus travels through this sign it will upset and reorder many of the traditions and attitudes that have held sway in the past. Conservative religious and social ideologies could come under attack. Even the foundations on which societies are established could be altered significantly. Those of you with this planetary position in your birth charts may believe in destroying all traditions and structures, and might embrace anarchy. You believe that the individual is more important than society and are an advocate of personal rights and freedoms. In the extreme, however, you could rebel against all types of social responsibility and duty.

Uranus in Aquarius

Uranus was in Aquarius during this century from February 1912 through March 1919, and again from August 1919 until January 1920. In April 1995, it will enter Aquarius again and remain there until 2003. In its own sign, Uranus' energy is amplified, so that such periods usually are racked with turmoil, sudden and explosive change, revolts and conflicts that involve issues of independence and equality. Both Uranus and Aquarius are associated with progressive social change, freedom, human rights, unconventional attitudes and behavior, new and revolutionary discoveries and ideas, modern technology and scientific advances; therefore, your Uranus-group will be involved with and instrumental in affecting changes and upsets in these areas.

World War I took place during Uranus' last passage through Aquarius. For the first time in history, aircraft—ruled by Aquarius and Uranus—played an important role in warfare. Authoritarian governments around the globe toppled and new political systems were established. The Russian Revolution, which overthrew the ruling czars and set up a government of the people, occurred during this period. In China, the Ch'ing dynasty, which had been in power since 1644, was ousted and a republic was set up in its place.

Other social equalizing forces were also at work during this period. In the United States, the women's suffrage movement was gaining strength and in Great Britain women achieved limited voting rights. New York health care worker and social activist Margaret Sangar began her birth control crusade, which was intended to give women greater independence. Workman's Compensation, the first social insurance program in the U. S., was established in some states, and the American income tax system was made law by the 16th amendment to the Constitution.

Those of you who have this Uranus placement in your birth charts have a strong sense of independence, individual rights and social equality. Labor leader James Hoffa, for example, had Uranus in Aquarius. The birth charts of liberal American politician Eugene McCarthy and former Egyptian President Anwar Sadat also feature Uranus in Aquarius. You could be involved in implementing social reforms or making breakthroughs in the established order that create more equitable situations. For example, Jackie Robinson, the first black to break the color barrier in professional baseball, had Uranus in Aquarius.

You also are curious, inventive, unconventional, perhaps a bit eccentric, and willing to try anything new and different. Perhaps you will be responsible for important discoveries or changes in scientific fields, as was true of physician/scientist Jonas Salk, who developed a polio vaccine; his Uranus was in Aquarius. Or, your curiosity and desire for excitement could lead you to discover new worlds. Captain John Smith, who was instrumental in founding the Virginia colony in the New World, is another good example of Uranus in Aquarius. The new "mini-generation" of Uranus-in-Aquarius people who will be born at the turn of this century will experience and be involved with significant, revolutionary changes in the areas of human rights, technology and science, new age thought. Perhaps they will even travel to other Universes or establish contact with other-world beings.

Uranus in Pisces

During this century, Uranus was in Pisces from April to August 1919, again between January 1920 and March 1927, then from November 1927 until mid-January 1928. Pisces is the sign of higher consciousness, and thus it is associated with spirituality, peace, art and music. It also is connected with anything that is unknown or hidden (including such things as the oceans' depths, outer space, prisons and mental institutions), the unconscious, dreams, fantasy, drugs and alcohol. Therefore, those of you with Uranus in this sign will experience and/or be responsible for changes in these areas.

Uranus' last passage through Pisces coincided with a period of relative peace, following the devastation of World War I.

In the art world, this position of Uranus heralded new and unconventional forms and movements. Surrealism, which was inspired by Sigmund Freud's recent work with dreams and the unconscious, and cubism were two new imaginative and unusual styles being explored by artists like Pablo Picasso, Joan Miró, Jean Arp, Paul Klee and Giorgio de Chirico. The music world, too, was undergoing significant changes with the introduction of a popular new musical form: jazz. In typical Uranian fashion, these revolutionary art movements shocked and outraged traditionalists.

While Uranus was in Pisces, Americans experienced another radical change related to Pisces: Prohibition. Suddenly alcohol was illegal and drinking became a rebellious, counterculture act.

Those of you who have Uranus in Pisces in your birth charts might be concerned with affecting changes that liberate, revolutionize or awaken public awareness in one of these areas. Perhaps you are active in trying to bring peace to the world, as was true of brothers Daniel and Philip Berrigan, Catholic priests and antiwar activists who both have Uranus in Pisces. You might be involved in making changes in religious organizations or teachings. One of your purposes may be to bring about more openness, individuality, freedom and/or equality in your religion, and you could find your spiritual convictions suddenly become political ones. Unconventional spiritual beliefs, such as metaphysics, may interest you more than orthodox faiths.

Or, you could be instrumental in developing or popularizing new art and/or musical forms. Musicians/composers Wolfgang Amadeus Mozart and Peter Ilych Tchaikovsky, and impressionist painters Claude Monet and Pierre Auguste Renoir all had Uranus in Pisces. Another possibility is that you might be responsible for opening up formerly hidden or unknown places. For example, astronauts Gus Grissom, John Glenn, Scott Carpenter and Gordon Cooper, who initiated exploration of the mysterious realm of outer space, have Uranus in Pisces. So does Timothy Leary, who was among the first to experiment with psychedelic drugs as a way of probing the secret territory of the subconscious mind.

Chapter Eleven

Neptune

Neptune takes about 165 years to travel through all twelve signs of the zodiac, and it remains in each sign for approximately fourteen years. Each fourteen-year period, therefore, has a special tone or theme that relates to Neptune's sign position, and everyone born during that time will resonate to the same tone. Generations are defined by the sign positions of Neptune and Pluto. Each generation has a common Neptune denominator which makes it distinct from all other generations, and every individual who is a member of a particular Neptune-group has certain beliefs, feelings, ideals, behaviors and responses that are similar to those of everyone else in the same generation.

The outer planets affect us at a deep, unconscious level, and though we witness their influences in our daily lives and in the world around us, we usually cannot control or direct their energies consciously. Rather, we respond and adapt to their influences, often *en masse* and frequently without realizing it or understanding why. These "transpersonal planets" seem to be more concerned with large-scale social and universal conditions and issues than with individual ones.

Neptune is the planet of idealism and fantasy. Its sign placement shows what your generation idealizes and has trouble being realistic about because your dreams and illusions of perfection get in the way. What you want most but have the greatest difficulty achieving is indicated by Neptune's position in your birth chart. Neptune also is associated with sacrifice, and the sign in which it is placed reveals the areas in which an entire generation will experience some sort of sacrifice. You might have to make sacrifices of some kind in order to achieve your ideals, or you may need to sacrifice your ideals before you can appreciate "reality." There is always some conflict between the physical and the ideal when Neptune is involved.

Neptune is not concerned with the physical world; its domain is the divine realm, and this planet has a way of dissolving everything it touches on the Earth plane. The more you try to hold on to the things represented by the sign in which Neptune is placed, the more likely you are to lose them. It seems that the only way you can attain something connected with Neptune is to be willing to sacrifice it, to give it up completely.

The planet's influence is not linear or rational. Instead, it operates on an unconscious level, and is related to dreams, intuition, psychic ability and deep emotions. (Interestingly, the first major operation in which anesthesia was used to render the patient unconscious was performed in 1846, the year Neptune was "discovered.") Neptune's sign position indicates what an entire generation responds to unconsciously, and therefore, what a large group of people finds pleasing and/or desirable without realizing why. Whenever Neptune passes through a sign, those things associated with that sign suddenly become fashionable.

Neptune's energy is very subtle, operating in the shadowy, other-worldly planes just outside conscious perception, and the planet tends to cloak reality in a fog of illusion. You may be able to understand Neptune intuitively or emotionally, but your intellect can't fathom it; therefore, the planet often is connected with confusion, delusions, mystery and deceit. The sign in which Neptune is placed shows what areas a generation is likely to be confused about, where large numbers of people will experience deceit and losses as a result of their illusions and lack of clarity. Usually there is a great deal of fantasy and imagination in these areas, too, which can manifest either as creative inspiration or delusions.

What we can't understand we often attempt to avoid. Such is the case with Neptune. The planet is associated with escapism, and an unwillingness to face up to the demands, responsibilities and harsh truths of physical existence. The sign in which Neptune is positioned indicates the things a generation doesn't want to deal with responsibly and realistically, and thus tries to avoid.

The mystical, other-worldly energies of Neptune find perfect expression through spirituality and religious pursuits. Divine love, perfect harmony and unity, the dissolution of physical barriers, and sacrifice of personal desires for a greater, universal good are all part of Neptune's—and many religions'—teachings. Therefore, the planet's sign placement suggests where and in what a particular generation will seek the divine.

Neptune in Gemini

Neptune was last in Gemini from 1887 until July 1901, and again from January to May 1902. Gemini is the sign of communication, language, the written and spoken word, and during this period there was an unconscious mass attraction to communication and the world of ideas. Reading, writing and other forms of communication became popular and fashionable. In the United States, education was highly valued and literacy was considered important; more public schools were built during Neptune's passage through Gemini than ever before. C. J. Rhodes founded the Rhodes Scholarship to help the brightest students further their educations. Newspapers proliferated and gained tremendous power, led by the publications of William Randolph Hearst and Joseph Pulitzer. The International Copyright Law was passed to protect the written word.

During Neptune's earlier passage through Gemini, between approximately 1724 and 1737, the collective unconscious also was attuned to all things related to communication, and this mass response resulted in the founding of the world's first circulating library, the first modern newspapers in England and the United States, and the first magazine. Even the physical process of disseminating ideas was improved. Benjamin Franklin began his printing business and produced his famous *Poor Richard's Almanac.* He also became the postmaster of Philadelphia and established America's first lending library.[1]

Your generation idealizes literacy, intelligence, education and communication skills. Perhaps you were unable to get a good education yourself, and might have had to sacrifice your dreams of being well-educated in order to fulfill more

At the time of this writing, there is virtually no one alive with Neptune in Aries, Taurus, Aquarius or Pisces. Therefore, these signs are not discussed in this chapter.

"practical" concerns such as working to feed yourself and your family. As a result, you desperately wanted your children to be properly schooled and worked hard to make this ideal a reality. You view education through "rose-colored glasses" and might believe that if everyone had an education the world would be a better place.

Those of you who have Neptune positioned in Gemini in your birth charts are interested in communication of every kind. You probably admire people who have writing and/or speaking ability and may be talented in this area yourself. Writers William Faulkner, John Steinbeck, Henry Miller, Dashiell Hammett, F. Scott Fitzgerald, Vladimir Nabokov and Pearl S. Buck are some examples of Neptune in Gemini. Neptune is associated with music, therefore, you might be able to communicate best through this medium. The birth charts of Cole Porter, Louis Armstrong and George Gershwin, for example, feature Neptune in Gemini.

Neptune also rules motion pictures, and while it was last in Gemini the first movie projection machines were used in Europe and the United States. Those of you with Neptune in Gemini have a fascination with the "silver screen" and its stars, and you might entertain fantasies of being in pictures yourselves. The movies not only were a source of entertainment and escape for you, however, but a way of receiving information as well—movie house newsreels provided news from around the world to your generation before the advent of television.

Short journeys and travel in and around your community also are related to the sign Gemini. Neptune's most recent trip through this sign brought about the invention of the automobile, the bicycle and America's first practical electric streetcar. Those of you who are members of the Neptune-in-Gemini generation have a fascination with travel. However, Neptune represents gradual dissolution and insidious losses, and your generation also is responsible for the disintegration of some forms of public transportation—especially passenger trains and trolleys—in the United States.

Neptune in Cancer

Neptune was in Cancer this century between July and December 1901, from May 1902 until September 1914, and from December 1914 to July 1915. The sign Cancer is associated with the mother, children, family, nurturing, food, home and country, so while Neptune is in this sign the collective unconscious is attuned to these areas and they became fashionable. Those of you who have Neptune in Cancer in your birth charts could be described as the "god and country, mom and apple pie" generation.

World War I, which brought about the collapse of some nations and a redefining of others, began while Neptune was in Cancer. In the United States (a country whose Sun is in Cancer) patriotism ran high, and former President Theodore Roosevelt (whose Moon was in Cancer) sought U. S. domination of the Western hemisphere. During this period, Hawaii, Guam, Puerto Rico and the Philippines became American territories, and the Panama Canal was built.

Those of you who have Neptune in Cancer in your birth charts idealize your homeland and are very patriotic. Former U. S. President Ronald Reagan and actor John Wayne are two good examples of this planetary position. However, your "my country right or wrong" attitude makes it hard for you to acknowledge any flaws in your nation's policies or behavior, and you prefer to ignore situations that are less than perfect rather than working to correct them. During the Nazi reign, for instance, many Neptune-in-Cancer Germans were aware of Hitler's cruelties, but chose to look the other way rather than admit that such things could happen in their country.

During Neptune's passage through Cancer, the home was glorified. During the mid-1700s, successful merchants and ship's captains in seaport towns in Europe and America built magnificent, sumptuously decorated mansions to show off their wealth, and one of the most graceful and enduring furniture styles, Queen Anne, was introduced. When Neptune again entered Cancer at the beginning of the twentieth century, the Vanderbilts and other wealthy industrialists constructed their palatial "cottages" in places like Newport, Rhode Island and the Hamptons in New York.

Food, another of Cancer's concerns, was emphasized when Neptune passed through this sign. In the mid-eighteenth century, sleek, speedy sailing ships opened trade between the East and West and introduced an array of new culinary delights to the Western world. The pineapple even became a popular symbol of hospitality. When Neptune again entered Cancer, the focus on food in the United States resulted in the passage of the Pure Food and Drug Act of 1906.

Those of you who were born while Neptune was in Cancer may be especially interested in food and cooking; famous chefs James Beard and Julia Child, for example, have this planetary placement in their birth charts. However, you might have a tendency to overindulge, particularly in sweets. It is hard for you to accept the relationship between nutrition and health, and you could suffer from diet-related illnesses as a result of poor eating habits that you are extremely reluctant to change. Your generation also is responsible for the introduction of chemical food additives, poisonous pesticides and highly-processed foods.

Neptune-in-Cancer periods focus attention on children, too. The first English books published for children and the translation into English of popular fairy tales Cinderella, Sleeping Beauty and Little Red Riding Hood occurred in the mid-1740s. When Neptune again traveled through Cancer, *The Wizard of Oz, Peter Pan, Wind in the Willows* and *Peter Rabbit* were published. The teddy bear was born, and the Girl Scouts, Boy Scouts and Campfire Girls were founded.[2]

Those of you who have Neptune positioned in Cancer in your birth charts idealize the family, children and motherhood. Pediatrician and author Dr. Benjamin Spock and children's book writer Dr. Suess are two good examples of Neptune in Cancer. However, you entertain such unrealistic illusions and fantasies about what the perfect family should be that you cannot acknowledge troubles in your parent/child relationships. Rather than deal realistically with less-than-ideal situations, you prefer to ignore them and hope they'll go away. Your generation never discussed sex with your children, for example, and if there was alcoholism, child abuse, infidelity, mental illness, etc. in your family you probably denied it or tried to cover it up.

Neptune in Leo

During this century, Neptune was in Leo between September and December 1914, from July 1915 until September 1928, and from February to July 1929. Leo is the sign of self-expression, artistic creativity, theatre and drama, entertainment and glamor. It also is associated with self-aggrandizement, ego, self-centeredness and individuality.

Neptune's trips through this sign coincide with periods of great creativity in all artistic fields, when self-expression becomes fashionable and the masses value art, especially that which is showy, overstated and larger than life. The most recent Neptune-in-Leo period may have marked the true beginning of "modern art," when expressing the artist's inner state became more important than attempting to reproduce reality. Many of the giants in the world of architecture were working at this time, too, including Frank Lloyd Wright, Le Corbusier, Gaudi, Saarinen, Mies van der Rohe, Gropius and Hoffman.[3]

Earlier Neptune-in-Leo transits also brought about peaks in artistic creativity and grandeur. During the period from approximately 1751 to 1765, one of the finest and most famous cabinetmakers of all times—Thomas Chippendale—opened his salon in London.[4] Neptune's previous trip through Leo corresponded to the Italian Baroque period and the one before that with the beginning of the Renaissance. Giovanni Bernini, principle architect and artist of St. Peter's Church in Rome, had this planetary placement in his birth chart.

In the United States, Neptune's most recent passage through Leo brought about a lively and dazzling new musical form: jazz. The planet's previous trip through this sign coincided with the popularity of grandiose operas in Italy, Austria and Germany. One of history's greatest operatic composers, Wolfgang Amadeus Mozart, was born while Neptune was in Leo.

Those of you who have this Neptune placement in your birth charts idealize creativity and artistic expression. Whether or not you have talent yourself you at least enjoy art and admire people who are creative. Most of you who were born while Neptune was in Leo, however, grew up during difficult times—the Depression and World War II—when art was viewed as a luxury or a frivolity, and you may have had to shoulder your responsibilities and sacrifice your dreams of being an artist. If you were not able to pursue your artistic yearnings yourself, you might have pushed your children to take music, dancing or art lessons. Women, in particular, who were not encouraged to develop their talents might view their children as the fruits of their creativity. Or, you could go to the opposite extreme, as did Mozart, and sacrifice everything else for the sake of your art.

Whenever Neptune is in Leo, styles become flamboyant, elaborate and glamorous, for there is nothing subtle or restrained about this sign. During "The Roaring Twenties," for example, everything from clothing to automobiles was flashy and designed to attract attention. In the mid-eighteenth century, ostentatious wigs and attire were typical expressions of this planetary placement. French king Louis XVI and Marie Antoinette, known for their elaborate dress and lifestyle, both had Neptune in Leo in their birth charts.

Leo also is associated with drama, Neptune with film, so it is fitting that this combination should have marked the tremendous popularity of movies in the 1920s. Talking films were introduced during this transit and lavish movie houses were constructed to show them. Actors and actresses became idols to a public that was searching for heros and heroines, and those of you who have this planetary position in your birth charts could be called the "star-struck generation." During an earlier Neptune-in-Leo period, theatre was born in America; the first theatres were build and the first play was written by an American dramatist.[5]

People who have Neptune in Leo in their birth charts idealize fame, beauty and glamor. You long to be famous yourself, fantasize about meeting important people and can be something of a name dropper. Vain and status-conscious, you badly want to impress others, to be praised and have attention focused on you. However, in your fascination with glory you overlook the perils of notoriety, and if you manage to achieve your dreams you might find the reality of fame is quite different from your illusions. Actress Marilyn Monroe is one such example of Neptune in Leo. You also have a tendency to look only at surfaces—of people and situations—and are easily "wowed" by a glitzy exterior or superficial charm. To your generation, image is often more important than inner substance.

Neptune in Virgo

Neptune was in Virgo this century from September 1928 to February 1929, between July 1929 and September 1942, and from April until July 1943. Virgo is associated with work, service, health and nutrition, ordinary everyday life and the "common man." Whenever Neptune passes through this sign, the public becomes sensitized to these things and they take on special significance.

Neptune's most recent trip through Virgo coincided with the Great Depression in the United States, a period of economic instability and disintegration unparalleled in this country. Twenty-five percent of the population was unemployed and finding work became the most important thing in life for the average person. In the American prairie states, the Dust Bowl reached peak proportions, wiping out crops and bankrupting farmers. To provide some sort of relief for the millions affected by loss of income, the government instituted the Social Security Act of 1935, Unemployment Insurance and the Works Projects Administration. Europe's economy, too, was undermined at this time and in Germany inflation was devastating. Those of you who were born during this period of economic disaster idealize work, and job security is extremely important to you.

An earlier Neptune transit of Virgo between approximately 1764 and 1779 corresponded with the American Revolution, a revolt of the common people against the British Crown, which was based in part on the colonists' dissatisfaction with the economic situation. This same period saw France's economy decaying due to a large public debt and government inefficiency, and the underprivileged were growing increasingly unhappy with the extravagances of the royalty. In both countries, food played a role: France's bread famine, America's boycott of British goods, and particularly the Boston Tea Party.

For people born with Neptune in Virgo in their birth charts, nutrition and health can be areas of much concern. British chemist Humphrey Davy, who isolated potassium, calcium, sodium and other minerals that are necessary for good health, had his Neptune in Virgo. Perhaps you dream of a time when all people have enough to eat, as does Rev. Jesse Jackson, national director of Operation Bread Basket. Your generation was in the forefront of health consciousness in the late sixties and early seventies. Or, you might hold misconceptions and illusions about diet and health, or worry incessantly about germs and disease. Perhaps poor eating habits have caused your health to deteriorate.

Neptune also rules chemicals and while it was in Virgo chemical fertilizers and food additives were introduced into the food chain. Although the manufacturers of these products intended to improve food quality and quantity, in typical Neptunian fashion their good intentions were misguided and led to environmental pollution and illnesses in people and animals. Neptune's most recent trip through Virgo also brought new discoveries in the area of medicine, most notably the introduction of penicillin in 1939. However, some of the drugs developed during this period were found to cause bigger problems than they relieved. Those of you who have this planetary placement in your birth charts could have a fascination with the medical field, and the use of drug therapy in particular. Your idealization of the medical profession and your desire for quick cures might cause you to avoid responsibility for your own health and rely too heavily on doctors and drugs to remedy your ills.

Finally, Virgo's relationship with everyday life was highlighted when Neptune passed through this sign, and suddenly, ordinary household objects were idealized. The Art Deco movement of this period glorified common items, and artists and manufacturers paid special attention to the design of such things as toasters, vacuum cleaners, dishes and cigarette trays. For those of you who have Neptune in Virgo in your birth charts, function is probably more important than form. You idealize efficiency and practicality, and see beauty in usefulness. For example, nylon, one of the first synthetic textiles introduced to make clothing care easier, was developed in 1938, and as your Neptune-group reached adulthood the use of synthetic fabrics in clothing and household products proliferated.

Neptune in Libra

In this century, Neptune was in Libra from October 1942 until April 1943, again between August 1943 and December 1955, and finally from March to October 1956. Libra is the sign of love and relationships, and in the postwar years, while Neptune was positioned here, record numbers of couples married. Marriage was idealized as never before and thought to be the answer to everyone's dreams.

Those of you who were born with this Neptune position in your charts idealize love, as did romantic poets Lord Byron and Percy Bysshe Shelley (who had Neptune in Libra). However, you hold unrealistic expectations of your relationships and your partners. You are seeking the perfect love, fully believe you'll find it one day if you look hard enough, and will settle for nothing less. You look to your partners to be everything to you—provider, nurturer, friend, lover, parent—and to fulfill your fantasy image in each of these roles. In typical Neptunian fashion, you have trouble accepting reality when it conflicts with your illusions, and may feel confused and deceived if a relationship doesn't turn out the way you'd imagined. As a result, your Neptune generation has experienced an unprecedented divorce rate, for although you idealize relationships you find satisfaction within them to be nearly impossible. Those of you who have Neptune in Libra are faced with the dilemma of either sacrificing your fantasies to achieve lasting partnerships or sacrificing relationships that don't fulfill your ideals. Though love and relationships are extremely important to you, they are perhaps the hardest thing for you to obtain.

The sign Libra is associated with women, and Neptune in this sign signaled changes in women's roles and images. During the war years, large numbers of women entered the workplace, filling jobs vacated by fighting men. "Rosie the Riveter" became a feminine ideal in America, and many Rosies found they were not only capable of doing "men's work," they also enjoyed their changed status and identities. But after the war was over, the image of the perfect woman returned to that of wife, mother and homemaker.

When the women who were born with Neptune in Libra in their birth charts reached adulthood in the 1960s and '70s, they were confronted with the same issues—and confusion—regarding their position in society. Your generation was in the forefront of feminism and has been responsible for dissolving the old myths of a "woman's place." As women's roles became blurred, however, many Neptune-in-Libra women adopted unrealistic expectations of themselves; those of you with Neptune in Libra not only believe you should be perfect wives, mothers and homemakers, but successful career people, too. Perhaps no group of women has ever had such high ideals, or been more confused about its place in life.

Libra also is the sign of peace, and in the United States the Neptune-in-Libra group was known as the "peace and love" generation who protested for peace and refused to fight in Viet Nam. Your generation, though, was born during World War II and the Cold War years that followed, when peace and harmony between nations seemed to be elusive, and throughout your lives your hopes for peace have been clouded by the threat of nuclear annihilation. The peace you idealize always seems to be just beyond reach, muddled by confusion, misconceptions and hidden issues. Peace is one of your fondest dreams, but may be the most difficult thing for your generation to achieve. While Neptune was in Libra, however, new relationships and alliances between nations such as NATO were formed, and the United Nations was established as an international peacekeeper. Under the presidency of Dwight D. Eisenhower (whose Sun was in Libra), which began near the end of Neptune's passage through this sign, the United States experienced a period of relative peace and prosperity.

Neptune in Scorpio

Neptune was in Scorpio this century from December 1955 to March 1956, between October 1956 and December 1969, and from May until November 1970. Scorpio is associated with power, control, anything secret or hidden, the occult, the unconscious, transformation, death and rebirth, destruction, obsession and sex. Whenever Neptune passes through this sign the public is sensitized to these areas and they become emphasized.

Neptune's most recent trip through this sign during the tumultuous sixties brought about transformations on many Scorpionic fronts. This was a time when the balance of power was being questioned throughout the world. Many African nations gained their independence from foreign domination during this period. In Cuba, Fidel Castro overthrew Batista and established the first Communist state in Latin America. In the United States, desegregation of the public schools was ordered and Civil Rights was an important issue. The struggle between the U. S. and the U. S. S. R. escalated and both world powers built up awesome arsenals of nuclear weapons.

Those of you who were born while Neptune was in Scorpio have lived your entire lives in the shadow of the bomb and fully expect the Earth to be destroyed by nuclear war. Your generation feels powerless in the face of such a devastating possibility and is, perhaps, the most pessimistic of all Neptune-groups. To you, the future looks dismal and you believe that almost everything is beyond your control. This is the bleak message conveyed by some punk songs, a musical style that reached popularity with your generation.

Nuclear power plants designed to produce electrical energy proliferated during this period, too. Though at first, the new technology promised to provide unlimited cheap power, this idealized picture turned out to be an illusion (as is typical whenever Neptune is involved); hidden dangers included environmental pollution from nuclear wastes and the chance of nuclear contamination and massive destruction from a meltdown.

Whenever Neptune is in Scorpio, public awareness is focused on the subject of death. When this combination occurred from approximately 1792 to 1806, France was embroiled in the Reign of Terror and several thousand people were guillotined. Neptune's most recent transit of Scorpio coincided with the assassinations of John F. Kennedy, Robert Kennedy and Martin Luther King. And, of course, this was the era of the Viet Nam War, when death was in the forefront of many Americans' minds.

This planetary placement also brought about a change in attitude toward death and dying. The hospice movement, a humanitarian program that helps the terminally ill and their families deal with death, was established in the U. S. while Neptune was in Scorpio. During this time, the concept of reincarnation also became popular in the West. Those of you who have Neptune in Scorpio in your birth charts probably believe in life after death; at least, you don't discount the possibility and may be fascinated with such things as past-life regression, life in other worlds, ghosts, channeling, etc.

You also may be intrigued with the occult and with discovering the ancient mysteries. Salem, Massachusetts, a city connected with witchcraft, was founded in 1629, while Neptune was in Scorpio. As your generation becomes an influential part of society the occult is growing fashionable. (This also was true toward the end of Neptune's last trip through Scorpio.) Perhaps you want to master the hidden forces of the Universe in order to gain power. Or, you simply may want to understand core truths and learn the secrets of the unconscious mind.

During Neptune's most recent passage through Scorpio the use of mind-altering drugs became popular as a way of probing the depths of the unconscious. Those of you with this planetary placement in your birth charts may have a particular fascination with drugs of all kinds, for a variety of reasons. Your desire to reach the deepest recesses of your mind could make psychedelics attractive to you, and your deep-seated feelings of powerlessness might incline you toward cocaine. Neptune is associated with drugs and alcohol, Scorpio with obsession and extremes; therefore, your generation is more susceptible to drug excesses and addiction than other Neptune-groups.

Scorpio is the sign of subterfuge, secret knowledge and undercover intelligence organizations. While Neptune was in Scorpio espionage became fashionable and books, television programs and movies on the subject proliferated, with the adventures of James Bond leading the pack. People who have this Neptune placement in their birth charts see spying and detective work as glamorous and exciting. You idealize the person who knows what goes on behind the scenes, whether s/he is a government agent, a corporate spy or an independent investigator. A bit of a snoop yourself, you want to know everything about everyone else, but may not be so willing to reveal yourself. Your generation might be responsible for the expansion of computer data banks that allow access to personal information about many thousands of people to anyone who knows the code.

Scorpio also is connected with sex, and while Neptune was in this sign sex became more relaxed and fashionable. The sixties were a time of "sexual revolution" when birth control became more accessible, abortion was legalized in many European countries, the U. S. S. R. and Japan, and many of the taboos about sex were destroyed.

Those of you whose birth charts contain Neptune in Scorpio probably entertain many fantasies and illusions about sex. Perhaps you see it as glamorous and fashionable, and you might even enjoy wearing overtly sexy clothing. Rock singer Madonna, for example, has her Neptune in Scorpio. You have a tendency to idealize sex and believe that sexual compatibility is all that's needed in a relationship. Your unrealistically high expectations of sex are likely to result in disappointments, however. The Neptune-in-Libra generation is searching for perfect love, your generation wants perfect sex.

Neptune in Sagittarius

During this century, Neptune was in Sagittarius between January and April 1970, from November 1970 to January 1984, and from June until November 1984. Sagittarius is associated with expansion of all kinds, and with things that broaden your knowledge and experience: long distance travel, foreign countries and people, higher education, publishing and journalism, religion and philosophy. Recreation, entertainment and freedom of movement also are related to this sign, so the great outdoors and sports—particularly those involving the legs, horses and/or gambling—are Sagittarian in nature.

Neptune's most recent trip through this sign attuned the collective unconscious to things related to Sagittarius and expanded many Neptunian areas. In the United States, for example, enrollment in colleges expanded as "baby boom" students sought higher education. Interest in Eastern religions and spiritual self-awareness increased. So did the passion for gambling; legal, state-run lotteries proliferated and Atlantic City was revived as a gambling center. The price of oil (a Neptune-ruled commodity, needed for Sagittarian travel) skyrocketed, and the use of credit cards expanded dramatically.

Physical fitness became fashionable (as did athletic clothing) and sports that involved the legs—running, bicycling, roller skating—were the most popular of all. The public discovered the great outdoors and camping suddenly became chic (though with flashy, trendy "recreational vehicles" camping no longer meant "roughing it"). Texas, with its Neptunian oil and Sagittarian horseback-riding cowboy image, saw its economy and population expand at an unprecedented rate. Foreign-made products—Japanese cars, French jeans, Danish ice cream—were prestigious and fashionable. Long distance travel took on a new meaning as astronauts visited the Moon, and Voyager and Pioneer space probes explored the Universe beyond our solar system. Books, movies and television shows about outer space journeys became international hits.

During Neptune's previous trip through Sagittarius, between approximately 1806 and 1820, similar trends occurred. Long distance travel, particularly the expedition of Lewis and Clark, played a significant role in the expansion of America's horizons and its knowledge of the territory beyond the eastern seaboard. The first federal highway, built in 1806, and the first successful steamboat in 1807 helped facilitate travel. Poker was introduced to the United States from France.[6]

As is always true with Neptune, however, insidious problems, losses, deception and confusion surrounded areas related to Sagittarius. Most obvious were the debilitating effect high oil prices had on the world's economy, and the financial instability created by inflation, overextended credit and excessive debt.

Those of you who have Neptune in Sagittarius in your birth charts idealize travel, freedom of movement and the world beyond your doorstep. You want to see and do everything, and one of your favorite fantasies might be to explore unknown lands or take a trip around the globe. You also want to share your knowledge and experiences with others, and could utilize your imagination to write colorful, mythological or philosophical tales about your adventures that satisfy others' desire to learn about foreign places and people. Writers Herman Melville, Charles Dickens, Edgar Allan Poe and Henry Wadsworth Longfellow are some examples of Neptune in Sagittarius.

Knowledge and education are also important to you. However, Neptune always requires sacrifice of some kind and your generation might find your dream of being learned denied you. As the oldest members of this Neptune-group reach college age many are discovering that higher education is beyond their financial grasp. Perhaps your generation will have to give up on the traditional channels and acquire your knowledge through other means.

Your Neptune-group is especially fond of all forms of recreation and entertainment including sports, music, movies and television, social interaction, gambling and/or drugs. As a group, you idealize "good times" and can be rather lazy and indulgent. Though you desire wealth you don't want to work very hard for it, and this inclination causes you to be attracted to—and deceived through—get-rich schemes, illegal activities, gambling, etc.

Spiritual development and moral and ethical principles are of great concern to many in the Neptune-in-Sagittarius generation. Reformationist Martin Luther, for example, had this planetary placement in his birth chart. You are seeking higher knowledge and ultimate truths. Your generation could be instrumental in raising the world's consciousness and bringing enlightenment to the masses. However, it is also possible that the deception and confusion inherent in Neptune might cause you to misinterpret religious teachings, follow false gods, persecute others for their religious beliefs or be deluded in some way about spiritual issues.

Neptune in Capricorn

Neptune entered Capricorn in January 1984 and will remain in this sign until November 1998 (except for brief periods between June and November 1984, and February to August 1998). Capricorn is connected with conservatism, traditions, the past, business, materialism, work and career success, banking, government, stability, realism and practicality. Therefore, these are the issues that become important and fashionable during Neptune's passage through this sign. They also are the areas, however, where illusions, confusion, disintegration, disillusionment and deception are likely to occur.

As Neptune moved into Capricorn, the collective unconscious became attuned to conservativism and materialism. This mass response resulted in a return to traditional values and attitudes, and a renewed emphasis on financial growth and material success. Conservative politicians gained control, liberal social programs and issues were pushed aside, and laws and policies that benefitted big businesses were implemented. International banks expanded their power. In the United States, making money was more desirable than ever, and how much you were paid for your work became more important than what you did. Investment plans and tax shelters proliferated, "networking" parties to make business contacts became chic, and finances, real estate profits, stocks, etc. were popular topics of conversation. Greed was fashionable, being poor became a disgrace, and the Reagan administration epitomized this attitude.

This trend toward traditionalism also brought about a resurgence of fundamentalist religions, and a renewed interest in the past was reflected in historical movies and books. Antique furniture and even traditional, classic clothing became fashionable again.

Neptune was last in Capricorn from about 1820 to 1834. This coincided with the Classic Revival period in architecture and furniture[7] when ancient Greek, Italian and Egyptian motifs were incorporated into current designs. Historical novels became popular, too, and in the United States there was increased interest in preserving and edifying the nation's historic buildings and sites. This also coincided with the founding of F. C. Lowell's textile mills in Massachusetts and the beginning of America's Industrial Revolution. Materialism was rampant and fashionable, leading Washington Irving to coin the phrase "the Almighty Dollar."[8]

However, unseen and insidious ills were obscured by the rosy haze of Neptunian fantasies and glory. Unchecked capitalism destroyed small businesses and undermined the free enterprise system itself. Relaxed regulations allowed corporations to damage the health of their employees and the environment. Tax breaks for businesses and the rich forced greater burdens on the poor and middle classes. Unsound economic policies created financial instability in many wealthy and developing countries, and produced a dangerously inflated national debt in America.

Those of you who have this planetary placement in your birth charts idealize all things associated with Capricorn. Writer Horatio Alger, who glorified hard work, the "self-made man" and material success, is a good example of Neptune in Capricorn. Your generation dreams of great wealth, success, social status and stability, but although you desire these things very much, they seem to elude you and are, perhaps, the most difficult things for you to achieve. Or, if you do achieve success you may find it's not all that you'd expected. When those of you who have Neptune in Capricorn reach adulthood, you may be confronted with financial burdens and a worldwide shortage of natural resources that are the legacy of earlier, wasteful generations. Because of declining birthrates in the developed countries, there will be fewer working people in the future to support a larger number of elderly, and maintaining social services might require individual monetary sacrifices. Economic stability—personal and/or national—could become an unattainable dream.

Neptune always involves some sort of sacrifice and signifies a conflict between ideals and reality. Those of you with Neptune in Capricorn might have to sacrifice your ideals and illusions of wealth and accept more conservative, practical and realistic lifestyles in a time of material scarcity. Or, you may come to an understanding that the physical world is just an illusion, that money doesn't bring happiness, and find contentment through relinquishing your desire for material things.

Notes

1. Stan Barker, *The Signs of the Times: The Neptune Factor and America's Destiny* (St. Paul, MN: Llewellyn Publications, 1984), p. 82-86.
2. Ibid., p. 117.
3. H. H. Arnason, *History of Modern Art* (Englewood, NJ: Prentice-Hall, Inc., and NY: Harry N. Abrams, Inc.), pp. 139-153.
4. Helen Comstock, *American Furniture* (Exton, PA: Schiffer Publishing Ltd.), p. 120.
5. Barker, p. 144.
6. Ibid., pp. 232-239.
7. Comstock, p. 191.
8. Barker, p. 263.

Chapter Twelve

Pluto

The most distant known planet in our solar system, Pluto takes about 248 years to complete its trip through all twelve signs of the zodiac. Its journey, though, is highly irregular and Pluto remains in each sign for varying lengths of time. Since the mid-nineteenth century, Pluto's movement through the signs has been accelerating; the planet was in Taurus for approximately thirty-one years, in Gemini for thirty, in Cancer for about twenty-five, but it will stay in Scorpio (where it is at the time of this writing) for less than twelve.

Because Pluto remains in one sign for many years, millions of people are born with the same Pluto-sign in their birth charts. The sign positions of Pluto and Neptune define the different generations. Each generation has a common Pluto-theme, based on the planet's sign placement, and everyone born with the same Pluto position resonates to the same tone or vibration.

Like Neptune and Uranus, Pluto affects us on an unconscious level; we usually cannot direct its energy consciously, but instead *respond* to it emotionally and intensely, often *en masse.* Although we experience its influence in our personal lives, Pluto is not concerned with individual matters so much as it is with universal conditions and large-scale social and cosmic issues. In fact, Pluto has no qualms about destroying the individual—or an entire society or life form—in order to bring about a necessary evolution; thus it is sometimes called "the destroyer."

Pluto is associated with values and transformation. According to astrologer Noel Tyl, its accelerated speed in recent years relates to the increased rate with which our values are transformed. "New values cover old values more swiftly."[1] The sign in which Pluto is placed shows what a generation values, but also what must be transformed. However, Pluto also is the planet of obsession and its sign position indicates what things a generation is obsessed with and clings to stubbornly. As a result, the transformation that Pluto demands often is painful and traumatic because changing our attitudes and attachments to those things is extremely difficult.

Pluto's message, though, is change or die, and it is willing to wreak absolute devastation in order to affect those changes. The "dead wood" must be cleared away before new growth can sprout, and that is what Plutonic transformations are all about: death and rebirth. Pluto's placement in the birth chart shows areas where death and rebirth (not always on a physical level, however) are needed and are likely to occur because the attitudes, emotions and behaviors associated with those areas have outlived their purpose. Thus, Pluto often is thought of as the planet of death.

Pluto also represents the dark side, that which is hidden, secret, unconscious, repressed, feared, taboo. When the planet moves through a sign, however, it brings those secret fears and repressed emotions to the surface and forces humankind to look them in the eye. Often what we see is terrifying and disgusting; we don't want to admit that it is part of us, our own underbelly, and prefer to project those Pluto-characteristics onto others, especially our enemies. It is easy to see why this planet is connected with sex, death, violence, cruelty and the occult. However, Pluto also symbolizes the desire to know what exists beneath the surface and to probe the depths in search of ultimate truths. The knowledge obtained from such investigation can then be used for personal, social and universal growth. Consequently, Pluto is associated with psychology, parapsychology, secret intelligence organizations, mining and surgery.

Finally, Pluto is the planet of power. The sign in which it is placed indicates where a particular Pluto-group focuses its power and from what that generation derives a sense of power. The planet's sign position also shows where and how a generation attempts to wield power, where power struggles are likely to arise, and where manipulation, domination and oppression—of people, situations or the forces of the Universe—might occur. For this reason, Pluto is often linked with dictators and tyrants. Its discovery in 1930 corresponded with the rise of cruel and powerful dictators, the most notorious being Adolf Hitler, and with the development of the most powerful destructive force known to humankind: the bomb.

The planet of extremes, Pluto represents the highest and the lowest, the greatest saint and the vilest villain—as well as the power to transform ourselves from one level to the other. It has long been considered to embody both the forces of good and evil, as does the god Abraxis, and to signify the good and evil that exist within each of us. Interestingly, scientists are now considering the possibility that Chiron, the body that orbits Pluto, is actually a twin planet to Pluto rather than its Moon. If so, perhaps one body symbolizes the forces of "good" and the other "evil."

Pluto in Gemini

Pluto was in Gemini from 1882 until July 1913, and between January and May 1914. Gemini is associated with communication, early education and short journeys, therefore, these things are foremost in the minds of the public and are transformed during Pluto's transit of this sign. Those of you who have Pluto in Gemini in your birth charts feel strongly about these areas, and you experience and/or are responsible for significant changes in things related to Gemini.

During Pluto's most recent trip through this sign, education was considered important. In order to ensure that everyone had access to at least a basic education, governments in Western Europe and the United States decided to establish state-supported, public elementary school systems. Pluto always brings about transformations and its passage through Gemini transformed education from an option available only to those who could afford to pay for it into something that was mandatory for all. In England and France, public primary schools were established in the 1880s, and France even went so far as to set up state-funded secondary schools which admitted girls as well as boys. Between 1885 and 1896 France also founded fifteen state universities. In the

Virtually no one is alive today who has Pluto in Aries, Taurus, Sagittarius, Capricorn, Aquarius or Pisces, therefore, these signs will not be discussed in this chapter.

United States, compulsory education was instituted widely during this period and by 1918 every state had some sort of requirements for school attendance. More schools were built at this time than ever before and literacy was highly valued. Pluto has a dark side, however, that involves fear and suspicion, especially of anyone or anything "different." Here this dark side showed itself in the Supreme Court's "separate but equal" ruling in 1896 that upheld racial segregation in U. S. public schools.

Those of you who have Pluto in Gemini in your birth charts are obsessed with education and may believe that if everyone were educated there wouldn't be so many problems in the world. Some of you born during this time were immigrants or poor children who had to forego schooling and go to work; as a result, you made sure your own children got an education. However, you are likely to support an educational system that is restrictive, authoritarian and regimented rather than one that is loosely structured or encourages free thinking. By teaching children what to think rather than how to find answers for themselves you can control their understanding of the world.

Gemini is associated with all forms of communication. During Pluto's most recent passage through this sign telephone communication developed rapidly. Newspapers proliferated and became influential and powerful. In an earlier Pluto-in-Gemini period, the first postal system in America opened at Richard Fairbank's Tavern in Boston. Those of you who have this planetary placement in your birth charts might be obsessed with communication—writing, speaking, teaching. For example, William Faulkner, Ernest Hemingway, Lillian Hellman, John Steinbeck, Evelyn Waugh, Vladimir Nabokov, e. e. cummings, Isak Dinesen, James Michener and Dashiell Hammett are only a few of the writers with this Pluto placement. Or, you may have been responsible for the creation or expansion of communication systems, television, radio, etc.

Since Pluto's energy often operates in a hidden or undercover manner, you might have been involved with secret communications or some sort of information-gathering operation. Perhaps you see knowledge as power, and may use—or misuse—information and language to mislead, manipulate or dominate people and situations. The FBI, for instance, was founded while Pluto was in Gemini, and the Bureau's long-time head J. Edgar Hoover had this Pluto position in his birth chart. So did former U. S. Senator Joe McCarthy, whose unsubstantiated accusations of communism ruined the careers and lives of many citizens. Fascist leaders Adolf Hitler and Benito Mussolini, and former U. S. Presidents

Richard Nixon and Ronald Reagan—all masters of "doublespeak"—are some other examples of Pluto in Gemini.

Your fascination with hidden knowledge and deeper truths could inspire you to pursue occult studies and/or psychology. When Pluto was in Gemini, there was a revival of interest in metaphysical matters and many secret orders, including the influential Golden Dawn, were formed during this time. Occultists Manly P. Hall and Francis Israel Regardie, astrologers Marc Edmund Jones, Dane Rudhyar and C. E. O. Carter, and psychologist Wilhelm Reich all had this Pluto placement in their birth charts.

Pluto in Cancer

During this century, Pluto was in Cancer from July to December 1913, between June 1914 and July 1938, and from February until June 1939. Cancer is the sign of mother, nurturing, family, home, country and security. While Pluto is in this sign these areas become extremely important, and all things connected with them are forced into the light and transformed. Those of you who have Pluto in this sign in your birth charts are strongly attached to these things, but are likely to experience or be responsible for their destruction; at your core, you have a deep, unconscious—perhaps karmic—need to learn to let them go.

Pluto's passage through Cancer coincided with a period of unparalleled devastation, upheaval and annihilation that left few untouched. World War I and part of World War II, which toppled or reordered entire nations and claimed the lives of millions of people, were fought under this transit. The end of the Chinese Empire, the Russian Revolution and the Great Depression in America also took place during this period. Homes and homelands were wiped out, families were torn apart, races and sects (the extension of family) were exterminated, multitudes went hungry. All things related to Cancer were caught up in a life-and-death struggle and the issue of security was foremost in the minds of people around the world.

Those of you who were born during this time are extremely patriotic. Many of you saw your nations ruined by war, others desperately feared the loss of your homeland, and millions died fighting for their countries. Your country provides your foundation and your sense of security, therefore, you are willing to sacrifice personal freedoms to ensure your security and protection. Anything that endangers it awakens your deepest, secret fears, thus, your generation was most threatened by the anti-war movement of the 1960s in the U. S. Your attachment to "national security" and your obsession with "the enemy" keep you from confronting problems in your own country. Pluto's sign position signifies areas where a particular generation is intransigent and unwilling to look at its own "minotaur." Perhaps your Pluto-group has lessons to learn about living with others on this planet, and needs to find ways to break down the barriers that separate people and countries from each other.

Family, as a microcosm of society, is also inordinately important to those of you who have Pluto in Cancer in your birth charts. Being part of a family makes you feel you are not alone, that you belong to something larger than yourself that connects you with the past and the future. You derive a strong sense of security from your family and are obsessed with maintaining a rigidly defined, carefully controlled family structure; without this you feel adrift in the world. Consequently, you attempt to hold your family together regardless of whether the situation is beneficial to those concerned. You tend to be possessive of family members and intransigent in your attitudes about family matters.

However, Pluto requires transformations, thus, your generation has witnessed the destruction of the "traditional" family and its rebirth into many new and varied forms. For you this transformation has been especially traumatic and painful. Many of you still can't cope with such ideas as divorce, unmarried couples "living together," single parents, childless couples and other alternate lifestyles. And although you wanted to keep your children near you forever, you instead find yourself in a highly mobile society that scatters family members far and wide. In this area, your generation has been forced to become more flexible, less domineering, less attached.

Finally, Cancer is the sign of mother, and the image of woman as mother. The Pluto-in-Cancer generation is deeply attached to the idea that "a woman's place is in the home" and that a woman's role is that of mother. Other options are difficult for you to comprehend and accept, for they conflict with your unconscious archetypes. Many women with this planetary placement have found it hard to compete in the business world because of deep-seated attachments to this image. Many men with this placement feel their security—as well as their power—is threatened by women who don't conform to this archetype. The transformation Pluto demands has forced your generation to adjust to changing women's roles in recent years, but this adjustment has not been easy for most of you.

Pluto in Leo

This century Pluto was in Leo from August 1938 to February 1939, from June 1939 until October 1956, and between January and August 1957. Leo is the sign of individuality, self-expression, creativity, love and entertainment. Whenever Pluto is in this sign these areas are brought into the light and transformed, and to people born during this time these things are extremely important.

During Pluto's passage through this sign, a major transformation took place in the entertainment business and a revolutionary creative and dramatic medium was introduced: television. The advertising field was radically changed by television and became a new "art form." Rock 'n' roll, a musical style that would eventually transform the music world, also had its beginnings during this period.

Those of you who have Pluto in Leo are obsessed with self-expression and need to be creative in some way. Unlike the previous generation, which was concerned principally with job security, your Pluto-group wants work to be exciting, fulfilling, creative—an expression of self. You are less likely than people of other Pluto-groups to stay in a position that doesn't actualize your talents or where feel you aren't appreciated, and unless your self-expressive needs are engaged you can be rather lazy and sullen. Nor are most of you willing to devote yourself entirely to your career—unless you really enjoy it—and you make time for your other interests and leisure activities. Entertainment and having fun are extremely important to Pluto-in-Leo people, and as your generation reached adulthood the recreational industry boomed. Your generation is more concerned with what others do for fun than what they do for work.

Your focus in life is *you,* and your generation suffers from a severe case of self-centeredness. Aptly nicknamed the "me generation," you are obsessed with improving yourself and engage in all sorts of self-actualization projects, psychotherapy, exercise programs and inner-development studies so you can "find yourself" and make yourself better, more beautiful, happier.

Many of you also have a deep desire for attention, love, recognition and fame. Leo is the sign of ego, identity and self-worth, and those of you with this planetary placement have a fundamental optimism, self-confidence and even arrogance. You believe that you know best and have little respect for people in other generations. Even if other personal factors in your individual birth charts make you more humble or insecure, at your core you have faith that everything ultimately will turn out alright—if not for everyone, then at least for you. You also believe that you are special in some way, or that you have an important calling in life. Jeff Green describes it as "a deep feeling of specialness" and a desire "to actualize this special destiny."[2]

Pluto requires transformation, often destroying things connected with a particular sign as it passes through it. Therefore, your generation has experienced a world where individual importance is being challenged and where society's needs and demands frequently conflict with personal ones. According to Liz Greene, "During the lifetimes of those with Pluto in Leo, half the nations of the world have espoused a form of socialism or communism which frustrates . . . the Leonine conviction of the sanctity of . . . individual worth."[3] Perhaps your generation needs to learn to value others and society as well as yourself, and to transform your egocenteredness.

Leo also is associated with love—self-love, love given to others and to the fruits of your creativity. Those of you who have Pluto in this sign were born during a time when there was little love in the world. World War II was raging during the early part of this transit, followed by the Cold War years. The world had witnessed heretofore unknown horrors and cruelty toward others—the Nazi concentration camps, Stalin's destruction of the Ukrainians and the bombing of Japan.

Your Pluto-group has experienced and been responsible for transformations in the way we look at and express love. As your generation reached adulthood, reliable birth control and abortion diminished the fears, restrictions and pressures that surrounded lovemaking. "Living together" without marriage became commonplace and socially acceptable. The Women's Movement made it possible for women to support themselves, and thus choose partners for love rather than financial security. Your generation desperately longs for love and believes that "all you need is love." Perhaps those of you who once proclaimed "make love not war" will have an opportunity to affect or witness the transformation of humankind through love, or at least be able to transform yourselves in this way.

Pluto in Virgo

Pluto was in Virgo this century from October 1956 to January 1957, between August 1957 and September 1971, and from April until July 1972. Virgo is associated with work, service, health and nutrition, analysis, precision and humility; therefore, these things are brought into focus and transformed during Pluto's passage through the sign. To people born while Pluto is in Virgo, these things are extremely important, and your generation will experience and/or be responsible for affecting major changes in these areas.

Pluto transits of Virgo metamorphose the way people work and earn their livelihood. Pluto's previous passage through this sign in the early 1700s coincided with the development of shipping and trade between continents. During the planet's most recent trip through Virgo, the United States' economy began shifting to a service-oriented one after being based on industrial productivity for more than a century. The same sort of transformation also took place in other developed countries. As those of you who were born during this period reached adulthood and entered the work force, this trend accelerated. "Business services (which range from word processing to cleaning offices), health care services (in hospitals, nursing homes, and social welfare agencies), and food catering services have all expanded enormously in recent years in both Western Europe and North America."[4]

For the Pluto-in-Virgo generation, work is vitally important and as a group, you are diligent and conscientious, concentrating much of your energy and attention on your careers. Many of the so-called "yuppies" are members of this Pluto-group. Those of you with this planetary placement in your charts often are employed in some type of service, technical or support capacity, and you are more concerned that the work you do has practical application than that it is creative, entertaining or self-aggrandizing. The Pluto-in-Leo generation might originate the ideas, but your generation finds ways to implement them.

To you, the purpose of education is to develop specific skills in preparation for a particular job, and during your generation's college years many schools began changing their focus from liberal arts to technical and "useful" career programs. According to Donald Kennedy, president of Stanford University, your generation is more adept in technological areas but less proficient in languages and writing skills than your predecessors.[5] You are not particularly interested in the arts, philosophy or learning for its own sake; you want to be able to utilize what you know directly and see immediate and quantifiable results from your efforts.

Health and nutrition also are important to the Pluto-in-Virgo generation. As Pluto neared completion of its most recent trip through Virgo, the public became increasingly concerned with the quality of the food they ate. Millions changed their diets, turned to "health foods," vitamins, low-salt or low-cholesterol diets, or vegetarianism, and attention was focused on the detrimental effects of chemical preservatives, fertilizers and pesticides. Those of you with this planetary placement in your charts tend to be attentive to the purity and nutritional value of your food, and as your generation reached adulthood, a plethora of health-conscious food products appeared on the market.

Virgo's connection with health links it to the medical profession. The sign also is associated with analysis and specialization, as opposed to synthesis and wholism; therefore, it is interesting to see how Pluto's passage through Virgo instigated a major shift in the medical field toward specialization. Virgo's obsession with purity and germs has led to a focus on viruses in medical research and treatment. While Pluto was in Virgo immunization programs became widespread, as did the use of antibiotics to treat everything from syphilis to the common cold. Those of you who have this placement in your birth charts may worry excessively about diseases, infections and germs; your obsession with illness might incline you to visit doctors and/or take medications more readily and frequently than members of other Pluto-groups.

Virgo is a modest, self-effacing sign. Those of you with this planetary placement in your charts are interested in job security, being productive members of society and making money, but fame is of lesser importance to you than to the preceding Pluto-in-Leo generation. You don't feel a compulsion to "set the world on fire," nor do you think you have some special mission in life. As a group, you tend to have a rather pessimistic and resigned attitude, believing that things will only get worse in the future, and that you'd better not set your hopes too high. Whether this stems from a fundamental pragmatism or from discouragement over your own inability (and everyone else's) to achieve perfection is debatable. You are more likely to see what's wrong with the world instead of what's right, and to feel victimized by situations beyond your control. According to Jeff Green, those of you who have Pluto in Virgo are "learning essential humility, but also a necessary self-purification that purges all traces of self-glorification and delusions of grandeur" in preparation for future growth.[6]

Pluto in Libra

This century, Pluto was in Libra from October 1971 to April 1972, between August 1972 and October 1983, and from May until August 1984. Libra is associated with relationships, women, art, balance and the law, therefore, these areas are forced into public awareness and transformed when Pluto passes through this sign.

Perhaps most significant of the changes which occurred during this time was the Women's Movement. Pluto in Libra brought to light the inequities between men and women in American society and tore down the old, restrictive, outworn attitudes about "a woman's place." In true Plutonic style, issues of power and control were important, and the movement was plagued by extremism, fear, resistance and turmoil. Pluto's entry into Libra saw the legalization of abortion in the U. S. (January 1973), the publication of *Ms.* magazine (January 1972), the introduction of the Equal Rights Amendment (1972) and the expansion of the National Organization of Women (NOW) into a formidable political force. By the time Pluto left this sign, a woman had run for vice president on the Democratic ticket and women's economic, professional, political and educational opportunities had increased dramatically. Most importantly, women's self-confidence, and their vision of themselves and their role in society had been transformed by this Pluto transit.

Laws concerning things that affected women's personal and professional lives, such as credit, ownership of property, equal job opportunities and pay, sexual harassment, divorce and medical care, were brought into the light and changed.

Those of you born during this time have a deep, abiding belief in the power of women and are obsessed with the issue of equality between the sexes. Women with this planetary placement in their birth charts may be strong, dominant, shrewd, even ruthless and manipulative; men with this placement may see women as being more powerful than they are and fear both women and the female (or yin) side of themselves. However, both men and women in the Pluto-in-Libra generation have the opportunity to eliminate sexual inequity once and for all and establish balance in society and interpersonal relationships.

Along with the changes in women's status came fundamental and unavoidable changes in personal relationships. As women achieved greater professional and economic power, they demanded more power in their relationships as well. The pattern that had been established by earlier generations of the man as unquestioned authority and provider, woman as nurturer and passive dependent, was revised. Improved birth control and the legalization of abortion allowed women to control reproduction, and thus exercise more control over the rest of their lives. This also enabled women to express their sexuality more freely. Predictably, Pluto's transit through Libra brought an end to many individual relationships as it destroyed the old concept of relationships. The divorce rate skyrocketed, "living together" without marriage became popular, and many people grew jaded about the institution of marriage.

Many of you who were born while Pluto was in Libra have seen your parents divorce. Even if your parents stayed together, you still have experienced the turmoil and instability inherent in this transformative period of redefining roles, rights and responsibilities. As a result, you are obsessed with maintaining strong, lasting relationships yourselves. You have a deep need for love and partnerships, are possessive of your partners and may be unhappy when you are not involved in a relationship. There is no such thing as a casual love affair for you. Your generation feels compelled to form committed relationships quickly and early, and to stay in those relationships despite problems that would have caused members of earlier generations to bale out. Relationships provide a sense of deep, emotional security for you and one of your greatest fears is being alone. However, this planetary placement suggests that, of necessity, you probably will go through many transformative, traumatic relationship experiences and perhaps losses that will force you to relinquish your attachment to partners and partnerships. Some of you may become involved in destructive relationships where domination, manipulation, sexual control and power plays are common. Others might submerge individuality and independence in the relationship. Your generation needs to learn to find the balance between self and others.

Pluto in Scorpio

Pluto entered its own sign, Scorpio, at the end of 1983 and stayed there until May 1984. The planet returned to this sign in September 1984, where it will remain until November 1995 (except for a brief period between January and April 1995). Both Pluto and Scorpio have similar characteristics, so when the planet is positioned here its expression is intensified.

It is interesting, though not surprising, that George Orwell chose the title *1984* for his famous novel; that date corresponds to Pluto's entry into Scorpio and the book aptly depicts the dark Plutonic forces at work. Though Orwell's portrayal of this Pluto-in-Scorpio period is perhaps an extreme one, we nonetheless see an increase in government domination and pervasiveness at this time, and a public willingness to sacrifice freedom to "Big Brother" out of fear. In the United States, mandatory drug testing is one example of Plutonic/Scorpionic prying. The expanded power of multi-national corporations and banks, and the effect this has on the world's financial situation, is another example of Plutonic/Scorpionic domination.

At the opposite end of the spectrum (for this planetary position indicates extremes) are the political and social reforms now taking place in the U.S.S.R. and The People's Republic of China. Known for their controlling, restrictive governments, these two nations show signs of opening up and interacting with the rest of the world.

Power issues of all kinds are connected with Pluto and Scorpio, therefore, those of you who have this planetary position in your birth charts may be obsessed with having power. You might attempt to control and manipulate other people—or the forces of nature. When your generation reaches adulthood, we may experience a time of government oppression, cruel and powerful dictators, or other conditions that strictly limit freedoms.

Nuclear power and nuclear weapons are also associated with Pluto and Scorpio, and this planetary combination forces this issue into public awareness. Power struggles between nations and the buildup of nuclear arsenals have been highlighted during this period, as we begin to realize we must change our attitudes about war or face annihilation. The reactor incident at Chernobyl, U.S.S.R. forced the world to reconsider the issue of nuclear power. (Interestingly, the Soviet Union has its Sun in Scorpio.) During Pluto's transit of Scorpio, nuclear and toxic wastes can no longer be ignored either, and the problem of what to do with these wastes, as well as the threats to health and the environment become more poignant and pressing.

These issues could be of major significance to those of you with this planetary position in your birth charts. Perhaps your generation will establish peace in the world and do away with war and power struggles. Or, you may be the survivors of a nuclear holocaust and be responsible for reconstructing life on Earth. Quite likely, your generation will face the problem of cleaning up the environment and getting rid of nuclear and toxic wastes. Or, you could suffer plagues, famine and pestilence as a result of damage done to the environment. On the brighter side, your Pluto-group might discover a problem-free source of power and energy for the planet, making nuclear power unnecessary.

Sex, and the taboos, fears and secretiveness surrounding it, are related to Scorpio and Pluto. Both the planet and the sign also are linked with death. Therefore, the connection between this planetary placement and the appearance of the venereal disease AIDS is obvious. In true Pluto-in-Scorpio fashion, fear of this mysterious and devastating disease has led to cruelty, suspicion, and attempts to isolate AIDS victims and deprive them of their rights, especially the right to privacy. Pluto always drags skeletons out of the closet and makes us take a good, hard look at our secret fears. AIDS has forced us to deal with the issue of sex and the taboos surrounding it—particularly homosexuality. Attention has been focused on other Plutonic problems during this period, too, such as the sexual abuse of children, the connection between such abuse and violent criminal behavior in adulthood, sex and violence in movies and television, rape, sex education and pornography.

For those of you born during this time, sexuality will be extremely important. Perhaps you will harbor intense fears about your sexuality or see sexuality as an instrument of power. Or, your generation could be responsible for transforming negative attitudes toward sexual expression. You might find a link between sexual repression and illness and be able to eliminate certain diseases like cancer as a result. By the time you reach adulthood it may be essential to limit population growth and your sexual and reproductive freedom might be curtailed sharply. More frightening is the opposite possibility: that a devastating war could make it necessary for your Pluto-group to re-populate the Earth. Or, your generation could be plagued by sterility or birth defects as a result of nuclear and/or toxic pollution.

One of Pluto and Scorpio's principal themes is death and rebirth, and public awareness has been attuned to this subject during the Pluto-in-Scorpio period. Reincarnation is more widely accepted in the West now than ever before, and past-life regression and channeling are popular. Concerns about the right to die have led many states in the U. S. to pass laws that allow individuals to make decisions about medical intervention in life-or-death situations *before* the fact.

Those of you who have this planetary placement in your birth charts are practically obsessed with the issue of death and the possibility of life after death. Your generation will be intrigued with the concept of reincarnation and, as you reach adulthood, we may see a period of intense interest in all matters pertaining to death and the hereafter. Your Pluto-group might make startling discoveries about life after death and other worlds beyond this one, or even witness the "Second Coming." Your generation also could be responsible for discovering new "miracle" cures that will extend the human life span significantly. Or, you might restore the death penalty and legalize euthanasia. It is also possible that you will experience cataclysmic events during your lifetime that destroy much of the Earth's life, such as the one that killed the dinosaurs, or the Biblical flood, or the sinking of Atlantis. Perhaps you could be responsible for a nuclear accident or war that brings us to the brink of destruction. It is difficult to predict how this energy will manifest, but undoubtedly, death will be an important issue for your generation.

Notes

1. Noel Jan Tyl, *Holistic Astrology: The Analysis of Inner and Outer Environments* (McLean, VA: TAI Books, 1980), pp. 59-60.
2. Jeff Green, *Pluto: The Evolutionary Journey of the Soul* (St. Paul, MN: Llewellyn Publications, 1986), p. 101.
3. Liz Greene, *The Astrology of Fate* (York Beach, ME: Samuel Weiser, Inc., 1984), p. 54.
4. Sylvia Ann Hewlett, "A Lesser Life," *Utne Reader,* May/June 1987, p. 88.
5. "Are Our Universities Letting Us Down?" *Parade Magazine,* January 24, 1988, p. 8.
6. Green, p. 116.

Sources for Data

Rodden, Lois M. *The American Book of Charts.* San Diego, CA: Astro Computing Services, 1980.

Moore, Moon. *The Book of World Horoscopes.* Birmingham, MI: Seek-It Publications, 1980.

The Boston Globe. Boston, MA: The Globe Newspaper Co.

Maynard, Jim. *Celestial Guide.* Ashland, OR: Quicksilver Productions, 1981.

________________. *Celestial Influences, 1987.* Ashland, OR: Quicksilver Productions, 1986.

Erlewine, Stephen. *The Circle Book of Charts.* Ann Arbor, MI: Circle Bookstore, Inc., 1972.

Collier's Encyclopedia. New York: Macmillan Educational Co., 1985.

The Concise Columbia Encyclopedia. New York: Avon Books, 1983.

Encyclopaedia Britannica, Inc. Chicago: William Benton, publisher, 1973.

Rodden, Lois M. *Profiles of Women.* The American Federation of Astrologers, Inc., 1979.

Who's Who in America, 44th edition. Chicago: Marquis Who's Who, Inc., 1986.

Who's Who of American Women, 14th edition. Chicago: Marquis Who's Who, Inc., 1984.

Who's Who in the World, 7th edition. Chicago: Marquis Who's Who, Inc., 1984.

The World Almanac and Book of Facts, 1988. New York: World Almanac, 1987.

About the Author

Felicity Skye Alexander has been a student, practitioner and teacher of astrology for about twelve years. She also edits metaphysical books, and has written for newspapers, magazines, radio and television. Ms. Alexander lives in Massachusetts with her husband and four cats, where she is currently writing a murder mystery and another astrology book.